International African Seminars
New Series, No. 1

THE PROFESSIONALISATION OF AFRICAN MEDICINE

THE PROFESSIONALISATION OF AFRICAN MEDICINE

EDITED BY
Murray Last and **G. L. Chavunduka**

Manchester University Press
in association with the
INTERNATIONAL AFRICAN INSTITUTE

Published by Manchester University Press
Oxford Road, Manchester M13 9PL, U.K.
and
51 Washington Street, Dover, N.H. 03802, U.S.A.

British Library cataloguing in publication data
The Professionalisation of African medicine.—
(International African seminar studies; v. 1)
1. Folk medicine—Africa
I. Last, Murray II. Chavunduka, G. L. III. Series
615.8′82′096 GR350

Library of Congress cataloging in publication data applied for

ISBN 0–7190–1851 X *cased only*

Photoset in Linotron Plantin by
Northern Phototypesetting Co., Bolton
Printed in England by
The Alden Press Ltd, Oxford

CONTENTS

ILLUSTRATIONS

Professional Signs

NOTES ON CONTRIBUTORS AND PARTICIPANTS

G. L. Chavunduka: Professor of Sociology, University of Zimbabwe; President, Zimbabwe National Traditional Healers Association; Chairman, Zimbabwe Government Traditional Medical Council. Author of *Traditional Healers and the Shona Patient* (Gweru, 1978), *A Shona Urban Court* (Gweru, 1980), *The Zimbabwe National Traditional Healers Association* (Harare, 1984). Address: University of Zimbabwe, PO Box MP 167, Mt Pleasant, Harare, Zimbabwe.

Steven Feierman: Professor of History, University of Wisconsin. Author of *The Shambaa Kingdom* (Madison, 1974), *Health and Society in Africa: a working bibliography* (Waltham, 1979), 'Change in African therapeutic systems', *Social Science and Medicine*, 1979. Field work in Tanga, Tanzania 1966–8 and 1979–80. Address: Dept of History, University of Wisconsin, Madison, Wisconsin 53706, USA.

Murray Last: Reader in Anthropology, University College London; formerly Professor of History, Bayero University, Kano, Nigeria 1978–80. Author of *The Sokoto Caliphate* (London: Longmans Green, 1967); 'The presentation of sickness in a community of non-Muslim Hausa' (in Loudon, ed., *Social Anthropology and Medicine*, London, 1976); 'The importance of knowing about not knowing', *Social Science and Medicine*, 1981. Fieldwork: Nigeria, 1961–7; 1969–72; 1978–80. Address: Dept of Anthropology, University College London, Gower St, London WC1E 6BT, England.

Carol MacCormack: Senior Lecturer in Social Sciences, London School of Hygiene & Tropical Medicine. Co-editor of *Nature, Culture & Gender* (Cambridge, 1980, with M. Strathern) and (with T. Vaskilampi), *Folk Medicine and Health Culture* (Kuopio, 1982); editor of *Ethnography of Fertility & Birth* (London, 1982), and author of 'Primary health care in Sierra Leone', *Social Science and Medicine*, 1984. Fieldwork in Sierra Leone, Tanzania, Jamaica and Burma. Address: Evaluation & Planning Centre for Health Care, London School of Hygiene & Tropical Medicine, Keppel St, London WC1E 7HT, England.

Jerome Msonthi: Dean of the Faculty of Science, University of Malawi; Co-ordinator, Herbalists' Associations of Malawi on Traditional Medicine; Member, Scientific Technical Committee, Italo–Africano Institute/WHO Centre for Traditional Medicine, Rome. Editor of *The Physical Scientist* (The Chemical Society of Malawi); author of over fifteen scientific papers and inventor of a new glucoside. Address: Chancellor College, PO Box 280, Zomba, Malawi.

D. D. O. Oyebola: Reader in Physiology, University of Ibadan. His MD thesis (Ibadan, 1977) was on traditional medical care among the Yoruba; subsequently he has published several papers on traditional midwifery (eg. *East African Medical Journal*, 1980; *International Journal of Gynaecology and Obstetrics*, 1980; *Journal of Tropical Paediatrics*, 1983) and on healers' training and organisation (eg. *Social Science and Medicine*, 1980, pp. 23–9 and 31–7; 1981, pp. 87–102: 'Professional associations, ethics and discipline among Yoruba traditional healers of Nigeria'). Address: Dept of Physiology, College of Medicine, University of Ibadan, Ibadan, Nigeria.

Tola Olu Pearce: Medical Sociologist, Dept of Sociology and Anthropology, University of Ife, Nigeria. Author of 'Political and economic changes in Nigeria and the organisation of medical care', *Social Science and Medicine*, 1980; 'Integrating Western orthodox and indigenous medicine', *ibid.*, 1982; 'Medical systems and the Nigerian society' (in Erinosho, ed., *Studies in Third World Societies*, Williamsburg, vol. 19, 1984; editor (with S. A. Afonja), *Social Change in Nigeria*, London, 1984. Address: Dept of Sociology & Anthropology, University of Ife, Ile-Ife, Nigeria.

Pamela Reynolds: Research Fellow, University of Zimbabwe (currently Dept of Land Management; formerly Dept of Psychology). Fieldwork on urban, suburban & rural healers in Zimbabwe, 1982–3; previously on Xhosa children in Crossroads, Cape Town (PhD thesis, 1984) and on fathers (*Men without Children*, Carnegie paper no. 5, 1984); currently on child labour in Harare and among rural Tonga (northern Zimbabwe). Address: Dept of Land Management, PO Box MP 167, Mt Pleasant, Harare, Zimbabwe.

Carolyn Sargent: Assistant Professor, Dept of Anthropology, Southern Methodist University, Texas. Author of *The Cultural Context of Therapeutic Choice: obstetric care decisions among the Bariba of Benin* (Dordrecht, 1982). Fieldwork: Atakora & Borgou provinces of the People's Republic of Benin, 1976–7, 1981–2. Present research: health issues in an urban Bariba population. Address: Dept of Anthropology, Southern Methodist University, Dallas, Texas 75238, USA.

I. A. J. Semali: Research Fellow, Traditional Medicine Research Unit,

University of Dar es Salaam. Medically qualified, Dr Semali carried out fieldwork in Kinondoni District of Dar es Salaam in 1983. Address: Traditional Medicine Research Unit, Muhimbili Medical Centre (Faculty of Medicine), University of Dar es Salaam, PO Box 65001, Dar es Salaam, Tanzania.

Harriet Ngubane (alt. Sibisi): Rural Sociologist, London. Author of *Body and Mind in Zulu Medicine*, London, 1977; 'Aspects of clinical practice and traditional organisation of indigenous healers in South Africa', *Social Science and Medicine*, 1981 and more than ten other papers on Zulu society and medical thought. Her more recent work and writing has focused on agriculture in Swaziland, under the auspices of the Overseas Development Administration, London. Address: 31 Ellesmere Road, London W4.

Frants Staugard: Head of the Epidemiology Unit, Ministry of Health, Botswana; formerly, Senior Regional Medical Officer, Botswana. After postgraduate clinical training, he wrote a Master's thesis on 'Traditional medicine in rural Botswana' (Gothenburg, Sweden, 1982); publications include 'Traditional medicine in a developing country' in T. Vaskilampi, C. MacCormack, eds., *Folk Medicine and Health Culture* (Kuopio, 1982), and 'Traditional birth attendants in Botswana', *Botshelo*, 1983. Three monographs, on traditional health care, medicinal plants and maternity care, are in press. Fieldwork was carried out in Botswana, 1978–83. Address: Epidemiology Unit, PO Box 10004, Gaborone, Botswana.

Patrick Twumasi: Professor of Sociology, University of Ghana. Presently Visiting Scholar, Cambridge University; formerly co-ordinator, Community Health Research Unit, Lusaka, Zambia. Author of *Medical Systems in Ghana* (Accra, 1975) and *Catholic Church Hospitals in Ghana* (Catholic Press, Accra, 1982); 'Colonialism & international health', *Social Science and Medicine*, 1981. He has now completed a research report on 'The professionalisation of traditional medicine in Zambia'. Address: c/o Dept of Social Anthropology, Free School Lane, Cambridge CB2 3RQ.

Dennis Michael Warren: Professor of Anthropology, Iowa State University; team leader of USAID-funded Zambia Agricultural Training, Planning & Institutional Development Project, Lusaka. Co-editor of *African Therapeutic Systems* (Los Angeles, 1979) and *Indigenous Knowledge Systems and Development* (Lanham (Maryland), 1980), and author of some sixty articles etc, including 'Ghanaian national policy towards indigenous healers', *Social Science and Medicine*, 1982. Fieldwork has been mainly in Ghana and Zambia, in the course of some twelve years in Africa. Address: Dept of Sociology & Anthropology, Iowa State University, Ames, Iowa 50011, USA.

The following participated in the seminar but their papers could not, regrettably, be included here:

Dr Alya Baffoun, Centre d'Études et de Recherches Economiques et Sociales, Université de Tunis, 23 rue d'Espagne, 1000 Tunis RP, Tunisia. Her paper: 'Ebranlement de la médecine traditionelle et effets "reductionnistes" sur le rituel de la circoncision: cas de la Tunisie'.

Professor Bernardo Bernardi, Universita' di Roma 'La Sapienza', Dipartimento di Studi Glottoantropologici, 00185 Roma, Piazzale Aldo Moro 5, Italy. His paper: 'The human aspects of professionalisation: what should not be lost'.

Dr Christopher Davis-Roberts, Center for Afro-American & African Studies, Dept of Anthropology, University of Michigan, Ann Arbor, Michigan 48109, USA. Her paper: 'Dawa ya kinchi, dawa ya kizungu: the politics of knowledge among the Tabwa of Zaire'.

Professor Kambu Kabangu, Université de Kinshasa, Faculté de Pharmacie, BP 212, Kinshasa XI, Zaire. His paper: 'Contribution à l'étude du savoir médico-pharmaceutique du tradi-practicien Zairois'.

Dr F. M. Mburu, Dept of Community Health, University of Nairobi, Box 30588, Nairobi, Kenya. His paper: 'Professionalisation and differentiation of traditional medicine in Kenya'.

FOREWORD

The International African Seminars and the seminar volumes based upon them are widely regarded as the most important contributions of the International African Institute to African studies. We are thus delighted to present the results of the seminar on 'The Professionalisation of African Medicine' which was held at the University of Botswana, Gaborone, in September 1983, which we hope will be the first of a new series examining topics which are both of academic and practical importance in contemporary Africa. The generally inadequate provision of 'Western' medical services in Africa contributes to the continuing vitality of 'traditional' African medical practices whose role in modern African states is a subject of lively controversy. Traditional African medical practices have thus been examined from many different points of view and not least that of the efficacy of the treatments provided. In treating this subject, therefore, we have been careful to select what we believe to be a neglected and very relevant issue: the professional structure and organisation of traditional medical practitioners and how this is affected by 'Western' medical institutions. The topic is treated comparatively, with contributions ranging geographically from Nigeria to Botswana, and includes extensive documentation on associations of traditional healers which is not readily available elsewhere. We hope that this volume will arouse interest and debate not only among academic Africanists but also among doctors, administrators and politicians with direct responsibility for medical care in Africa.

The Institute is indebted to all the seminar participants who assembled in Botswana and contributed to the lively discussions whose spirit is, I believe, well captured in this volume. We are particularly grateful to the editors and especially to Murray Last, without whose enthusiasm and energy the seminar could scarcely have taken place. The Institute is also deeply grateful for the warmth and skill with which Professors Michael Crowder and Leonard Ngcongco organised the seminar, for the co-operation of the University of Botswana, the Vice-Chancellor, Professor John Turner, for the staff of the two departments most involved, namely the Department of History and the National Institute of Development Research and Documentation. Their support and encouragement made the meeting – so the participants said – almost unique in their experience, and thus greatly enhanced the success of the seminar.

Finally, I wish to thank those organisations without whose financial support the seminar would not have taken place. Through the good offices of Sir Leslie Kirkley, a grant from the Voluntary and Christian Services encouraged the Swedish Agency for Research Co-operation with Developing Countries (SAREC) to add its welcome support, and here we are particularly grateful to Dr Gerhard Hultcrantz. The World Health Organisation and the Commonwealth Foundation provided additional support. Those familiar with the Institute's earlier seminars may recall that the previous programme of seminars was financed largely by a generous grant extending over several years from the Ford Foundation. The situation today is very different. It is proving necessary to seek support from a variety of organisations to cover the costs (moderate though they are) of a single seminar. Our thanks are therefore due to all those who value this work of the Institute and are concerned to maintain the highest standards of research co-operation in African studies inside and outside Africa by supporting us in these aims.

I. M. Lewis
Hon. Director
International African Institute

Introduction Murray Last

THE PROFESSIONALISATION OF AFRICAN MEDICINE: AMBIGUITIES AND DEFINITIONS

Ten years ago the Dingaka Society of Botswana was reported as having received official recognition from the Government, with a mandate to regulate the practice of traditional healing and issue licences to those whom its officers judged to be competent. This prompted Dr Priscilla Ulin, in a short study of Botswana medicine, to comment at the time: 'structurally at least, the organisation of traditional medical practice in Botswana is moving in an increasingly rational direction' – the implied goal then being, I suggest, the status of a profession.[1] Yet apparently the Dingaka Society did not in the event ever perform its expected role. It thus seemed appropriate to hold a conference in Botswana to take stock of developments (and failures) in the organisation of traditional medicine during the last decade – a decade which in Africa perhaps more rapidly than elsewhere has seen the growth of a movement in support of traditional medicine.

Though the various reasons for the movement's success do not concern us here, it is clear that it has drawn together some remarkably diverse interests into a sort of consensus or coalition: Governments (whether parties, bureaucracies or military men) who need both to cut costs and maintain popular support; WHO (or a section within it) urging these governments on with ideas and international pressure; psychiatrists puzzled by solutions to patients' problems in other cultures and pharmacologists on the look-out for new compounds; idealists seeking to develop a truly national medicine and sceptics weary of the medical profession, its claims and its drug companies; radicals of varying persuasion, backing for example the countryside against the town or the 'folk' against the bourgeoisie; or realists who simply remark that 'primary health care' is already, *de facto*, the province of traditional medicine and therefore want local knowledge and skills recognised for what they are. Not surprisingly, then, at conferences no less than in policy debates, there is a danger for discussion to be at cross purposes; and the danger for anyone reading later the printed record of those debates is to be baffled by the apparent contradictions. Though a cynic might suggest that a certain confusion is essential for any coalition (or conference?), in this brief introduction to the conference papers I wish to set out some of the ambiguities and suggest some definitions before the reader embarks on the substantive issues presented in the chapters that follow. For quite apart from any political differences, many have quite divergent assumptions underlying their use of such terms as 'traditional medicine' or 'profession'.

Essentially, such ambiguities arise out of the ambiguous position of traditional medicine itself in most states in recent years. The present position – one of more or less benign neglect – can, I think, be summarised as follows: healers have been left to practise as before, unregulated and unfunded by Government, and largely unaccountable in law for malpractice, manslaughter or fraud. Even where regulations for licensing practitioners and pharmacists have been in existence for several years, the effect nation-wide has been minimal. During this time, academic medicine has used specific healers on an *ad hoc* basis for referrals, for giving medical students an insight into traditional methods of medicine and for carrying out scientific studies on healers' therapeutic techniques or, more often, on their pharmacopoeia with a view to their possible application in hospital clinics. Some would advocate that the position of traditional medicine should be kept ill-defined in this way though its use encouraged and extended piecemeal as conditions suggest. I doubt, however, whether this will prove medically, administratively or politically practicable for much longer now. Governments are being increasingly urged to go beyond merely extending the present *ad hoc* system; instead, they are to incorporate the traditional medical practitioner into some sort of national health service.

AMBIGUITIES

It is at this point that the ambiguities over what people really mean by 'traditional medicine' become apparent. For certain crucial choices have to be made by Government; yet to make these choices requires an unambiguous understanding of what 'traditional medicine' in any one region stands for. As regards the subject of this volume, some of the most important areas of ambiguity are, I suggest, as follows.

1 The initial decision whether:

(*a*) Government should use its own Ministry of Health as the sole regulating, training and managing body, and if necessary dissolve or limit such embryonic professional bodies as have already come into existence; or

(*b*) it should use (or if necessary establish) formal professional institutions.

If the policy is to retain professions, then the second decision a Government has to make is: what niche should practitioners of traditional medicine occupy – are practitioners to be (*a*) subordinate members of health teams within the existing medical profession, or (*b*) autonomous members of a new and independent profession of traditional medicine? If traditional practitioners are to be subordinate, perhaps functioning like extension workers for such departments as Community Medicine, Obstetrics, Orthopaedics, then inevitably they will be given some additional training, with medical and legal responsibility for management lying ultimately with the consultant. In short, the traditional practitioner will at best be 'traditional' only in some 'moonlighting' role; and it is difficult to see how 'traditional medicine' in this context could ever be taught to the next generation except as some 'home remedy'.

2 Underlying the choice between a subordinate or an autonomous role for the traditional practitioner are divergent assumptions as to how or why traditional medicine works. One assumption is that

(*a*) traditional medicine is useful both because it has techniques and drugs that can be usefully added to the stock already in use and because it has personnel who have valuable local insight and experience. By 'useful' here it is usually being implied either (i) that traditional medicine works because it has pharmacologically effective drugs (and therefore these can be used outside their immediate cultural context after evaluation away in a laboratory), or (ii) that the techniques of traditional medicine work particularly well, for example, in psychiatric cases, but are largely ineffective in serious disease. Therefore the assumption here is that the traditional healer has a place locally either in primary health care or for handling specific cases under supervision.

The alternative assumption is that

(*b*) the biomedical model is inadequate, or at best only partially equipped for treating the whole range of illness to be found in Africa; and that what is required, alongside bio-medicine, is a more 'holistic', alternative system, which recognises, for example, both the importance of the mind's control over the body and the effect of the social on the individual. In which case, only an autonomous traditional medicine can develop and sustain this second approach to health. Implied here is that traditional medicine works through a heightened placebo effect (to use a biomedical explanation!) and therefore cannot readily be divorced from its cultural context without losing its efficacy.

3 Underlying these assumptions are assessments of traditional medicine which apparently reflect experiences of widely different medical cultures. No one would seriously expect traditional medical cultures, especially

where ritual and symbolism are important aspects of therapy, to be uniform throughout a continent the size of Africa. Furthermore, it is acknowledged that these medical cultures are, and have been for decades, adapting, adding as well as dropping practices and theories – just as has medical culture elsewhere. At the very least one has to differentiate, for instance between those areas with and without:

(*a*) organised medical 'guilds', with strongly systematised theories of anatomy, illness and treatment, or in some places specialist groups (often mistakenly identified as a sort of 'tribe') which provide medical services over a wider region;

(*b*) complex herbal traditions based either (i) primarily on extensive observation and experimentation, or (ii) primarily on an extensive symbolic system;

(c) complex psychiatric traditions, often using 'spirit possession' as the idiom of therapy;

(d) cultures where sickness is a matter of such paramount concern that it is *the* idiom for articulating disaster and conflict, quite irrespective of the local epidemiology of disease;

(*e*) cultures where sickness is conventionally minimised (again, irrespective of local epidemiology), and illness as well as conflict is expressed in other ways.

Though within most nations there are usually a large number of medical sub-cultures, each with its own characteristics and structure, policy-makers often have in mind apparently a single, paradigmatic culture from which they generalise about 'traditional medicine'. Inevitably such stereotypes are likely to reflect political conditions – as of course happened under colonial rule when traditional healers were categorised as 'witches'.[2] Yet hopes for a rational assessment, performed centrally by Government, of all the variety of medical expertise in a nation are unrealistic. If drugs alone were assessed for their safety, let alone their efficacy (and therapies were left to be reviewed later), the task would still be enormous. Even in Britain 11,000 of the 43,000 drugs on the market still require review.[3]

As if the varieties of traditional medicine did not provide complications enough, in discussions of efficacy it is clear that the analyst tends to have a specific disease, problem or speciality in mind (favourite ones, it seems, are TB, childbirth, bone-setting & psychiatry!). Obviously a person's assessment of traditional medicine will vary according to which paradigmatic illness he has tacitly in mind.

4 Finally, while the term 'traditional medicine' is full of ambiguities, meaning different things to different people, the same is true, of course, of such concepts as 'health'. Conventionally one distinguishes between:

(a) the WHO-style concept of the whole person cured and well in all aspects of life; or

(*b*) the much more limited concept of the individual 'coping' with various impairments and problems, adjusting as best as can to circumstances and avoiding actually ever being 'disabled'.

But others might argue that Government priorities should lie with generating wealth (on the assumption that that leads to health) rather than promoting health *per se*. This in turn may reflect the analyst's political preferences or merely a pragmatic assessment of his nation's manpower, finances and 'political space'. In which case 'traditional medicine' may be used simply as an ill-defined, rag-bag term for what people have always resorted to when left to their own devices.

Ambiguities are, alas, easier to set out than to clear up; and the reader will be quick to point out that what are here presented as stark alternatives are not in practice so clear cut. People can hold contradictory views, propose inconsistent policies – and call it compromise. But in the case of 'traditional medicine', the ambiguities are also, I suspect, essential to its efficacy and its survival, enabling it to adapt to new conditions yet still retain its legitimacy. Ambiguity, then, in analysis may merely reflect the essential ambiguity of the object analysed. If so, professionalisation, in the formal sense, may prove incompatible with 'traditional medicine' as many of us think of it now.

One ambiguity is intentional, however: by 'African medicine' I mean medicine of whatever kind available to the patient in Africa – including, therefore, not only all the varieties of 'traditional medicine' but all the varieties of non-traditional medicine, too, whether Islamic, homoeopathic or 'Western'. For though conventionally one considers 'Western' medicine as a single strictly disciplined system and its practitioners as part of a single hierarchically-organised profession (with sub-divisions, however, like nursing etc.), in practice even this medicine is apt to present itself *to the patient* (at least in a country like Nigeria) as at best a coalition of rival practitioners of varying skill, accessibility and cost. Drugs may in fact be dispensed (albeit illegally, off the hospital premises) by a range of hospital personnel from ward cleaners upwards. Similarly, antibiotic and other drugs are available over the counter (as indeed they are in France), and traders have to learn to help diagnose and dispense imported medicines.

In this context, then, the contrast is not between professional and unprofessional medicine, but between a range of therapeutic systems which are to a varying degree 'professional'. Professionalisation, then, is an issue not only for 'traditional medicine' but for hospital medicine too, where all the usual defining characteristics of a formal 'profession' are not necessarily equally well established. Similarly, the problem is not whether 'traditional medicine' is or was 'professional', but rather why, and in what way, are some medically specialised groups within traditional medicine more 'professional' than others. So what is meant by 'profession'?

DEFINITIONS

As with 'traditional medicine', there are ambiguities in the way the term 'profession' is used; and these ambiguities derive from people's different assumptions about a 'profession' as an institution and their assessments of its contribution to patients' care. But there are, broadly speaking, two current definitions of 'profession', one colloquial, the other technical. The colloquial definition tends to distinguish between professional and amateur, between the profession and the lay public (as 'client' – not 'consumer'!) – in both cases there is implied a specialised skill and a distinct system of training which differentiates 'profession' from any other full-time occupation providing the main source of income. It is not, however, the colloquial definition I want to consider here, though the emphasis on skill and training is crucial, and common to both definitions.

The technical description of a profession lists four critical characteristics which together set a profession off from other less formally constituted occupations.[4] The characteristics are:

(*a*) autonomy: the profession retains a measure of independence through its right to regulate itself; both the profession as a whole and the professional as an individual are thus able to organise and carry out their work without undue interference from the employer or the clients.

(*b*) monopoly: the professional also has a statutory monopoly over a defined sphere of work; the monopoly is maintained by the profession's control over licences to practise its particular kind of expertise – some of the work, however, is divided out among subordinate groups under the profession's control. (Nonetheless, in the case of medicine, there is not necessarily a general monopoly over health care – one can still set up as a healer so long as no false claims are made; similarly self-medication with defined limits is still legal, of course.)

(*c*) ideology of service: a code of ethics governing relations between a professional and the client and limiting competition between professionals is formally set out and can be enforced by the profession's own institutions. Central to the code is an assumption that service should replace self-interest in the performance of professional duties. In return for social recognition of its special status, the profession is accountable to the public for providing the expected level of service.

(*d*) body of esoteric knowledge: a profession is responsible, as 'experts', not only for applying a body of knowledge and skills in practice on behalf of the community but also for teaching and examining recruits to the profession and for promoting research so that the profession can effectively reproduce both its membership and its claim to expert knowledge. The knowledge itself is normally structured in such a way as to be susceptible to standardised instruction and use.

Historically these are the defining characteristics of a select group of privileged occupations – the church, the law and medicine, primarily. Statutes and custom governing these professions have also been built up over time, but especially in nineteenth and twentieth century Britain and the USA, – more so than, say, in France. Developed out of 'guilds', the professions grew, in the case of medicine, through an amalgam of interests – the Royal Colleges and Societies, the hospitals, universities, trade-union-like groups such as the BMA. But the growing power of medicine as a profession should be seen alongside the creation of the newer professions like engineering, architecture, accountancy as part of a wider professional movement. Their history would not concern us here, being, it seems, specific to a period and place in European history, were it not that 'secondary professionalisation' – local professional associations developing out of, or on the lines of, metropolitan professions – is a central issue in the history of African medicine.

One consequence of the particular historical importance of professions in Britain and America is that the literature on professions outside those two countries is sparse.[5] Recent sociological interest in the professions is usually dated back to Carr-Saunders [1933] in Britain and to Talcott Parsons [1951] and Everett Hughes [1958] in America – with the medical profession being a major focus of study.[6] By the late 1960s, professionalisation had become synonymous with modernisation, and it was assumed that everyone would be a professional sooner or later. But just as modernisation theory fell into disrepute, so too the professions became the target of increasingly critical analysis throughout the 1970s: the 'disabling professions' they were called in a popular book.[7] Today the subject of professionalism still rouses sufficient emotion and distaste to inhibit support for it as a conference topic.

Criticism of the medical profession has focused on each aspect. First, its monopolistic position has been reduced, for example by the public's recognition of alternative systems of medicine; as a result, in Britain many 'fringe' therapies are now readily available, including some practised by doctors on the NHS. Second, its autonomy has been undermined by a Government concerned about the costs, whether trying to curtail doctors' freedom to prescribe the drugs they choose, or influencing the way hospitals and services are managed. In consequence, within the profession, the hierarchy has been challenged by subordinate groups such as the nursing profession, the hospital administrators and even the hospital workers' unions. Furthermore, malpractice suits and litigation generally suggest an erosion of confidence, too, while the code of ethics has had to be updated and circulated again.[8] Scepticism over the ideology of service is fuelled in the USA by criticisms of the profits made out of people's sickness. Not surprisingly academic studies are in keeping with this new attitude: concern with institutional order and ideals of service have given way to analyses of 'interests' and conflict.

Far from predicting the professionalisation of everyone, academic forecasts are now for de-professionalisation.[9] The assumption is that video and computer systems will increasingly enable the patient to be diagnosed by machine, and in consequence the specialised skill and expertise will no longer be the province of a medical elite. In practice, certain specialities, such as surgery, are unlikely to be much affected, and the limitations of self-help are well known. But Tanzania's experience (in its Village Health Workers programme) with a non-technological version of this approach to medicine is evidence of its relevance.

The point, here, is that 'professional' is not a simple, changeless attribute – it is politically negotiable. The other important point, however, is that critics object as much to the mystification of medical expertise as to the privileges or costs of the professional system – for it is knowledge that gives medical practitioners their power over patients and patients' kin.

Knowledge as the source of power or authority is central to the notion of 'professional', whether he be a hospital specialist or a practitioner of traditional medicine. If anything, traditional practitioners are usually considered to be more jealous of their craft secrets than are scientists, whose ways of understanding the body, disease etc. are openly taught in schools and published in books (albeit in somewhat abstruse terminology!). The way this specialist knowledge has been built up, almost as a discrete entity outside the common run of learning, and how it continues to be maintained, modified and passed on, has been the other main area of academic research over the last twenty years. Michel Foucault's *Birth of the Clinic* (*Naissance de la Clinique*, 1963), like his earlier *Madness & Civilisation* (*Folie et Déraison*, 1961), pioneered the analysis of the social conditions and processes which enabled the construction of these particular kinds of medical knowledge.[10] Similarly, it is as systems of knowledge that some of the most influential studies have analysed traditional medicine.[11]

Just as in the literature on the professions, so in the last twenty years analyses of systems of knowledge and how they alter over time have undermined the solidity of scientific 'truth' or fact. The result is a certain convergence of the scientific with the traditional: no longer can a facile contrast be made between 'primitive' and 'scientific', at least in the sphere of thought.[12] The privileged possession of 'knowledge' and the potential for power that it offers have been seen in all kinds of medicine as means for extracting advantages and manipulating the rest of the community.

Although much of the literature may be written in, and about, Europe and America, the issues are of course debated quite as fiercely in Africa, in universities and elsewhere. In Nigeria, for example, television drama serials (like *Hospital*, scripted in Yoruba) are explicitly raising the same problems, though from the public's perspective and with greater ambivalence than *Dr Kildare*.[13] Likewise there is considerable discussion in the press, as when for example the Association of Nigerian Medical Practitioners in the USA, in a forty-page letter to the Nigerian President, demanded less 'hard conditions of service' as a pre-condition for any of them agreeing to return to practise in Nigeria.[14] I have heard Nigerian doctors argue that the professional ethic of public service can no longer be taken for granted and anyway cannot really be enforced, whilst elsewhere it is the profession's autonomy that is said to be at risk.

Given the debates within the medical profession, it was inevitable that traditional healers would become involved in these issues too. Indeed, healers' associations, though they may have made little headway at the time, have been in existence in countries like Nigeria and Ghana since the 1930s and thus ante-date some of their hospital colleagues' organisations; in some areas, too, practitioners have been organised, since before the colonial period, into what might be called a profession (though more often they are referred to as guilds or corporations).[15] But when healers' associations award their members PhDs, MAs etc., and healers start using, and are given publicly (for example on TV), the title of Doctor, – it is then that the importance of professional qualifications, the restrictions on the use of titles and the question of the public's confidence in them become subjects of urgent debate. For titles are symbols and guarantors of expert 'knowledge'; and it is by its 'knowledge' that a profession ultimately defines itself.

PROFESSIONALISATION IN AFRICA: A HYPOTHESIS

Here I would like to put forward a general hypothesis that arises out of the definitions of professional medicine discussed above. Much of my thinking, of course, is based on West Africa, and specifically on Nigeria, where I have worked intermittently since 1961.

For most of the colonial period the medical profession *as a profession* scarcely existed in either anglophone or francophone Africa.[16] Doctors were appointed and worked as virtual civil servants, and though, like other technical staff, they may have been often in confiict with administrative personnel, they equally often assumed official powers (sometimes, but not always, in an 'emergency') as *de facto* members of the colonial government. In some francophone areas, and particularly in the early period, they were often under military discipline. The ambiguous position of doctors, in government service and with limited professional status, is perhaps most acutely (notoriously?) shown by the dilemma of prison doctors. Missionary doctors were anomalous in a different way – but they too have at the very least a divided allegiance to medicine. In addition, particularly again in francophone areas, it was the colonial authorities (and not the profession) who decided whether or not a doctor's professional qualifications, if derived from somewhere other than the metropolitan power, were acceptable in that colony. For most of the colonial period, too, doctors in African countries were too few to constitute a local autonomous professional association (only Sierra Leone stands out as a possible exception, outside the settler-dominated territories), and too cut off from colleagues in the metropolitan countries to be within the otherwise pervasive professional structure. Certainly in the eyes of the public, doctors in the colonial period were not recognised as members of some autonomous organisation called a 'medical profession'!

By contrast the African members of the 'learned professions' during the colonial period relied on their professional status to overcome (with varying success, it should be said) the racial discrimination against them. For them, from a very early period, professionalisation was of paramount importance – and it did not matter whether the profession was medicine, the law or the church. In consequence, their emphasis was more on local unity among professionals than on the organisation of a particular profession itself (and in this their position was closer to that of professionals in France or Germany).

If this analysis is correct, the medical and ancillary professions, as self-conscious *professions* in Africa, are relatively new, dating back to the 1950s for the most part, when African doctors greatly increased in numbers, when private practice outside government or mission hospitals became increasingly common, when university medical schools and teaching hospitals were established – and indeed the whole paraphernalia of a formal profession of medicine (including often a version of the 'British Medical Association') were gradually instituted and won formal recognition from the government and public alike. The process of professionalisation became part of decolonisation; it coincided with the Africanisation of staff and curriculum; it was to prove, proudly, that the new independent states were not content with second best, with having only 'sub-standard' para-medicals as their doctors. In short, it accompanied the establishment of a middle class whose legitimacy was based on educational attainments, a meritocracy to be open to all yet independent of commercial wealth or traditional power. The impetus and rationale, however, behind this new professionalisation were not just applied modernisation theory, etc., but, more importantly, that old, original professional tradition which had been maintained despite the odds, in some cases ever since the nineteenth century, by the families who pioneered higher education.

In this context traditional medicine was viewed initially with some suspicion. Whereas some of the earliest African doctors wrote their medical theses explaining and sometimes defending traditional treatments, now in the 1950s and 1960s their descendants tended largely to ignore the traditional healers – unless the direr consequences of their ministrations directly affected out-patients' clinics; perhaps more sharply antagonistic to traditional medicine (and much closer to the generality of patients) were the nurses and dispensary attendants. It seems too that the public began to take more eagerly to experimenting with the new, much extended facilities that were becoming available in rural as well as urban areas, not least because they cost very little and were staffed by people who understood them.

As a result, what we are now seeing, is a kind of 'second generation' of traditional healers who have adapted their methods to meet the competition, and organised themselves to defend their right to practise against criticism from an expanding medical profession.[17] The prize is recognition from the government, and ultimately a share in the salaries, supplies and buildings provided by government. Their moves have coincided with a crisis in the medical profession, a crisis among whose symptoms are doctors' strikes, shortages of equipment, a sharp rise in the unofficial costs to the public of obtaining treatment and a realisation on the public's part that hospital medicine might not cure everything. For some doctors, particularly those from the older professional families, the crisis threatens all that they have stood for and, if unchecked, might result eventually in a form of de-professionalisation. On the other hand, the expansion in numbers and the rising assertiveness of the new doctors make them an even more formidable opponent for any potential rival.

It is at this juncture that the incorporation of traditional healers into a national health service has become a possibility. Obviously, to incorporate healers as subordinates within an expanding medical profession is an attractive solution for some (in Britain, the official term is a 'profession supplementary to medicine'). But given the way healers' associations have grown again in response to a more assertive medical profession, it was likely that these associations would become a focus of resistance to any policy of absorption, and claim instead that they might fulfil the functions of a fully independent profession. The danger, however, is that they would be called upon to be no less professional than the medical profession; and this, as we have seen, means a formal systematisation of 'knowledge'.

If, as the price for such recognition, it was demanded that the credentials of their members should be examined to a uniform standard, that the efficacy and safety of their treatments should be tested, and practice sufficiently standardised to guarantee, at least in theory, a uniform quality of care, then of necessity colleges of traditional medicine would have to be organised, with a curriculum incorporating both the theoretical and the empirical basis of the particular traditional medical system being taught – but it would still have to be taught in a way that would satisfy the ambitions and intellectual expectations of school-leavers who were of sufficient calibre to ensure that traditional medicine remained a viable, respected calling. Obvious models for such a college are the Indian Ayurvedic and Unani schools of medicine, some of whose problems have been examined sympathetically by Charles Leslie in a series of papers over the last fifteen years.[18]

But whereas Ayurvedic and Unani (Islamic) medicine both have a large corpus of ancient literature in which their formal theories and practices have been set out, few if any systems of traditional medicine in Africa have such a corpus. Furthermore, some of the more efficacious treatments may not be part of a *system* at all. The prospect, then, of formal colleges of traditional medicine is daunting – I would say unrealistic on this scale: for no less than a fundamental construction of what will in effect be a new medical system is required. Yet unless something like that happens – so the argument goes – traditional healers will be marginal, potentially suspect as quacks and unable to attract adequate recruits. Their status in courts of law will be problematic, whether as expert witnesses or as defendants in malpractice suits, and as such always open to the risk of being legislated out of existence.

Healers' associations, of course, need not be caught in such a trap. One alternative is not to seek national status as a profession but rather to set up local schools limited to specialising in teaching and perfecting a specific technique (of bone-setting, for example) or in a specific field (like psychiatry), much as osteopathy, acupuncture or psycho-analysis are taught elsewhere. And no doubt in some countries an alternative model for therapy, based on a radically different understanding of, say, the properties of herbs, might be developed in a systematised way and proved efficacious outside its cultural context – much as homoeopathy has proved popular in Brazil, and effective too in as unlikely, culture-free a setting as veterinary medicine.

CONSTRAINTS

One final area of ambiguity concerns the law. Broadly speaking, under the several Medical Practitioners Acts herbalists have not been forbidden to practise 'native medicine' (as it used to be called). By contrast, under the various Witchcraft Suppression Acts (many of which have been re-enacted since independence), healers are committing a criminal offence if for example, in diagnosing the cause of illness through divination or the use of ordeals and oaths, they identify a specific 'witch' or sorcerer as the agent responsible.[19] The legal logic for these Acts which simply made the whole matter of witchcraft potentially criminal was to avoid many of the complications of proving slander or fraud and restrict the consequences arising from debates over what was 'reasonable belief' or what evidence was required to prove that a 'witch' had indeed caused some disaster. But knowing the statutes governing traditional medicine is one thing – it is quite another to discover the current policies of the local police, the prosecuting authorities or the different levels of courts towards cases of witchcraft.

Nonetheless, in areas where beliefs in witches and sorcerers – and not just ancestors or spirits – are an integral part of traditional diagnosis and therapy, the law is perhaps the most significant among many factors external to traditional medicine which are determining what constitutes acceptable practice (if not acceptable 'knowledge'). As attempts to repeal the law have tended to show, the law has sufficient symbolic importance to unite the opponents of traditional medicine, whose grounds for opposition are otherwise very varied. The main grounds are:

(*a*) political ideology – especially for Marxisant governments such as Mozambique's on the grounds that healers were, and potentially still are, part of the old 'feudal' system, unproductive, giving support to chiefs, furthering 'superstition' and liable to exploit the poor in their need;

(*b*) religious doctrine – held not only by Christians (in certain West African Aladura churches for example, as well as in missions) but also by strict Muslims who oppose particular types of traditional medicine as basically Satanic;

(*c*) scientific and practical reasons – most obviously by members of hospital-based professions, but also by others of a strictly rationalist persuasion (not necessarily all members of the educated elite), who object not only to the delays in effective treatment but also to the deaths or serious injuries caused by misplaced attempts at healing.

(*d*) opposition to the 'underworld' of traditional medicine. Popular culture (and not merely colonialist mythology) has a marked suspicion of medicine misused – as attendance at local law courts or regular reading of the popular press will demonstrate; similarly, an air of outrage (and anxiety) surrounds politicians who are widely assumed to make use of dubious healers in their pursuit (and exercise) of power.

While the first two sets of arguments would seek to have traditional medicine outlawed, the last two more often lead to demands for stricter control over healers. An important consequence of this opposition is that potential leaders of professional associations require more than therapeutic skills: they are functioning perforce in a political arena where the odds are weighted against them. In these circumstances, professional organisation becomes more a matter of self-defence than a claim to monopoly.

The very ambiguity of the law as it is operated in practice to-day is but one element in the wider political debate. For any profession of traditional medicine, no less than the law, has to be seen to have an interest in curbing the criminal element among healers, whether as 'quacks' or as 'trouble-makers'. The difficulty, of course, lies not in the rhetoric but how (or whether) to specify who exactly constitutes this criminal element in practice.[20]

'Medicalising' the relevant, previously religious terminology becomes thus a conscious attempt to shift the ground of this often sterile yet heated debate and make us re-think our categories. It also reflects what has long been happening already in many parts of Africa. Thus the term 'healers' now has to include diviners, mediums, 'witch-doctors' as well as herbalists; 'therapy', 'treatment' includes rituals and symbolic instruments as well as various potions, lotions, inhalants (of the sort that in earlier accounts of anointing ceremonies might have been called unguents, incense). To medicalise the vocabulary in this way is more than mere semantic piracy: it marks a serious redirection of interest away from the causes of illness and misfortune and towards the patient and his body; away from a preoccupation with 'primitive thought' and towards the individual quest for therapy, the problems of efficacy and coping; towards, too, what policies governments should espouse in the field of health.

Similarly, in the field of law, illness and misfortune are apt to be labelled, especially in southern Africa, as offences against a person or his property; the diviner is seen as a detective, the witch as a criminal, the patient as victim; the penalties are paid, restitution made. Indeed, given the extraordinary concern to use 'law' as the main means of social control in southern Africa (and as a consequence, the traditional preoccupation of social anthropologists in that region with law), one might argue that it is the language of law – and not religion – that is being replaced by medicine as the idiom of misfortune. Thus the importance given to debates over repealing Witchcraft Suppression Acts, and the significance of professionalisation as conferring on traditional medicine the whole structure of legality, may be a reflection of the pervasiveness culturally of the legal idiom in central and southern Africa – and the need there now to narrow down for people the intellectual space allowed to sources of social conflict. Thus the ambiguities in 'traditional medicine' may continue to play in certain states a peculiarly significant role – in politics if not in academic analysis!

IN CONCLUSION

The questions, then, that I have sought to prompt by this introduction are:

1 What, in any particular state, exactly *is* the 'traditional medicine' (or the aspect of it) that is to be organised, possibly as a 'profession'; and what precisely are policy-makers' assumptions about this traditional medicine?

2 What will be the consequences for the very varied expertise within traditional medicine if it is the expertise too – and not just the experts – that is to be rationally organised, as a 'profession' apparently requires, at least in the long term?

3 What have been the pressures – historical, political, medical; local and international – for advocating in Africa *now* the professional organisation of medicine (of whatever kind)?
4 What social constraints are there on the form that professional organisation (and its construction of professional knowledge) will take in any particular state? What, in short, is the particular compromise now being worked out for each kind of 'traditional medicine'?

I have sought here only to set out the ambiguities in the use of the terms 'traditional medicine' and 'profession'. I am aware that they are also used as ideology, embedded within an actual political process. The danger, it seems to me, is that the politics of professionalisation will overshadow all other issues – principal of which is the problem of how best to give patients the care that cures them. Though power undoubtedly has its place in therapy, effective traditional medicine, as I understand it, is usually more subtle and uncertain (if not more fragile) than the politicians of medicine seem to remember in the heat of debate.

That there exists at present some 'political space' for all the varieties of traditional medicine is clear. However, any purely political solution to how to accommodate traditional medicine may prove in the long term deceptive. For though 'professionalisation' is at one level all about power (and thus offers immediate scope for political solutions), at another level it is about the long-term structuring of a specific kind of knowledge, and about how to transmit what is still relevant of it to the next generation. The ultimate test of this knowledge will be not in its political successes, however – though these should not be discounted – but in its success with patients as therapy. And that is much harder to judge.

NOTES

1 Ulin, P. R., (1975) 'The traditional healer of Botswana in a changing society', *Botswana Notes & Records*, 7, p. 101. The article is also in *Rural Africana*, 26, 1974, pp. 123–30, and in Ademuwagun, Z. A., et al. (eds.) (1979) *African Therapeutic Systems*. Waltham: Crossroads Press, pp. 243–6. In Lesotho similarly, the Natural Therapeutic Practitioners Association was granted in 1976 powers to certify traditional healers as qualified to practise under the Natural Therapeutic Practitioners Act (no. 14, 1976, sect. 4.1.a) but nothing apparently came of it (cf. the amending Act, no. 6, 1978); homoeopaths, osteopaths, etc also came under this Act. I am grateful to Professor Michael Crowder for sending me Ulin's article. I am also very grateful to Professors J. F. A. Ajayi and M. G. Smith and to Dr Richard Rathbone for their help in revising this chapter.

2 Stereotypes can alter subtly over time. For example, 'witch-doctor' means, and meant in the past, a doctor to cure witchcraft (on the analogy that an eye doctor treats eyes). The term, however, has gradually come to mean a doctor who is also a witch – that is, a 'witchdoctor' (cf. 'barber-surgeon'). There is yet to be a detailed analysis of how this semantic shift came about. It is tempting to link the shift to the rise of missionary-run medicine and its allies, but there was a strong political

element too in the campaign against 'witch-doctors' (e.g. in southern Africa in the 1840s, and in East and West Africa in the early 1900s).

3 Goldberg, A., *et al.* (1983) 'A prescribers' guide to the approval and surveillance of medicine'. *Prescribers' Journal*, 23, 3 (June), p. 54.

4 It is important to recognise that a 'profession' is itself a continuing compromise, and the 'characteristics' are but key items in that compromise.

For a new work on the professions (with a useful bibliography), see Dingwall, R. and Lewis, P., (eds.) (1983) *The Sociology of the Professions*. London: Macmillan.

The main recent texts on the subject are: Freidson, E., (1970) *Profession of Medicine*. New York: Dodd, Mead; also his *Professional Dominance*, New York, Atherton Press, 1970; Johnson, T. J., (1972) *Professions and Power*. London: Macmillan; Berlant, J. L., (1975), *Profession & Monopoly*. Berkeley: Univ. of California Press; Parry, N. C. A., and Parry, J., (1976), *The Rise of the Medical Profession*. London: Croom Helm; Larson, M. S., (1977), *The Rise of Professionalism*. Berkeley: University of California Press. On the medical profession and its politics, *cf.*: Eckstein, H., (1960), *Pressure Group Politics*. London: Allen & Unwin; Starr, P., (1982), *The Social Transformation of American Medicine*, New York: Basic Books.

Collections of essays include: Jackson, J. A., (ed.), (1970), *Professions and Professionalisation*. Cambridge: University Press; Lorber, J., and Freidson, E., (eds.), (1972), *Medicine Men and their Work*. Chicago: Aldine; Freidson, E., (ed.), (1973), *The Professions & their Prospects*. Beverly Hills: Sage; Halmos, P., (ed.), (1973), *Professionalisation and Social Change*, Keele: Sociological Review; Stacey, M., *et al.* (eds.), (1977), *Health and the Division of Labour*. London: Croom Helm.

5 An exception is the essay by Johnson, T. J., 'Imperialism & the professions', in Halmos, P., (ed.) (1973) *Professionalisation & Social Change*. Keele, pp. 281–309. On the new medical professions in Zaire see de Craemer, W. and Fox, R. C., (1968), *The Emerging Physician*. Stanford: Hoover Institution; for Ghana, see Bennell, P., 'Professionalisation: the case of pharmacy in Ghana', *Social Science & Medicine*, 16, 1, 1982, 601–7. The legal profession in Africa, by contrast, has been studied: *cf.* Adewoye, O., (1968), *The Legal Profession in Southern Nigeria. 1863–1943*, PhD thesis, Columbia University; and the recent work of Robin Luckham and others on the Ghanaian legal profession (e.g. in Dias, C. J., (ed.), (1981), *Lawyers in the Third World*. Uppsala: Scandinavian Institute of African Studies.

6 Carr-Saunders, A. M., (1928), *Professions: their organisation and place in society*. Oxford: Clarendon; &, with Wilson, P. A., (1933), *The Professions*, London: Oxford University Press; Parsons, T., (1951), *The Social System*. Glencoe: Free Press, (esp. ch.X); Hughes, E., (1958), *Men and their Work*, Glencoe: Free Press.

7 Illich, I., (1977), *Disabling Professions*. London: M. Boyars.

8 General Medical Council (1983), *Professional Conduct & Discipline: fitness to practise*, London.

9 Haug, M. R., (1973), 'Deprofessionalisation', in Halmos, P., (ed.) (1973) *Professionalisation & Social Change*. Keele, pp. 195–211.

10 Foucault, M., (1961), *Folie et Déraison*. Paris: Plon, (re-issued, 1975, as *Histoire de la Folie*: English translation, *Madness & Civilisation*, 1965); *Naissance de la Clinique*, Paris, Presses Universitaires de France, 1963 (English translation, *Birth of the Clinic*, 1973). *Cf.* Leonard, J., (1981), *La Médecine entre les Pouvoirs et les Savoirs*, Paris: Aubier Montaigne.

For a recent collection of essays using this approach, see Wright, P., and Treacher, A., (eds.), (1982), *The Problem of Medical Knowledge*. Edinburgh: University Press.

11 *Cf.* the studies of V. Turner on the Ndembu of Zambia (1967) *Forest of*

Symbols, Ithaca: Cornell U.P.; (1968), *Drums of Affliction*, Oxford: Clarendon; Buxton, J., (1973), *Religion & Healing in Mandari*, Oxford: Clarendon; or the classic by Evans-Pritchard, E., (1937), *Witchcraft, Oracles & Magic among the Azande*, Oxford: Clarendon.

In works of this 'school', the boundary between religion and medicine is often so slight that studies in the anthropology of religion, ritual and symbolism contain much that is relevant to traditional medical thought (e.g. Middleton, J., (1960), *Lugbara Religion*, London: OUP for the International African Institute, ch. III.1).

12 *Cf.* Robin Horton's re-appraisal, 'Tradition & modernity revisited' in Hollis, M., and Lukes, S., (eds.), (1982), *Rationality & Relativism*, Oxford: Blackwell.

13 Adejobi Theatre Company (1982), *Ile Iwosan*. Ibadan: Television Service of Oyo State. I am grateful to Dr Karin Barber for discussions on this serial of 13 half-hour episodes.

14 *Cf. West Africa*, issue 3439, 11 July 83, p. 1609. More general moral issues in Nigeria (e.g. strikes by doctors) were discussed in 1982 at a workshop at the College of Medicine, Lagos and published as Akpata, E. S., (ed.), (1982), *Medical Ethics*, Lagos: Lagos University Press.

15 *Cf.* Ojo-Cole Institute of National Therapeutics (Lagos, *ca.* 1926); Society of African Herbalists (Accra, 1931). For an example of a pre-colonial organisation of healers, see Maier, D., (1979), 'Nineteenth century Asante medical practices', *Comparative Studies in Society & History*, 21, pp. 63–81.

16 This is the general assessment too of T. J. Johnson in his essay (pp. 287–93) quoted in note 5 above. Before 1902, when there was formed a separate West African Medical Staff (from which African doctors were effectively barred), African and European doctors in anglophone areas had been directly employed by government agencies, with the African doctors often proving more popular – because more professional – with European patients than their European colleagues. But since 1878, African Doctors had been paid less, and usually confined permanently to the rank of Assistant Surgeon. The new Colonial Medical Service, from the mid-1930s on, may have served to make the European colonial doctor more a professional and less a local civil servant by enabling him to move from one colony to another. But this 'internationalisation' of medical practice was apparently not permitted to the African doctor: instead, medical schools were set up to give local, 'licentiate' qualifications to African medical staff (as had been done in francophone West Africa since 1918 at Dakar). Otherwise, perhaps the major issue in colonial medical politics was whether or not government doctors should be permitted also to practise privately – an issue the profession still clings to as evidence of their autonomy (and of their entrepreneurial rather than merely bureaucratic role). The distinction for the medical profession between 'government service' and 'a state service' is crucial; for this reason, fees, for example, had to continue to be charged in colonial government hospitals.

Some of the more accessible histories of colonial medicine in West Africa are Schram, R., (1971), *A History of the Nigerian Health Services*, Ibadan: University Press; Patterson, K. D., (1981), *Health in Colonial Ghana*, Waltham: Crossroads Press; Adeloye, A., (1971), *Nigerian Pioneers of Modern Medicine*, Ibadan: University Press; Sabben-Clare, E. E., *et al.* (eds.) (1980), *Health in Tropical Africa during the Colonial Period*, Oxford: Clarendon; Gale, T. S., (1973), 'Official Medical Policy in British West Africa', PhD thesis, London University; Lasker, J., (1976), 'Health Care & Society in the Ivory Coast', PhD thesis, Harvard University.

17 It is the international aspect of the healers' lobby in the 1960s and 1970s that is most visible – not least because its activities are recorded in print! See for example the First Inter-African Conference on Medicinal Plants (Dakar, 1968), the Pan-

African Conference on Research into Medicinal Plants (Ife, 1974; proceedings published as Sofowora, A., (ed.), (1979), *African Medicinal Plants*, Ile-Ife, the AFRO Technical Report Series, 1 (1976), *African Traditional Medicine*, (Brazzaville), and WHO Technical Report Series, 622, (1978), *The Promotion and Development of Traditional Medicine*, (Geneva). Local lobbying, though much less well documented, is probably more significant, and therefore urgently needs recording.

18 Leslie, C., (1968), 'The professionalisation of Ayurvedic and Unani medicine', reprinted in Freidson, E., and Lorber, J., (eds.), (1972), *Medical Men & their Work*, Chicago: Aldine, pp. 39–54; 'The professionalising ideology of medical revivalism', in Singer, M., (ed.), (1973), *Entrepreneurship & the Modernisation of Occupational Cultures in South Asia*. Durham: Duke University Press; 'The modernisation of Asian medical systems', in Poggie, J., and Lynch, R., (eds.), (1976), *Rethinking Modernisation*. Westport: Greenwood, pp. 69–108; 'The ambiguities of medical revivalism in modern India', in Leslie, C., (ed.), (1974), *Asian Medical Systems*, Berkeley: University of California Press, 356–67; 'Pluralism and integration in the Indian and Chinese medical systems', in Kleinman, A., *et al.* (eds.), (1976), *Medicine in Chinese Cultures*, ch. 24, pp. 401–17, National Institutes of Health.

I am grateful to Professor Leslie for a discussion of his views. The literature on the medical profession in China is also relevant, especially the work of Unschuld, P., (1971), 'Medico-cultural conflicts in Asian settings', *Social Science & Medicine*, 9, pp. 303–12; (1979), *Medical Ethics in Imperial China*, Berkeley: University of California Press). But the recent context is very different: during the cultural revolution, the All China Association of Traditional Chinese Medicine was dissolved, along with other professional bodies, only to be revived in 1978 (Hillier, C. M., and Jewell, J. A., (1983), *Health Care & Traditional Medicine in China 1800–1982*. London: Routledge and Kegan Paul, 326).

19 For example: Nigeria – Medical & Dental Practitioners Act, 1963, no. 9, section 14(6); Tanzania – Medical Practitioners & Dentists Ordinance, 1959, no. 1, section 37. On witchcraft: e.g. Nigeria – Criminal Code Ordinance 1916, section 210; Northern Nigeria, Penal Code Law, 1960, ch. XVII; Tanzania – *Revised Laws*, 1961, chap. 18, supp. 56.

In southern Africa the Natal Code of Native Law (1891; *cf.* the draft section 137 of the Native Territories Penal Code for Transkei, 1883) – unlike Cape Colony law – had recognised traditional herbal medicine and required practitioners to be licensed. While Zimbabwe inherited the basic Cape law on this matter, East and Central African states apparently were more influenced by practice in Natal. The Acts, however, against witch finding, ordeals and witchcraft were more or less uniform. Though these Acts date back in Africa specifically to a Cape statute of 1895 (no. 2), they are drawn ultimately from English laws of 1736 and 1824. In the 1840s there was apparently a concerted drive against 'witch-doctors': the Sotho King, Moshweshwe, himself banned independently the killing of supposed 'witches', while D'Urban's treaties of this period include specific clauses against 'witch-doctors'; this general attitude was then carried over into the new penal codes for 'native territories'. The slight but curious variations in the colonial Acts, and the ideas behind the Acts themselves, were strongly criticised in 1934 by Orde Brown, G. St J., 'Witchcraft & British colonial law', and Roberts, J. C., 'Witchcraft & colonial legislation', in *Africa*, VIII, 1935, pp. 481–7 & pp. 488–93. A much earlier, indigenous objection was written, necessarily pseudonymously given the law, by 'Ngxakaxa': 'On Witchcraft', *Cape Law Journal*, VIII, 1891, pp. 210–18. More recent discussions are: Mutungi, O. K., (1977), *The Legal Aspects of Witchcraft in East Africa*, Nairobi: East African Literature Bureau; Chavunduka, G. L., (1980),

'Witchcraft & the Law in Zimbabwe,' *Zambezia*, VIII, ii, pp. 129–47. A recent brief discussion of contemporary medical legislation is by Stepan, J., (1982), 'The pattern of legislation concerning traditional medicine', ch. 27 in Bannerman, R. H., *et al.* (eds.), *Traditional Medicine and Health Care Coverage*, Geneva: WHO, pp. 290–313.

20 The issue is further complicated by the argument – to be heard in both western and southern Africa – that whereas the healers of old were genuinely therapeutic, the present generation are ignorant of past skills and thus necessarily 'charlatans'. This raises the hoary problem, of course, of what is 'traditional' in the context of knowledge, and calls into question from the very outset the possibility of reconstituting a 'traditional' profession and ensuring for it an expertise that will be widely recognised, even on its own terms, as truly 'professional'.

1 Headquarters: the original ZINATHA head office in Harare (Zimbabwe).

MBUYA NEHANDA
AND SEKURU KAGUVI

BUYA NEHANDA
AND SEKURU KAGUVI

FOR
TRADITIONAL
MEDICAL
PRACTITIONERS

TRADITIONAL
MEDICAL
PRACTITIONERS
Including
SPIRIT MEDIUMS

Certificate of Registration

This is to Certify that..
is a member of Zimbabwe National Traditional Healers Association and is Authorised to practice within the terms of the Traditional Medical Practitioners Act, No. 38 of 1981.

To Whom it May Concern

This Certificate is issued within the Traditional Medical Practitioners Act, No. 38 of 1981, (Section 18) and the holder is entitled to the rights pertaining to privileges of that Act.

The Association's Constitution has been approved by the Minister of Health of the Republic of Zimbabwe.

Date.............................. Signed by..............................
President
THE ZIMBABWE NATIONAL TRADITIONAL HEALERS ASSOCIATION

2 Certificate: Zimbabwe National Traditional Healers Association. A formal register of certified practitioners is also published (the two figures shown at the top of the certificate were healers who led the resistance to British colonialism in 1897).

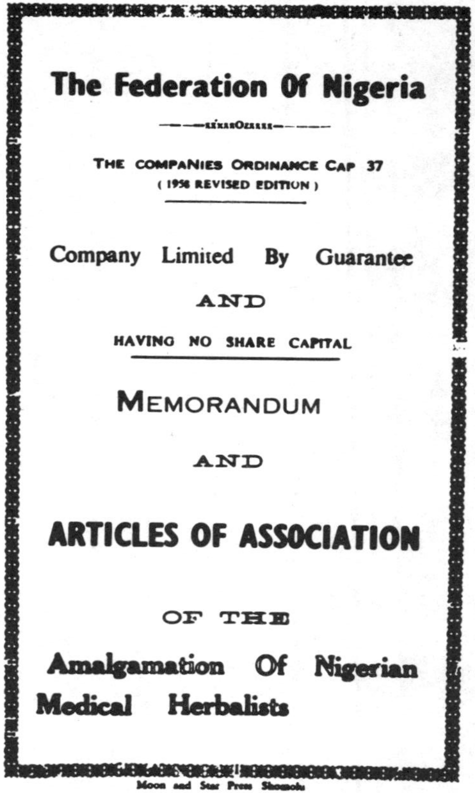
The Federation Of Nigeria

THE COMPANIES ORDINANCE CAP 37
(1958 REVISED EDITION)

Company Limited By Guarantee

AND

HAVING NO SHARE CAPITAL

MEMORANDUM

AND

ARTICLES OF ASSOCIATION

OF THE

Amalgamation Of Nigerian Medical Herbalists

Moon and Star Press Shomolu

3 Certificates: Amalgamation of Nigerian Medical Herbalists (Lagos) – *left*: Qualified membership certificate *right*: Formal documentation as a limited company

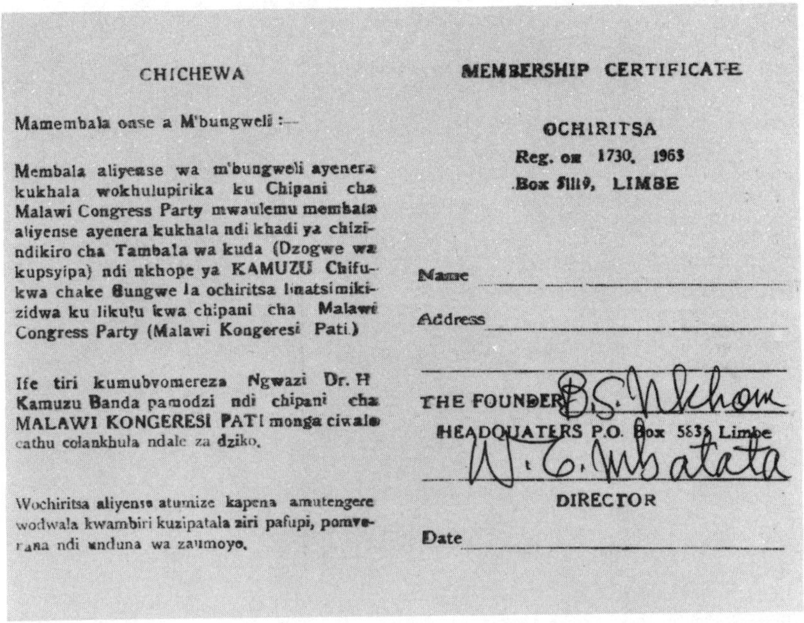

CHICHEWA

Mamembala onse a M'bungweli :—

Membala aliyense wa m'bungweli ayenera kukhala wokhulupirika ku Chipani cha Malawi Congress Party mwaulemu membala aliyense ayenera kukhala ndi khadi ya chizindikiro cha Tambala wa kuda (Dzogwe wa kupsyipa) ndi nkhope ya KAMUZU Chifukwa chake Bungwe la ochiritsa limatsimikizidwa ku likulu kwa chipani cha Malawi Congress Party (Malawi Kongeresi Pati.)

Ife tiri kumubvomereza Ngwazi Dr. H Kamuzu Banda pamodzi ndi chipani cha MALAWI KONGERESI PATI monga ciwalo cathu colankhula ndalc za dziko.

Wochiritsa aliyense atumize kapena amutengere wodwala kwambiri kuzipatala ziri pafupi, pomverana ndi unduna wa zaumoyo.

MEMBERSHIP CERTIFICATE

OCHIRITSA

Reg. on 1730, 1968

Box 5119, LIMBE

Name ______

Address ______

______

THE FOUNDER B.S. Nkhoma

HEADQUATERS P.O. Box 5835 Limbe

N. C. Mbatata

DIRECTOR

Date ______

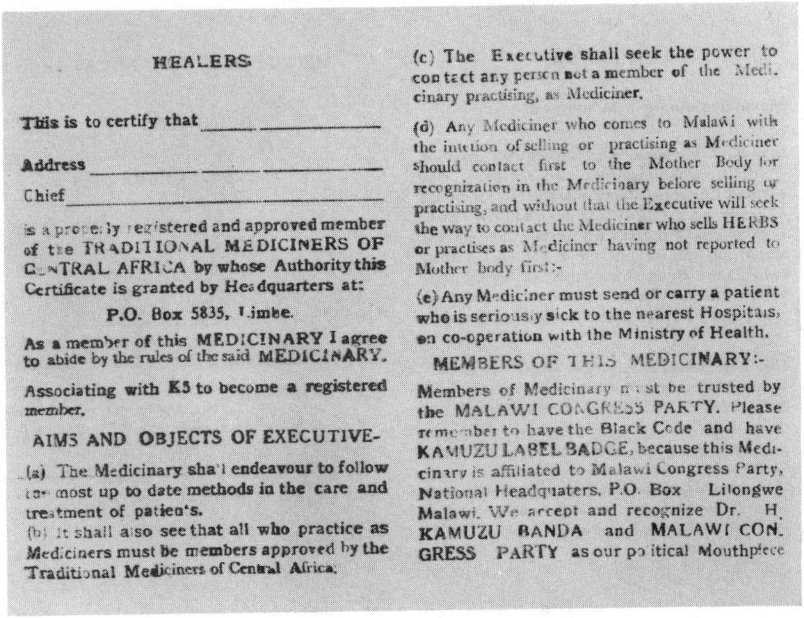

HEALERS

This is to certify that ______

Address ______

Chief ______

is a properly registered and approved member of the TRADITIONAL MEDICINERS OF CENTRAL AFRICA by whose Authority this Certificate is granted by Headquarters at:

P.O. Box 5835, Limbe.

As a member of this MEDICINARY I agree to abide by the rules of the said MEDICINARY.

Associating with K5 to become a registered member.

AIMS AND OBJECTS OF EXECUTIVE-

(a) The Medicinary shall endeavour to follow the most up to date methods in the care and treatment of patients.

(b) It shall also see that all who practice as Mediciners must be members approved by the Traditional Mediciners of Central Africa.

(c) The Executive shall seek the power to contact any person not a member of the Medicinary practising, as Mediciner.

(d) Any Mediciner who comes to Malawi with the intetion of selling or practising as Mediciner should contact first to the Mother Body for recognization in the Medicinary before selling or practising, and without that the Executive will seek the way to contact the Mediciner who sells HERBS or practises as Mediciner having not reported to Mother body first:-

(e) Any Mediciner must send or carry a patient who is seriously sick to the nearest Hospitals, on co-operation with the Ministry of Health.

MEMBERS OF THIS MEDICINARY:-

Members of Medicinary must be trusted by the MALAWI CONGRESS PARTY. Please remember to have the Black Code and have KAMUZU LABEL BADGE, because this Medicinary is affiliated to Malawi Congress Party, National Headquaters, P.O. Box Lilongwe Malawi. We accept and recognize Dr. H. KAMUZU BANDA and MALAWI CONGRESS PARTY as our political Mouthpiece

4 Membership card: Herbalists Association of Malawi *or* Ochiritsa ('Healers')

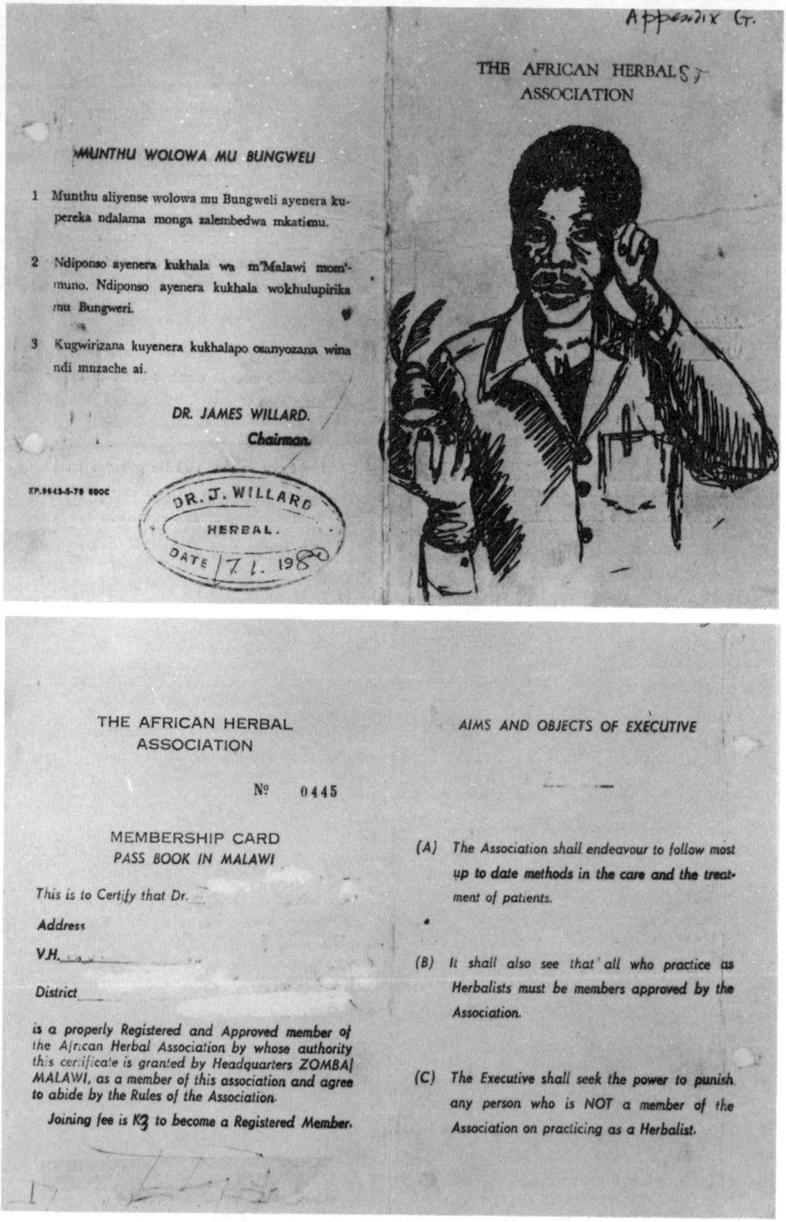

Appendix G.

THE AFRICAN HERBALS ASSOCIATION

MUNTHU WOLOWA MU BUNGWELI

1 Munthu aliyense wolowa mu Bungweli ayenera kupereka ndalama monga zalembedwa mkatimu.

2 Ndiponso ayenera kukhala wa m'Malawi mom'-muno. Ndiponso ayenera kukhala wokhulupirika mu Bungweri.

3 Kugwirizana kuyenera kukhalapo osanyozana wina ndi mnzache ai.

DR. JAMES WILLARD.
Chairman.

EP.9643-5-78 600C

DR. J. WILLARD
HERBAL.
DATE 7.1. 1980

THE AFRICAN HERBAL ASSOCIATION

№ 0445

MEMBERSHIP CARD
PASS BOOK IN MALAWI

This is to Certify that Dr.

Address

V.H.

District

is a properly Registered and Approved member of the African Herbal Association by whose authority this certificate is granted by Headquarters ZOMBA/ MALAWI, as a member of this association and agree to abide by the Rules of the Association.

Joining fee is K3 to become a Registered Member.

AIMS AND OBJECTS OF EXECUTIVE

(A) The Association shall endeavour to follow most up to date methods in the care and the treatment of patients.

(B) It shall also see that all who practice as Herbalists must be members approved by the Association.

(C) The Executive shall seek the power to punish any person who is NOT a member of the Association on practicing as a Herbalist.

5 Membership card: African Herbal Association (Malawi)

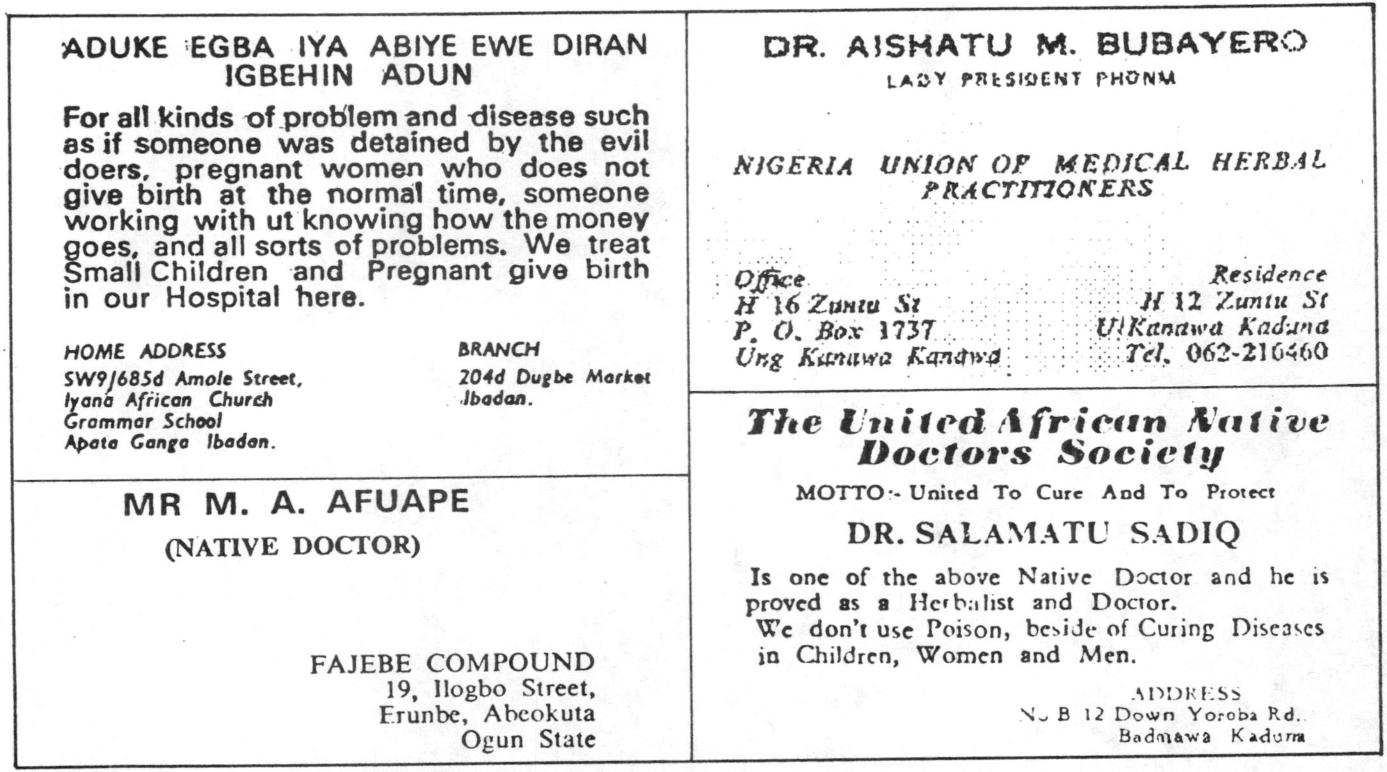

6 Trade cards: Nigerian practitioners and the titles they use in Kaduna, Ibadan and Abeokuta

7 Packaging: towards the standardisation of content and dose in south-western Nigeria. The labels are printed in Yoruba.

PART I
PROFESSIONAL ASSOCIATIONS AND GOVERNMENT

1 G. L. Chavunduka

ZINATHA: THE ORGANISATION OF TRADITIONAL MEDICINE IN ZIMBABWE

INTRODUCTION

Before the introduction of conventional or modern medicine at the turn of the last century, traditional healers were the only medical practitioners in Zimbabwe. This system of medicine is known today as traditional or indigenous medicine and the various practitioners are generally known as traditional healers or doctors of traditional medicine. A number of terms were used in the past to describe traditional healers, the most common terms being witch-doctor and herbalist. The term witch-doctor is no longer used because it is not correct. Although traditional healers believe that many illnesses are caused by witchcraft, they also recognise many other causes of illness as well, such as spirits, germs and bacteria. There are some traditional healers who are able to cure witches. But such traditional healers also handle illnesses and other social problems. There are a number of people who have practised or have attempted to practise witchcraft or believe that they are witches or have been accused by other members of the society as witches. Such people often come to traditional healers for help, help to remove what they believe is an evil spirit in them. Some churches perform this service as well. Although the term herbalist is still used a great deal, it does not describe the work of traditional healers adequately. The term is not strictly correct because traditional healers do not confine their remedies to herbs only. They also use other ingredients such as portions of animals, insects and birds.

On the whole, traditional healers enjoyed tremendous prestige in the past. Not only were they regarded as medical specialists; they were also expected to deal with a wide range of social problems as well. In fact much of the traditional healer's time was spent trying to help people to come to terms with their social problems. In the social field, the traditional healer was a religious consultant, a legal and political adviser, a marriage counsellor and a social worker. Although many traditional healers still perform these roles, much of their prestige and status was lost during the colonial years. This loss of status was due not only to advances in modern medical science but also to Christianity, western education and colonialism.

Colonial governments and early Christian missionaries despised and therefore attempted for many years to discourage the use of traditional medicine (Chavunduka 1978). They attempted to suppress the traditional medical system for a number of reasons. Firstly, many colonial Government officials and missionaries did not know that traditional medicines are effective in curing many illnesses. They believed that the traditional healer was just a rogue and a deceiver who prevented many patients, who would otherwise be treated effectively with modern drugs and surgery, from reaching government and mission hospitals.

Secondly, many early missionaries and Government officials felt that traditional healers encouraged the belief in witchcraft which was regarded as one of the greatest hindrances and stumbling blocks in the way of Christian missionary work. They were opposed to it too because they felt that traditional healers encouraged people to worship their ancestors instead of worshipping God. Worshipping one's ancestors was at that time regarded as a sin. Thus, because of their association with ancestral spirits, traditional healers were regarded as worshippers of devils. In fact, the patient seeking relief and the traditional practitioner attempting a cure were all treated alike. They were both regarded as worshippers of devils who were doomed to hell-fire unless they turned to Christianity. Then there was enthnocentrism, that is, the tendency to like what is familiar and to devalue the strange or the foreign. Ethnocentrism led many early Europeans to regard those who failed to act in accord with their own practices as being ignorant and superstitious. To them, the only medical system which worked was their own. It was the only system of medicine which they knew. The last important reason why attempts were made to suppress traditional medicine was an economic one. It was the desire on the part of colonial administrators to force Africans everywhere to depend entirely on medicines produced in western countries. Complete dependence on Western medicines would, of course, benefit Western countries and their pharmaceutical companies. Attempts are still being made to discredit traditional healers for this reason.

A number of measures were adopted in order to weaken traditional medical practice. Provision of Christian education was regarded as one way of weakening traditional medical beliefs and practices. It was hoped that Christian education would eventually force people to abandon their traditional religious ideas and their faith in traditional healers. Another way of breaking down traditional medical beliefs and practices which was attempted was the building of more mission and government hospitals; again it was hoped that in the future these hospitals would prove one of the greatest instruments for breaking down suspicion of the white man and a means of conversion and of keeping the people in touch with the spiritual life of the church. The schools, too, which until recently were largely controlled by the missionaries were used through teaching and books to discourage the use of traditional medicine. Then there was the Witchcraft Suppression Act.[1] This law was aimed, at least in part, at preventing the activities of the traditional healer. In the Witchcraft Suppression Act (see Appendix II), witchcraft is defined as, ' "the throwing of bones", the use of charms and any other means or devices adopted in the practice of sorcery'. 'Throwing of bones' is not necessarily done to identify or drive out witches. It is a means of divination, that is to say, a means by which a diviner or medical practitioner determines, or attempts to determine, who or what caused an illness or other misfortune complained of by an individual or a group of individuals. Many charms have nothing to do with witchcraft. A large part of the traditional healer's practice is concerned with prescribing remedies and preventive charms. Some of these charms confer or are believed to confer immunity against specific types of illness or to protect the individual against misfortune. Other charms confer or are believed to confer positive benefits such as physical strength, attractiveness to the opposite sex and other desirable qualities. There are other charms that are believed to protect an individual or a group of individuals against witchcraft.

The Medical Council (of modern medicine) also took part in these attempts to suppress the activities of traditional healers. This Medical Council did not recognise traditional healers as medical practitioners. Modern medical doctors were not allowed to refer patients to traditional healers or work with them in any way. If they did, they committed a breach of ethics and were liable to penalties through the Medical Council. Patients who went to hospitals and clinics after consulting traditional healers were often insulted by doctors and nurses for doing so. In commerce and industry some workers lost their jobs because they had been absent from work while consulting traditional healers. Workers who were absent from work while consulting modern doctors were not dismissed from work, provided of course, they produced a letter or certificate from such medical practitioners. Letters or certificates given by a traditional practitioner were not accepted.

Despite the attempts made by early missionaries and Government officials to suppress the activities of traditional healers, many people have continued to use their services. There are a number of reasons for this. One reason which accounts for the persistence of traditional medicine is that traditional healers are successful in curing a large number of illnesses. Many people know that. Some patients who consult traditional healers recover not because of the medicines given but because a number of illnesses are self-limiting and self-curing. When this happens credit is, of course, given to traditional medicine. Moreover, among those illnesses that are not self-limiting and self-curing, many are intermittent in the impact that the disease has on the patient. Thus lengthy treatments may lead to recovery (Turner 1964; Leeson 1967; Frankenberg 1969; Young 1974). Even where traditional medicine can be shown to be medically useless, many patients recover because of the attempts the traditional healers make in solving the patient's social problems. Furthermore, many traditional practices are empirically correct by scientific standards. For example, if an individual is bitten by a snake, the traditional healer might open the wound further and suck out the poison or what he believes to be the evil spirit which has entered. In doing this, he also extracts venom from the wound, thus accomplishing what is essential in objective scientific terms for curing the patient (Coe 1970).

The choice of whether one should consult a modern practitioner or a traditional healer depends on a number of factors such as the cost of each type of treatment, accessibility, knowledge of the probable effects of each kind of treatment, and the definition given to that particular illness at that particular time by the individual and members of his social group. This last factor is usually the most important one.

Most people tend to put illnesses into two broad categories (Chavunduka 1978). In the first category are those illnesses that people regard as normal or natural. In the second category are those illnesses people regard as abnormal or unnatural. Illnesses such as coughs, colds, slight fevers, stomach-aches, and headaches are generally regarded by many people as normal or natural since they occur from time to time in the life of individuals and are usually of a fleeting nature and disappear completely. But when an illness such as a headache or stomach-ache persists over a long period of time it ceases to be a normal illness because it is considered unusual for a headache or a stomach-ache to fail to respond to treatment. The illness is then regarded as abnormal. Many people agree that normal illnesses are caused by such things as germs, bacteria, bad food, accidents, poisons and so on. In the case of abnormal illness, however, many people believe that such illnesses are sent by ancestor spirits, angered spirits, alien spirits, witches or sorcerers. What are considered normal illnesses are treated with herbs or are referred to modern medical practitioners. Once the illness has been defined as abnormal, however, it is not inconsistent, as Mitchell (1960) points out, for patients to consult traditional practitioners alone since they know that modern doctors are unable to attack the ultimate cause of abnormal illness, namely, jealous neighbours and co-workers, spirits or malignant kinsmen.

TRADITIONAL PRACTITIONERS

In Zimbabwe traditional healers can be placed in eight main categories. In the first category are spirit mediums (spirit-diviners). Spirit mediums are those healers who have or are believed to have the ability to communicate with ancestor or alien spirits while in a state of spirit possession. Such healers have inherited or believe that they have inherited their healing spirit from a deceased healer in the family or have been possessed by an alien spirit. Some spirit mediums have both types of spirits. Many spirit mediums are only concerned with the cause of illness or other social problems presented to them. They do not handle medicines. They are expert at carrying out a diagnosis. In the case of illness the individual is then referred to those practitioners who handle medicines.

It is believed that when a spirit medium dies his spirit may return and possess one of his children or grandchildren. The possessed individual then begins his medical practice. We still know very little about spirit possession. However, the events that occur when an individual is about to become possessed have been described by a number of writers. The individual becomes ill. The illness may be defined as a normal one at first and attempts are made to cure it with ordinary medicines. Later it becomes clear to the people involved that the illness is abnormal. At this stage a traditional specialist is consulted, and if he discovers that a spirit is wishing to confer its healing power upon the patient, a ritual ceremony is held at which beer is offered to the spirit. The spirit is then accepted and honoured, and the individual begins his medical practice.[2]

There is another way of becoming a spirit healer. This is by living in a river bed or pool, usually for a few days. One healer who claims to have qualified in this way told me that one afternoon while standing near a pool, a hidden force pulled him into the water. He sank to the bottom of the pool and remained there for two days. At the bottom of the pool he found himself in a village peopled with spirits. He was told by the spirits that he would become a healer from that time. The man does not remember how he eventually left the pool. After the two days he found himself back at home. He told members of the community that he was now a medical practitioner and many people came to see him. He has been practising medicine since then. Although there are only a few healers who claim to have qualified in this way it is important that these claims be investigated by research workers. We know very little about this method of becoming a healer.

An alien spirit is the spirit of a person from some other clan or tribal group who died uncared for, or perhaps was not properly buried according to custom. It is believed that the spirit of such a person may wander restlessly until it settles on someone. An alien spirit can confer any kind of talent on a person it selects. It may be a talent for hunting, for fighting, for ploughing or for healing. Once the possessed individual has accepted such an alien spirit by honouring it in the customary way it usually remains with that person for life.

The second category of traditional healers consists of what are generally known as herbalists (pharmacists). These practitioners are not generally concerned with the cause of illness, but only the treatment of physical symptoms. Some of them have drug-stores where medicines are sold over the counter; others sell their medicines at the urban market-places. Many patients who go to herbalists are referred to them by spirit mediums, or other medical practitioners, but other patients with common symptoms go to them directly. Herbalists receive some form of medical instruction. An individual wishing to enter the traditional medical profession in this way is apprenticed to another healer for a number of years. Nowadays it is possible for individuals to acquire such medical knowledge and skill at a school of traditional medicine.

The third category of traditional healers consists of those spirit mediums who are also herbalists. Many spirit mediums, in fact, do both. They carry out a diagnosis while in a state of possession and also treat the patients.[3]

The fourth category of traditional healers consists of general diviners. These are also experts at carrying out a diagnosis. The most common method of divination in Zimbabwe besides spirit possession is the use of what are known as bones; these are small pieces of wood or stones. The number of bones used appears to vary from area to area and from individual to individual. The diviner throws the bones and quickly looks to see how they have fallen. He then explains the meaning in reference to the problem presented to him. Less common methods of divination include the use of a calabash, a looking-glass, a needle, a book and dreaming. Many general diviners also treat their patients, and this is our fifth category.

The sixth category of traditional healers consists of midwives. But there are midwives who are also herbalists; this becomes our seventh category. The eighth category consists of those who are generally known as faith healers. These are members of certain churches who rely mainly on prayer in their treatment of patients.

Within each category there are specialists. There are, for example, healers who are highly skilled in divination. Other specialists are noted for their skill in the treatment of children's diseases. Some specialise in women's illnesses, while another group are noted for their treatment of epilepsy. There are also specialists in the field of mental disorders and so on.

The majority of the practitioners have entered the profession through spirit possession (Table 1.1).[4] However, the percentage of such practitioners may be slightly lower than that shown in Table 1.1. I had a feeling at the time of the survey that some people who do not have a spirit claimed that they did because of the prestige in the traditional medical profession at present attached to spirit possession. Those who use spirit possession in carrying out a diagnosis form the elite group in this profession. They are considered by both practitioners and members of the public to be the most skilful of all practitioners. On the other hand, the number of people who

Table 1.1
Qualifications of Practitioners by Sex
Sample : 4,013

Qualifications	*Males*		*Females*		*Total*	
	N	%	N	%	N	%
Spirit possession	1365	75.7	2009	90.9	3374	84.1
Apprenticeship	438	24.3	201	9.1	639	15.9
Total	1803	100.0	2210	100.0	4013	100.0

enter the profession by apprenticeship and formal training may increase in the future because of the recent establishment of training schools for traditional medicine.

RELATIONS WITH GOVERNMENT

Traditional healers of Zimbabwe were legally recognised by the Government of Zimbabwe in 1981. This was the first time that such recognition was given by the government in the history of Zimbabwe. An Act of parliament was enacted which is known as the Traditional Medical Practitioners Act, No. 38 of 1981. The Act established a council known as the Traditional Medical Practitioners Council. Section 3(2) of the Act states that the function and purpose of the Council shall be:

(*a*) to supervise and control the practice of traditional medical practitioners;
(*b*) to promote the practice of traditional medical practitioners and to foster research into, and develop the knowledge of, such practice;
(*c*) to hold inquiries for the purposes of this Act;
(*d*) to make grants or loans to associations or persons where the Council considers this necessary or desirable for, or incidental to, the attainment of the purposes of the Council.

In the Act, the 'practice of traditional medical practitioners' is defined as every act, the object of which is to treat, identify, analyse or diagnose, without the application of operative surgery, any illness of body or mind by traditional methods.

The traditional medical council consists of twelve members. Seven members of council including the chairman and vice-chairman, are appointed by the Minister of Health after consultation with the Association of Traditional Healers. The other five members of Council are elected by all the registered traditional medical practitioners. Council members hold office for a period of three years. The Registrar of the Council is also appointed by the Minister of Health after consultation with the Council.[5]

Registration of traditional medical practitioners is now a legal requirement. It is the duty of the Registrar to enter in the Register, in relation to a registered healer, his name, address and date of first registration and such other particulars as the Council may from time to time determine. The Registrar is also required by law to make any necessary alterations in the name, address or other particulars of a registered traditional medical practitioner and to delete from the Register the name of a registered traditional medical practitioner who dies, and when required to do so by or under the Act:-

(i) to mark in the Register the registration of a person or, as the case may be, the suspension from practice of a registered traditional medical practitioner, and

(ii) to delete from the Register the registration of a registered traditional medical practitioner.

Although the new law was not being enforced at the time of writing, it is now an offence for any person who is not registered as a traditional medical practitioner to practise traditional medicine. Section 31(2) of the Act states that the person who, not being registered as a traditional medical practitioner,

(*a*) for gain practises or carries on business as a traditional medical practitioner, whether or not purporting to be registered; or

(*b*) pretends, or by any means whatsoever holds himself out, to be a registered traditional medical practitioner; or

(*c*) uses the title 'Registered Traditional Medical Practitioner' or any name, title, description or symbol indicating or calculated to lead persons to infer that he is registered as a traditional medical practitioner in terms of this Act;

shall be guilty of an offence and liable to a fine not exceeding two thousand dollars or to imprisonment for a period not exceeding two years or to both such fine and imprisonment.[6]

THE MEDICAL ASSOCIATION

The Traditional Medical Practitioners Act also encouraged traditional healers to establish a national medical association of their own. Before 1980 there were a few small associations of traditional healers in some parts of the country. Previous attempts to unite the various associations had been unsuccessful. There are a number of reasons why these associations remained weak and small in the past. Poor leadership was a factor. The other reason was lack of government support and encouragement. Then there was rivalry between the various associations. Each association claimed that it was the true medical association and attempts were made to discredit the others (Chavunduka 1978, pp. 79–86).

The present national body of healers, the Zimbabwe National Traditional Healers' Association (ZINATHA) was formed at a meeting of traditional healers held on 12 July, 1980. The meeting, which was organised by the then Minister of Health, Dr. H. S. M. Ushewokunze, was attended by about 100 traditional healers. Many of the traditional healers present at the meeting were leaders and office-holders of the various small associations that existed at that time. The main purpose of that meeting was to consider the possibility of establishing a single national organisation. This proposal was accepted and an interim National Executive Committee was elected on 13 July, 1980. All other associations of traditional healers were dissolved on that day.[7] The first congress of the new association was held on 6 and 7 September, 1980. Besides electing the national leaders the congress also approved a constitution for the Association.[8] (See Appendix 1.)

For about three years after the establishment of ZINATHA there was an increase in the number of people wanting the services of traditional healers. This increase was due, at least in part, to the growing awareness in Zimbabwe of some of the achievements of traditional healers. Furthermore, the stigma attached to traditional medicine during colonial times has largely disappeared. The end of the liberation war in Zimbabwe also led to an increase in the work-load of many healers. A large number of religious and family rituals which could not be held during the war were held after the war. In the majority of cases traditional healers are required at these rituals. They help to organise and preside at the ceremony. This is not the kind of work that people from other professions can perform satisfactorily.

The basic organ of ZINATHA is a branch; each branch consists of at least twenty members. A branch conference is held annually at which the Branch Executive Committee is elected. The Executive Committee has ten officials. Between the branches and the national leadership is the District Executive Committee. In every administrative district of Zimbabwe there is at least one District Executive Committee of ZINATHA. The District Executive Committee is responsible for supervising and co-ordinating the activities of branches in that district. It may also appoint such sub-committees as may be necessary for the better carrying out of the policies of the Association. Above the District Executive Committee is the National Executive Committee. The eleven members of the National Executive Committee are elected by all traditional healers at a congress of the association.[9] A congress is held once every five years. There are a number of special sub-committees of the National Executive Committee which have been formed in order to perform certain specific tasks such as finance, research, education and discipline. The National Executive Committee meets at least four times a year. Branch and District meetings are held very frequently. At these meetings the policies of the association are explained not only to healers but also to other people who attend. Most of the meetings are open to members of the general public. A few meetings were held in 1983 and 1984 consisting of representatives of modern medicine and ZINATHA delegates to discuss common problems.

The Zimbabwe National Traditional Healers' Association has a research department as well as a department of education. No research projects were carried out between 1980 and 1984 mainly because of shortage of funds and qualified research workers. The department of education has, however, been active since 1981. By 1983 the association had two medical schools and four clinics. At these schools students are taught the various uses of plants and other medicines. They are also taught hygiene and simple book-keeping. Spirit possession is not taught. The medical course lasts one year. Graduates who are interested in practising medicine on their own spend another three years or more working in the clinics run by the association where they gain further practical experience. A number of patients are already making uses of these clinics. Profits made, if any, are shared equally between students and their instructors. Instructors get an additional allowance from the Association.[10]

Other important functions of the association are to rationalise where possible traditional medical procedures, to eliminate incompetent healers and to prevent as far as possible abuse and quackery.

Section 9 of the constitution of the Zimbabwe National Traditional Healers' Association states as follows:

Disciplinary offences shall include:

(i) fraud or misappropriation of funds;

(ii) failure to abide by the constitution;

(iii) performing any act pertaining to the healing profession in a grossly incompetent manner.

(iv) improper conduct or disgraceful conduct or conduct which, when regard is had to the profession or calling of that person, is improper or disgraceful.

The need for discipline is also emphasised by speakers from time to time at meetings of the Association. In a booklet published by the Association in 1981 some of the things a healer may or may not do were spelled out:

1. No healer may advertise or promote his own competence.
2. Professional jealousy is discouraged; a healer may not criticise in public medicines and methods of healing used by another healer; he should not say anything derogatory about his colleague.
3. The sale of medicines in open spaces such as road sides and unauthorised market places is not allowed.
4. A healer must appeal to the Association if a patient refuses to pay his fees.
5. If a patient shows no sign of improvement he must be advised to seek another opinion.
6. A healer must be helpful to everyone.
7. The use of harmful medicines is strictly forbidden.
8. Medical fees must remain as low as possible.
9. No healer may attempt to try a case of witchcraft. This is a matter for the courts of Zimbabwe.
10. A healer must in every respect conduct himself in a respectable manner.
11. There are many diseases which the conventional medical profession is better at treating than traditional healers. These must be referred to hospitals and clinics without delay.

Many healers nowadays, particularly in the urban areas, tend to publicise their practice. This is not in accordance with normal traditional practice. There was in traditional society a definite code that no healer may advertise or promote his or her own competence. The healer's reputation depended and still depends a great deal on the success of his treatments. It was also not common practice for a healer to receive the fees for his services at the time of the consultation. Fees were collected after a cure had been effected and the patient's family was satisfied. In the rural areas most traditional healers still follow the normal practice of not publicising their practice and of not receiving the fees until the patient is fully cured.

The difference in behaviour between rural and urban healers is largely due to the difference in the social and demographic features of town and country. The major difference between the rural and urban communities is the heterogeneity of the towns. In the urban areas there is also a great deal of mobility and the population is by and large residentially unstable. On the other hand, rural villages are inhabited by people who are known to each other. Thus there is no real need for a healer to publicise his practice. His reputation depends on the success of his treatments which are generally known in the area. And because the rural population is generally stable, rural healers can afford to wait until the patient is fully cured before collecting their fees. Because of these changing social and demographic features in the country healers have now been permitted to use door plates on which their qualifications are indicated. Medical certificates and badges issues by the Association are also now in common use. These certificates are generally hung on the wall of the healer's place of healing. The Association also provides badges which may be pinned on the healer's jacket or dress. On the badge is the name of the healer and his qualifications. Many healers, particularly in the towns, also demand nowadays their fee or as much of it as possible during the treatment process.

PROBLEM AREAS

Concern has been expressed by many people regarding possible negligence and abuse of position on the part of many healers in dealing with their patients. This does not appear to be a serious problem. The problem is often prevented by social sanctions against the abuse of authority that exists in traditional medical practice. Traditional healers do not often abuse their power because of fear of their ancestors. This particularly applies to those healers who inherited their healing spirit. It is strongly believed that ancestors may withdraw the healing skill bestowed upon the individual if offended. Negligence, abuse of authority and other forms of deviance can offend the ancestors. Moreover, consultations are usually attended not by the healer and patient alone but by others such as the patient's relatives. Another sanction against the abuse of power is, of course, the fear of losing clients. A dissatisfied client has the right to a second opinion. Nowadays there is also the fear of being expelled from the Association or the danger of being stopped by the Traditional Medical Council from practising medicine.

It is difficult to exclude completely all fake healers from practising medicine. However, a number of measures have been worked out in an attempt to deal with this problem. The main mechanism of control in this respect is the Register of Traditional Medical Practitioners which is published from time to time. Copies of the Register are sent to community leaders all over the country. They are also sold to members of the public. Thus the Association relies very heavily on reports received from members of each community regarding the performance of resident healers shown in the Register. Reports from ZINATHA officials and other traditional healers practising in the vicinity have also proved to be useful. Many patients also write to the Association regarding the performance of traditional practitioners in the area. Individuals who are believed to have doubtful qualifications are made to appear before the National Disciplinary Committee which has power to cancel an individual's membership and remove his name from the Register of the Association. There is, however, a further problem. An individual whose name has been removed from the

Register of the Association may continue to practise medicine. This is a problem that many other systems of medicine face. ZINATHA attempts to deal with this by informing its officials, and all relevant government and other community leaders when a decision has been taken to expel a member, giving reasons for such expulsion, and asking for their co-operation. This measure has worked fairly well in the past in preventing fake healers from practising medicine. Another useful method used nowadays for preventing fake healers from joining the association is to ask the chairman and other officials of the local branch of ZINATHA to comment on applications for membership received from their area. This method was not used in the past because such large numbers of applications were received.

Many healers recognise their limitations in treating certain illnesses and refer some of the difficult cases to other traditional specialists and hospitals. A large number, however, do not refer cases to other specialists, believing that they can treat any kind of sickness. This attitude is being discouraged by the Association.

The complaint made by the early missionaries and others that traditional healers prevent people from becoming Christians has never been supported by evidence. In fact, a large number of traditional healers themselves are Christians. Some are preachers in Christian churches. Membership of the Christian church does not prevent an individual from practising traditional medicine or from participating in traditional religion. Many African Christians also take part in some aspects of traditional religion. In any case there is nothing wrong with traditional religion.

The major area of conflict at present between traditional and modern practitioners is the subject of witchcraft. Most traditional practitioners agree that witches exist and cause illness while most modern practitioners say witches do not exist. Thus traditional practitioners see their job (where witchcraft is believed to be involved) as that of naming the witch (if possible) and then advising on the steps to be taken to remove the disease. On the other hand most modern practitioners see their job as eradicating the belief in witchcraft which some people hold. To them the witch does not exist, and any person who purports to locate him and render him harmless is the real public enemy.[11]

Although traditional healers express a desire to co-operate with modern practitioners many of them are opposed to the idea of working alongside them in hospitals and clinics (Table 1.2). They prefer to continue working in their own homes as at present. A few now have clinics or hospitals of their own. They have no objection to exchanging patients and information. This is already being done.

There are a number of other unresolved issues. Proper registration of all healers is not going to be easy; many are illiterate, many are old men and

Table 1.2
Preferred Situation of Practice

	N	%
In favour of working in hospitals	771	19.2
In favour of working at home	2854	71.1
In favour of working both in hospitals and at home	388	9.7
Total	4013	100.0

women who are unwilling to travel long distances to register, and some spirit mediums argue that the spirit which they inherited will not allow them to register. Attempts to get Medical Aid Societies to include traditional healers on their lists of medical practitioners will also present problems. Besides lack of formal education on the part of many healers there are two other major problems; many do not have bank accounts and banking facilities are not available in many rural areas. Thus payment by cheque, as in the normal practice of Medical Aid Societies, will present some hardship to many traditional practitioners. Moreover, many practitioners live far from post offices. Another issue which will take time to resolve concerns the issuing of sickness certificates by traditional healers. These matters are being examined and discussed in the society at present.

REFERENCES

Chavunduka, G. L., (1978), *Traditional Healers and the Shona Patient*, Gweru: Mambo Press.

——(1980), 'Witchcraft and the law in Zimbabwe', *Zambezia*, VIII, ii, pp. 129–47.

Coe, R. M., (1970), *Sociology of Medicine*, New York: McGraw-Hill.

Frankenberg, R., (1969), 'Man, society and health', *African Social Research*, VIII, 1, pp. 573–87.

Leeson, J. N., (1967), 'Paths to medical care in Lusaka, Zambia', Paper for International Conference of Africanists, Dakar. Mimeo.

Mitchell, J. C., (1960), 'The meaning in misfortune for urban Africans', in Fortes, M. and Dieterlen, G. (eds.), *African Systems of Thought*. London: Oxford University Press for the International African Institute.

Turner, V. W., (1964), 'A Ndembu doctor in practice', in Kiev, A., (ed.), *Magic, Faith and Healing*. New York: Free Press.

Young, A., (1974), 'The practical logic of Amhara traditional medicine,' *Rural Africana*, 26, p. 82.

APPENDIX I
ZIMBABWE NATIONAL TRADITIONAL HEALERS' ASSOCIATION CONSTITUTION

1. NAME

The name of the Association shall be the Zimbabwe National Traditional Healers' Association, hereinafter referred to as 'the Association'.

2. AIMS AND OBJECTS

(*a*) To unite all traditional healers into one body.
(*b*) To promote traditional medicine and practice.
(*c*) To promote research into traditional medicines and methods of healing.
(*d*) To promote training in the art of herbal and spiritual healing.
(*e*) To supervise the practice of traditional medicine and prevent abuse and quackery.
(*f*) To co-operate with the Ministry of Health.
(*g*) To preserve and promote African culture.

3. MEMBERSHIP

(*a*) Membership of the Association shall be open to all traditional healers including spirit mediums.
(*b*) On enrolment each member shall pay a joining fee of $20.
(*c*) Annual subscription fees shall be $2 per member.
(*d*) Each member shall be supplied with a membership card, a badge and a certificate.
(*e*) Membership of the Association may be lost through:
  (i) Resignation.
  (ii) Expulsion.
(*f*) On resignation or expulsion no refund will be made of:
  (i) Joining fee.
  (ii) Subscription fee.

4. THE NATIONAL EXECUTIVE COMMITTEE

(*a*) The National Executive Committee shall consist of:
  (i) President
  (ii) Vice-President
  (iii) Secretary-General
  (iv) National Chairman
  (v) Vice Secretary-General
  (vi) National Treasurer General
  (vii) Deputy Treasurer General
  (viii) Four Committee members
  (ix) Four members appointed by the Minister of Health
(*b*) The above office bearers, except members appointed by the Minister of Health, shall be elected every five years.
(*c*) Meetings of the Executive Committee shall be held not less than six times in each year.
(*d*) At any meeting of the Executive Committee five members shall form a quorum.
(*e*) Disciplinary powers of the Association shall be exercised by the National Executive Committee.
(*f*) The National Executive Committee may appoint an Administrative Secretary and such other employees as it considers to be necessary or desirable.

5. DUTIES OF NATIONAL OFFICERS

(i) *President*

He shall be the head of the Association.

He shall ensure discipline and order in the Association.

He shall be the chief spokesman for the Association.

He shall ensure adherence to the Association's policy by all officials and members and is empowered hereby to discipline and suspend from office any person who acts or speaks contrary to the policy of the Association.

(ii) *Vice-President*

He shall assist the President in his duties and assume the responsibilities of the President in the latter's absence.

(iii) *Secretary-General*

He shall be responsible for running the Association under the direction of the President.

He shall be responsible for arranging all National Executive meetings.

He shall keep records of minutes of all meetings of the National Executive Committee and National Conferences.

(iv) *The National Chairman*

He shall preside over all National Executive Committee meetings and all other functions of the Association in the absence of the President and the Vice-President.

(v) *Vice Secretary-General*

He shall assist the Secretary-General in his duties and assume the responsibilities of the Secretary-General in the latter's absence.

(vi) *National Treasurer General*

He shall be in charge of the Association's financial affairs under the direction of the President.

He shall prepare and submit to the National Executive Committee a financial statement every month.

He shall ensure that the Annual Statement of Accounts, duly audited, is circulated to all delegates to the Annual General Conference.

(vii) *Deputy Treasurer General*

He shall assist the National Treasurer General in his duties and assume the responsibilities of the National Treasurer General in the latter's absence.

6. ANNUAL GENERAL CONFERENCE

(*a*) The Annual General Conference shall be composed of delegates as follows:

(i) All members of the National Executive Committee.

(ii) Three members from each District.

(iii) Three members from each Branch.

(*b*) The Annual General Conference shall be held every year at a place and date decided by the National Executive Committee.

7. FINANCE

(*a*) The funds of the Association shall consist of all fees paid in terms of regulations referred to in Section 3, donations and other moneys and assets as may vest in or accrue to the Association.

(*b*) All moneys shall be paid through the National Treasurer General.

(*c*) All moneys shall be deposited in a bank approved by the National Executive Committee.

(*d*) The Accounts of the Association shall be examined and audited annually.

(*e*) A member of the Association shall be paid from the funds of the Association such allowances as the National Executive Committee may fix to meet any reasonable expenses incurred by him in connection with the business of the Association.

(*f*) A District or Branch Executive Committee shall be paid from the funds of the Association such moneys as the National Executive Committee may decide to meet any reasonable expenses incurred in connection with the business of the Association.

8. DISTRICTS AND BRANCHES

(*a*) The Association shall establish District and Branch organs with Executive Committees consisting of:

(i) Chairman
(ii) Vice-Chairman
(iii) Secretary
(iv) Vice-Secretary
(v) Treasurer
(vi) Deputy Treasurer
(vii) Four Committee Members

(*b*) Each District and each Branch shall hold an annual general meeting.

(*c*) District and Branch officials shall be elected annually at the Annual General Meeting.

(*d*) At any meeting of the District or Branch Executive Committee four members shall form a quorum.

(*e*) Each Branch shall consist of at least 20 members.

9. DISCIPLINE

Disciplinary offences shall include:

(i) fraud or misappropriation of funds;
(ii) failure to abide by the constitution;
(iii) performing any act pertaining to the healing profession in a grossly incompetent manner;
(iv) improper conduct or disgraceful conduct or conduct which, when regard is had to the profession or calling of that person, is improper or disgraceful.

10. RESEARCH

(*a*) Research into medicinal herbs and methods of treatment by interested bodies, companies and individuals must be approved by the National Executive Committee and the Minister of Health.

(*b*) Any public statements made to the mass media in connection with any research about traditional medicine must first meet the approval of the National Executive Committee of the Association.

11. SALE OF MEDICINAL HERBS

The Association shall seek the co-operation of the competent authorities to prevent:

(i) the sale of medicine in open spaces such as road sides and unauthorised market places;
(ii) the sale of medicines by unauthorised persons.

12. AMENDMENT TO THE CONSTITUTION

Amendments to this constitution shall be by two-thirds majority of those members present at the Annual General Conference. Such proposed amendments must further have the approval of the Minister of Health.

13. DISSOLUTION

With the approval of the Minister of Health, the Association may, by a resolution passed by two-thirds majority of members at a special conference called expressly for that purpose, resolve that the Association be dissolved. All properties and funds of the Association after meeting all liabilities shall, in consultation with the Minister of Health, be distributed in such a manner as shall be determined by that Conference.

APPENDIX II
THE WITCHCRAFT SUPPRESSION ACT

To suppress the practice of pretended witchcraft (18th August, 1899) — Ord. 14 1899

1. This Act may be cited as the Witchcraft Suppression Act (Chapter 73). — Short Title.

2. In this Act 'witchcraft' includes the 'throwing of bones', the use of charms and any other means or devices adopted in the practice of sorcery. — Interpretation of term.

3. Whoever imputes to any other person the use of non-natural means in causing any disease in any person or animal or in causing any injury to any person or property, that is to say, whoever names or indicates any other person as being a wizard or witch shall be guilty of an offence and liable to a fine not exceeding two hundred dollars or to imprisonment for a period not exceeding three years, or to whipping not exceeding twenty lashes or to any two or more of such punishments.

4. Whoever, having so named and indicated any person as a wizard or witch, is proved at his trial under section three to be by habit and repute a witch doctor or witch finder shall be liable, on conviction, in lieu of the punishment provided by section three to a fine not exceeding five hundred dollars or to imprisonment for a period not exceeding seven years or to whipping not exceeding thirty-six lashes or to any two or more of such punishments. — Punishment for imputation of witchcraft by habitual or reputed witch doctor or witch finder.

5. Whoever employs or solicits any other person –

(*a*) to name or indicate any other person as a wizard or witch, or

(*b*) to name or indicate by means of witchcraft or by the application of any of the tests mentioned in paragraph (b) of section eight or by the use of any non-natural means any person as the perpetrator of any alleged crime or other act complained of; or

(*c*) to advise him or any other person how by means of witchcraft or by any non-natural means whatsoever the perpetrator of any alleged crime or other act complained of may be discovered:

shall be guilty of an offence and liable to a fine not exceeding fifty dollars or, in default of payment, to imprisonment for a period not exceeding six months.

6. Whoever, professing a knowledge of so-called witchcraft — Punishment for witch doctor or witch finder practising witchcraft or supplying witchcraft materials.

or of the use of charms, either as a witch doctor or witch finder, advises or undertakes to advise any person applying to him how to bewitch or injure any other person or property, including animals, and any person who supplies any other person with the pretended means of witchcraft, shall be guilty of an offence and liable to the punishments provided by section four.

7. Whoever, on the advice of a witch doctor or witch finder or any person pretending to have the knowledge of witchcraft or the use of charms, or in the exercise of any pretended knowledge of witchcraft or of the use of charms, uses or causes to be put into operation such means or processes as he may have been advised or may believe to be calculated to injure any other person or any property, including animals, shall be guilty of an offence and liable to the punishments provided by section four.

Punishment for applying means or processes of witchcraft for injury of persons or property.

8. Whoever

(*a*) by the exercise of any witchcraft, conjuration, use of charms or of any other unnatural means pretends to discover where or in what manner any property supposed or alleged to have been stolen or lost may be found or to name or indicate any person as a thief or perpetrator of any crime or any other act complained of; or

(*b*) in the pretence of discovering whether or not any other person has committed any crime or any other act complained of, applies or advises the application or causes to be applied to such person the 'boiling water test' (that is to say the dipping by such other person of any of his limbs or portion of his body into boiling water), whether such dipping is voluntary or compelled, or administers or advises or causes the administration of, to such other person, with or without consent, any emetic or purgative;

shall be guilty of an offence and liable to the punishment provided by section four.

Punishment for the naming or indicating of thieves, etc., by witchcraft, charms, etc.

9. Any money, animal or other thing received by any person by way of payment or reward for or in respect of any exercise or pretended exercise of so-called witchcraft or of the use of charms, or for or in respect of advising any person as to any mode or method of be-witching or injuring, by non-natural means, any other person or property, including animals, or for or in respect of indicating any person who by non-natural means is supposed to have bewitched or injured any other person or any property, including animals, or for or in respect of the performance of any of the acts mentioned in section eight, shall be deemed to have been obtained by fraud, and the person so receiving such money, animal or other thing shall be liable to be prosecuted for fraud and to suffer such punishment as is by law provided for such offence.

Money, etc., received as payment or received for practice of witchcraft, etc., shall be deemed to have been received by fraud, and punishment for such fraud.

NOTES

1 The Witchcraft Suppression Act 1899 (Chapter 73). The Act is aimed at five categories of persons. Firstly, any person who names or indicates any other person as being a witch or is guilty of an offence. Secondly, any person who names or indicates any other person as being a witch and is proved at his trial to be by habit and repute a witch-doctor or witch-finder faces a heavy sentence. Thirdly, it is an offence to employ or solicit any other person to name or indicate thieves and other wrongdoers by means of witchcraft; similarly, a person who employs someone to advise him or any other person how by means of witchcraft such thieves or wrongdoers may be identified, commits an offence. The fourth group of persons are those who claim to have a knowledge of witchcraft or of the use of charms. Lastly, anyone attempting to practise what the Act refers to as 'so-called witchcraft' is also guilty.

2 Studies being carried out in Zimbabwe at present seem to indicate that spirit possession can be learnt particularly in the early years of an individual's life. See chapter 8.

3 It appears that many healers who claim to have inherited their healing skill have, in fact, also had a long period of apprenticeship. Many of them have grown up in a family where there was a healer and learnt a great deal about medical practice before the death of the old man or woman, although healers themselves will deny that knowing the various medicines is a personal talent. (See Chapter 8.)

4 Midwives and midwife/herbalists were not included in the survey.

5 At the time of writing (October 1984), the names of members of Council had not yet been announced by the Government. The Council was, therefore, not in operation. However, much of the work of the Council was being done by the Association of Traditional Healers. The delay in establishing the Council has been due, at least in part, to the continued debate in the society over the role of traditional healers in modern Zimbabwe. A number of leaders still argue that the Government was wrong in granting traditional healers legal recognition. The Traditional Medical Practitioners Act recognises ZINATHA (Zimbabwe National Traditional Healers Association) as the Association of traditional healers. This is stated in section 2(1) of the Act which reads: 'Association in the Act is defined as the Zimbabwe National Traditional Healers' Association'. [Council members were named in mid 1985.]

6 Spirit mediums now use the title R.S.M. (Registered Spirit Medium). Herbalists, general diviners and midwives use the title, R.T.M.P. (Registered Traditional Medical Practitioner). Spirit mediums who are also herbalists use the title R.S.M. R.T.M.P. The title 'doctor' is used only by qualified doctors of modern medicine. The aim of the legislators was to prevent confusion in the society over the use of similar titles.

7 The author was elected President. Although I was not a practising healer at that time, a number of reasons helped me gain the leadership of the new association. Since the previous associations had failed to unite partly because of rivalry between them, it appears that the voters were now looking for someone who was not controversial; an outsider who was acceptable to all groups. During the past ten years I had worked among healers as a research worker from the University of Zimbabwe and got to know many of the leaders. I had demonstrated my respect and keen interest in their work. Traditional healers at that time also appear to have been looking for an educated leader who knew many of the Government leaders and could therefore fight the political battle for them for legal recognition. Another reason which may have influenced the voters to elect me was the desire to have someone as leader who can be trusted in financial matters. Previous associations had been weakened, at least in part, by poor financial management.

8 Members of the Association pay a joining fee of Z$20. Annual subscription fees were Z$2 per member. From January 1984 annual subscription fees were raised to Z$5 per member. By October 1984, 20,000 practitioners had already joined the Association.

9 At the time of writing there were 312 branches and 104 District Executive Committees. The Association had ten offices situated in all the major urban centres of the country. There are fifteen people employed by the Association, including clerks, secretaries, a messenger, a driver and two instructors. In addition to the eleven ZINATHA officials on the National Executive Committee, four members are appointed by the Minister of Health. However, at the time of writing (October 1984) the Minister had not yet appointed anyone to serve on the ZINATHA National Executive Committee. As in the case of the Council already mentioned, the delay appears to be due to the continuing debate in the society at present over the role of traditional healers in modern Zimbabwe.

10 The two medical schools have been closed down for the time being because of financial problems. This indicates the problems faced by associations that rely on joining fees and annual subscriptions for funding programmes of this nature. The Government of Zimbabwe does not at present assist ZINATHA financially in any way.

11 The controversy between traditional healers and modern practitioners over the problem of witchcraft has been discussed in detail elsewhere (Chavunduka 1980).

2 Frants Staugard

TRADITIONAL HEALTH CARE IN BOTSWANA

TSWANA MEDICINE IN A UNIVERSAL CONTEXT

During recent centuries representatives of modern medicine have stated that traditional medicine is not only of no value, but that it actually causes positive harm to the population which it is supposed to serve (Bø 1972; *Time Magazine* 1982). However, as serious doubts have recently been raised about the effectiveness of modern medicine in its predominantly curative form as an instrument for the attainment of the goal of health for all (McKeown 1972; Lalonde 1975), it might be timely to examine in some depth the question, whether we ought to re-evaluate traditional medicine universally and whether – especially in the developing countries – co-operation between modern and traditional medicine should replace the present confrontation?

Developed within the Tswana culture in southern Africa, Tswana medicine has a number of culturally specific characteristics. However, these specific characteristics are few compared to the features identifying Tswana medicine as part of the universal paradigm of traditional medicine.

When examining the Tswana healers' conceptions of causes of disease, their social role and significance in the society and their therapeutical armamentarium, a great number of parallel and even identical features with traditional medicine in other cultures far from southern Africa can be identified. Modern doctors often compare the curative effectiveness in certain cases of diseases of their own system with that of traditional medicine. Such comparisons in most cases result in demonstrating the shortcomings of traditional health care. Yet the whole concept of comparison is inadequate. Traditional medicine is far more than merely a system for the treatment of manifest disease.

Traditional medicine plays a prominent role in social control in the indigenous society. It represents the justice and stability in a community with no written laws or established judicial system. It is in this sense indispensable to the social stability of the local community, since it is integrated with the prevailing religious and moral views (Mead 1955; Chavunduka 1978).

The traditional healer in the Tswana village – in common with healers in other parts of southern Africa (*WHO* 1978) – is not only a medicine man. He is also a religious consultant, a legal and political adviser, a police detective, a marriage counsellor and a social worker.

From the above it will appear that modern and traditional medicine are to some extent not comparable systems. To discuss an *integration* of those systems in a comprehensive health care sector should thus be harmful to both. It would appear far more fruitful to examine the possibility of future *co-operation* between modern and traditional medicine in order to preserve and utilise the specific values of both systems.

TSWANA RELIGIOUS BELIEFS AND THE TRADITIONAL HEALER

The religious background to the practice of contemporary Tswana medicine in general, and the role of the Independent Churches in healing in particular, is of central importance.

Elements of magic and so-called *witchcraft* are still prevalent in Tswana medicine and must also be analysed in their proper social context, although it seems obvious that the majority of traditional healers in Botswana are gradually turning towards more *rational* elements of healing such as, for example, herbalism. This development – undoubtedly a response to the dominant influence of Western medical thinking at the official level in Botswana – is probably more an expression of a pragmatic attitude on behalf of certain traditional healers than a sign of a profound change of mind and conceptions.

The traditional Tswana religious beliefs were based on the existence of an omnipotent, transcendental principle called *Modimo* – the Great God.

Modimo was regarded as the creator of all things and reigned supreme over the most important events in life. He (in fact *Modimo* is always referred to as a male being) could withhold rain, send lightning and cause death in other ways and would often do so to punish members of the tribe if general laws and rules were not respected (Schapera 1976). The chief and his close family were considered direct descendants of *Modimo*, but He was too remote to be approached directly by either the chief or the people through prayers.

However the *Badimo* – the ancestral spirits – could act as mediators to *Modimo* and their role in the religious life of the tribe was central.

When members of the tribe died they were buried in their cattle kraal or in the backyard of the family compound. They were buried in a sitting position, equipped with their normal tools of work and dressed properly, their faces turned westwards. They were believed to rise immediately after the burial and to travel to the world of the ancestral spirits. This was considered to be situated close to the home village – usually behind the nearest high hill, underground or on the top of it. From here the ancestral spirits would continue their normal existences, doing the same work they did when still alive and present in the village.

The *Badimo* would continue to take a close interest in the destiny of their relatives in the village and would actually supervise and guide every aspect of their daily life. They could mediate between the will of *Modimo* – his anger or blessings – and the village, but could also reward or punish their earthly relatives themselves.

While major events like drought and rainfall – affecting all the members of the tribe – were ascribed to the *Modimo*, individual luck or misfortune were usually considered to emanate from the *Badimo*.

These would in general be the guardians of the tribal laws and moral taboos, guiding the everyday life of each member of the community and their influence could thus be seen as stabilising and conservative in a social and political sense. One of the commonest ways for the *Badimo* to express their disapproval of the behaviour of one of their earthly relatives would be to cast disease on him.

One of the main ingredients in the treatment of such a disease would consequently involve appeasing the *Badimo* in order to restore the good relationship, on which the welfare of any member of the tribe depended. While the *ordinary* ancestral spirits were only responsible for the individual welfare of their descendants, the *Badimo* of the chief held power over the destiny of the tribe as a whole. Thus the chief, as the earthly representative of his own *Badimo*, commanded great respect in the tribe and was responsible for a number of major rites. These included rain-making, which in an often drought-stricken area as Botswana, was of the utmost importance. During the rain-making – which contained a number of complex rituals – the chief would often be assisted by the tribal priest – the *Ngaka ya Setswana*.

Under the influence of Christianity and modern development almost all of the former important tribal rites, conducted by the chief, have disappeared from the Tswana culture. Prayers for rain, however, are still frequently conducted by the President and in the Christian churches in Botswana.

The role of the tribal priest – or traditional healer – was central to tribal life and his social role and significance is best understood against the background of his relationship with the transcendental powers of Tswana religious beliefs (Figure 2.1). The *Ngaka* was the personal adviser to the chief and the only person in the village who was capable of mediating

Figure 2.1. The social role and significance of the Tswana healer.

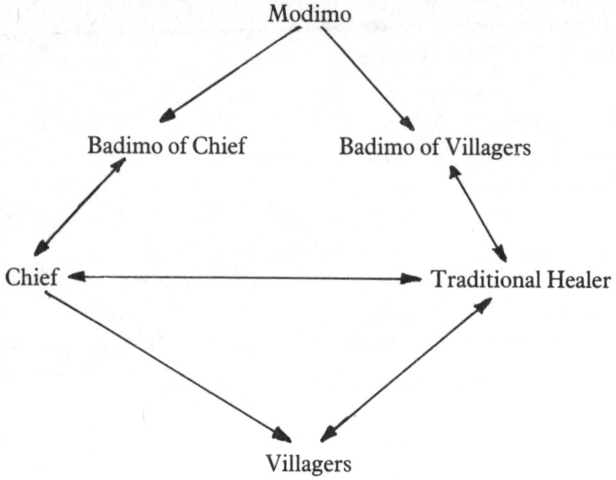

between the villagers and their *Badimo*. As the commonest way for the *Badimo* to express their dissatisfaction with their earthly descendants was to cast disease on them, the tribal priest logically also became the tribal healer, capable of interpreting the symptoms of disease and prescribing the correct treatment.

The advent of white Christian missionaries to the Tswana culture resulted in a wide variety of developments and changes.

The missionaries built churches, developed new rituals – which in some cases replaced the old tribal rites – and instituted partially new moral rules and sanctions for their violation. They taught the Tswana to wear European clothes and to sing Christian hymns. Some of them also engaged in teaching and in health care at mission clinics or hospitals.

The missionaries adopted the term *Modimo* for the Christian God and it is now generally used in the Christian churches. New social distinctions were created by this development, e.g. between Christian and Heathen (Schapera 1976). This distinction, however, is as much correlated to social and economic characteristics as to religious, and is probably just a reflection of the class structure of both the pre-Christian and the contemporary Tswana society.

The conversion of the chiefs to Christianity – explained in most cases by political pragmatism rather than by religious considerations (Bechuanaland Protectorate Administration 1908–1927, files 37/4 and 6/1) – had as one of its consequences the displacement of the traditional healer from his central position as an adviser to the chief. This position was then occupied by the Christian missionary.

The displacement of the *Ngaka* obviously had a profound influence on his position in the tribal community, but only at the official level. As white Christianity had not provided an alternative to the *Ngaka* at the local level, his influence and importance in the everyday life of the majority of the rural population remained almost unaffected by the official changes in society.

The traditional healers should thus be considered contemporary *local community leaders*. The importance of this fact becomes evident when it comes to the planning of the future co-operation between modern and traditional health care in Botswana.

Responding, presumably, to the influence of Western medical thinking which has gained a dominant influence in the affluent groups of the society, some Tswana healers demonstrate a high degree of adaptability and to an increasing extent seem to focus their interest on those elements of traditional healing which fit into the Western concepts of 'rationality', such as for example herbalism. The majority of Tswana healers, however, are still firmly basing their diagnostic and therapeutic activities on traditional concepts, in terms of which disease is considered the symptom of a social disruption in the broadest sense. As part of these traditional concepts the traditional healer would generally be trying to find a solution to a problem, presented to him in case of disease, through giving advice and finding cures which endorse popular sentiment and inspire a sense of justice and security in the traditional way of thinking and living in the village.

The advice of the traditional healer is therefore generally well integrated in the religious and moral concepts and beliefs prevailing in the society and the *Ngaka* thus assumes a stabilising role in social control.

THE VARIOUS TYPES OF TSWANA HEALERS

During the surveys which form the background for this paper, six main types of traditional healers were identified in Botswana. The Traditional Birth Attendants (TBAs) form a seventh group of traditional health workers. Sometimes a traditional healer would combine several of the functions described, for example a combination of herbalism with sucking and bone-throwing. An increasing tendency to specialise in one of the components of traditional healing has however been noticed during the survey.

The Herbalist or *Ngaka ya Ditshotshwa* has specialised in retail or wholesale of herbal drugs, most often gathered by himself. He has a small shop or stand, where the herbal drugs are sold to the customers, or he travels around in his district to distribute the medicines to customers or in some cases to other traditional healers.

In the majority of cases – but not obligatory – the herbalist would be closely related to another herbalist. He would have to go through a learning period of approximately two years and pay around P100 to his teacher for this training.

The information received from the traditional healers, on the length of their training period, is obviously not based on an eight-hour working day, but is just indicating the length of time, during which the apprentice is supposed to work under the guidance of the older healer and not to engage in independent diagnostic or therapeutic activities.

The herbalists might have chosen their profession because of the close relationship to another herbalist and claim to have 'inherited' the special gifts required of a successful *Ngaka ya Ditshotshwa*, but could also choose this profession from pure interest.

The Diviner-Herbalist or *Ngaka ya Ditaola* combines the art of making a diagnosis by means of the 'holy bones' with that of treating the diagnosed disease with herbal preparations. He would have to spend approximately six months at the cost of approximately P120 to learn about divination from another diviner in addition to the above training for herbalism.

The *Ngaka ya Ditaola* would in the majority of cases be closely related to another healer of the same type and would most often claim to have inherited the necessary qualifications from this relative. In some cases the art of divination would be conferred by the *Badimo* through a dream, according to the healer, but in any case he has to learn this part of healing through an apprenticeship. Like the *Ngaka ya Ditshotshwa*, the diviner-herbalist could also choose his profession from pure interest and without direction from the *Badimo* or through relationship.

Ngaka ya Di-Dupang (the Sucker) performs *go lomega* (sucking). This healer would in most cases combine divination and herbalism with *go lomega*, which in most cases would aim at removing *sejeso* (a special type of 'witchcraft' impurity in the body). *Go lomega* might also be applied in case of a diagnosis of the patient suffering from 'bad blood'.

The sucking could be performed by means of hollow horns, or simply by using the mouth (especially among the *Basarwa*). Apart from the training for learning divination and herbalism as described above, the sucker would have to learn this specialised type of healing for approximately twenty four months and pay approximately P130 for this training. The sucker thus achieves the status of 'specialist' among the healers. He would also in the majority of cases be closely related to another healer of the same type and often claim a close communication with the *Badimo*, who might have chosen him through a revelation in a dream.

Moprofiti (the Faith Healer) is distinctly different from other traditional Tswana healers. The Faith Healer would usually be the leader of one of the approximately 160 Independent Churches of Botswana. In order to rise to leadership in an Independent Church, a prophet must above all be able to heal (Sundkler 1970). In most cases the Faith Healer would claim that he had been chosen by *Modimo* (through a revelation in a dream) to perform healing. A substantial number of Faith Healers have a close relationship to another Faith Healer. As a Faith Healer is chosen by *Modimo* and given his power to diagnose and treat diseases, he considers questions on formal training to be irrelevant.

Sangoma is a type of healer rare in the surveyed area, but seems to be more common in other parts of Botswana. The *Sangoma* is a more 'holy' figure than the other types of *Dingaka* and invariably claims to have been chosen by the *Badimo* for her profession. In the majority of cases the *Sangoma* is a female, but some male *Disangoma* are found. The *Sangoma* would often, as a young person during a severe illness, be 'called' by the *Badimo* through a dream and then seek guidance and training from an elder *Sangoma*. Having been 'called' by the *Badimo* the individual has no option but to train. If an individual should try to resist the 'call' various symptoms of disease would develop, some of which according to description could be classified as those of psychosis (Boshill 1975).

The dream on which the individual is 'called' includes a multitude of scenarios and events but invariably involves a snake. The training of the apprentice comprises the arts of divining, herbalism and sucking, in most cases and follows the guidelines concerning length and costs described above. In some cases the *Sangoma* would specialise in some type of exorcism during which she would engage in singing, dancing and in some cases using her drum, often entering into a state of trance. A *Sangoma* may or may not have a relationship to another *Sangoma*. In earlier times, at puberty, a *Sangoma* had to go through special initiation ceremonies, which are still performed following the original pattern among Basuto and other tribes in Southern Africa, but seem to be uncommon at present among Batswana. Both the *Moprofiti* and the *Sangoma* are newcomers to the Tswana culture. They are to a certain extent related – both of South African origin and both with a distinct, religious profile. They are, however, integrated in the contemporary Tswana culture.

Recent times have seen the emergence of a new type of traditional healers in Botswana. These might appropriately be called *neo-herbalists* (Seeley 1973) and could in many ways be seen as Tswana representatives of the upsurge of alternative medical systems, which presently flourish in western Europe and North America. Such *neo-herbalists*, identified in Botswana, would be younger than the average traditional healer, they would be better educated and would have learned their skills through formalised training at an institute outside Botswana's borders, usually South Africa. Many of their ideas and conceptions would be influenced by homoeopathy and naturopathy.

In Botswana they would be found behind the counter of a small shop, from where they would sell their herbal drugs. Some of these would be bought from other local herbalist for resale, others they collect themselves but the majority of the items for sale in the *neo-herbalists'* shops would be ready-made and labelled homoeopathic and other alternative medical preparations, emanating from South African companies.

Expatriates, with a homoeopathic or other alternative medical training, who apply for a licence to practise in Botswana would not be granted any such permission according to the present regulations, but *Batswana* with a similar training abroad are not restricted from practising their skills and will only as a formality have to register with the District Council.

The *neo-herbalists* do not only sell herbal drugs across the counter and give advice on prevention and treatment of disease to their customers. They also as a rule have a small back-room to the shop, where treatment such as enemas and various types of massage and body-baths can be administered.

Only a few *neo-herbalists* or *alternative medical practitioners* were identified during the survey which provided information for this paper, but if the development in western Europe in this field – as in so many others – is going to be (uncritically) duplicated in Botswana, we might expect this special variety of traditional healing to be more common in the future.

The *Traditional Birth Attendants* (TBAs) are widely represented in the rural parts of the country. They are, however, culturally and socially distinctly different from the group of traditional healers, and it is questionable whether the TBAs should be described under the same heading as the *Dingaka* and the *Baprofiti*.

The TBA in rural Botswana would be an elderly woman, often concentrating on assisting close relatives in the extended family with their deliveries. She would be firmly integrated in the indigenous Tswana culture, but would not base her professional activity on the same platform of religious conceptions as other traditional health workers.

THE FAITH HEALER IN TSWANA MEDICINE

As already mentioned, the Faith Healers form a group, which is quite distinct from the group of *Dingaka tsa Setswana*. The Faith Healer is always closely linked to one of the Independent African Churches, while the *Ngaka* would not have any church affiliation.

Faith healing is a fairly new phenomenon in Botswana and not based on the centuries of traditions, habits and conceptions, which form the background for the function of the *Ngaka*. The Independent Churches are to some extent alien to the Tswana culture and represent an intermediary stage between the indigenous culture and European (colonial) conceptions. The socially and culturally significant historical role of the *Ngaka* as the adviser to the chief and the mediator between the ancestral spirits and the villagers – albeit nowadays diminished and in some cases almost extinct – gives his profession an aura which cannot be shared by the Faith Healer.

Faith Healers are not primarily health workers, although healing dominates their activity. Rather they might be considered religious workers, who utilise their presumed healing potential in promulgating their faith.

Faith healing is further a calling (from *Modimo*) and does not demand any training. It tends to emphasise the healer's individual relationship with medicine and the healing skills of the individual healer. It therefore may lend itself to individualism and ultimately cultism, which may be one of the reasons why Faith Healers generally seem reluctant to collaborate with each other (while they seem to accept co-operation with the *Dingaka* without any reservations).

From the reasons given above it might seem strange that for the purpose of this paper a choice has been made to treat Faith Healers as part of the system of Tswana traditional medicine. But the *Baprofiti* actually have more in common with, than differences from, other Tswana traditional healers.

All the Independent Churches in Botswana belong to the Zionist movement. The Zionist movement is theologically characterised as syncretic with healing, speaking in tongues, purification rites and taboos as the main expressions of its faith (Sundkler 1970).

Recruitment to the church is almost invariably made through healing, and rites concerned with the prevention and treatment of disease occupy almost all the time of the services in a typical Zionist Church.

In its function as a health care facility rather than a religious institution the Zionist movement has gradually adopted almost all of the conceptions and treatments used for centuries by the traditional healers in the Tswana cultures.

The Zionists might combat the use of the traditional healer's remedies and fight the traditional conceptions of demon possession and 'witchcraft', but 'the weapons with which they fight the struggle belong to an arsenal of old, tribal religion' (Sundkler 1970).

By 1983, 158 Independent African Churches – all of them belonging to the Zionist movement and offspring of churches in the Republic of South Africa – were represented in Botswana. Faith healing is a dominant feature in church life and by no means just secondary in importance to other congregational activities. The role of healing in the Zionist Church could be seen as an adaptation of Christianity to the social reality of the typical Tswana village in which the demand for health care is dominant in the population.

The Faith Healers – like the *Dingaka tsa Setswana* – find their followers and patients mainly in the underprivileged groups of the population. The Faith Healer applies the same holistic – or synthetical – model for the conception of causes of disease as the *Ngaka*, and his treatment has the same basic features. The Tswana Faith Healer is deeply rooted in indigenous culture and plays the same role as a local community leader as the *Ngaka*. For these reasons a choice is made to consider the Faith Healer a member of the group of traditional healers in Botswana.

TRADITIONAL HEALERS AND TRADITIONAL HEALTH CARE

The vast majority of Tswana people find themselves now living under the influence of two distinctly different cultures – the traditional tribal culture and the modern Western civilisation. This fact has implications for almost all spheres of life. Health care is one of the fields in which the contrasts resulting from this dual confrontation is most clearly demonstrated.

It has been said very illustratively (Makhurane 1980) that the *Motswana* is like a little boy standing on top of a hill with his thumb in the mouth, one leg in a black hole and the other in a white one and wondering which one to lift first. The white hole represents the beaten path of traditional methods of health delivery via our traditional doctors, nurses and midwives. The black hole represents the whole unknown world in health care via hospitals and clinics with their new-type doctors and nurses using strange tools and most of the time speaking a foreign language.

Every time a person falls ill he has to face the difficult dilemma of which leg to lift first – whether to seek help from the traditional health care system, culturally and socially integrated in the village life, or whether to go to the hospital or clinic – lying there more or less literally on a hill, conceptually and socially floating over the everyday realities of village life.

In this section an attempt will be made to describe briefly as well the practices of the traditional healers as the pattern of consumption of traditional health care in representative sample groups of the rural population of Botswana.

The following description is made on the basis of a number of surveys, performed in Botswana during the period 1978–82 and using the methods of descriptive epidemiology. A total of 369 traditional healers and 2,034 members of the general population in rural and urban Botswana were sampled for extensive interviews in accordance with structured and semi-structured questionnaires. A multi-stage sampling method (purposedly-stratified-random) was used.

A comprehensive description of the studies and their results is published as a monograph (Staugard in press).

The population of traditional healers in Botswana is dominated by men. The healers outnumber the modern healthworkers in all rural areas.

The group of Faith Healers constitute approximately one-third of all traditional healers in Botswana. The majority of the members of this group are illiterate and might even in terms of other socio-economic characteristics such as for example ownership of cattle be characterised as belonging to the underprivileged groups of the population.

The average traditional healer is of mature age, has a long experience of healing work and receives patients mainly from his own or the immediately neighbouring villages. He would in most cases be paid by the patient only if his treatment results in cure for the actual disease.

A comparatively large proportion of the healer's time is spent on preventative work in the traditional sense of this word, although an increasing tendency towards focussing on curative aspects of traditional healing has been observed during the surveys.

The attitude towards a future co-operation with the modern health sector is unanimously positive among the traditional healers. All of the healers appear firmly rooted in the indigenous Tswana culture and have maintained their beliefs in the importance of the *Badimo* when it comes to causing and curing disease. A fairly large proportion of the healers seem to have a (dangerously) high confidence in their own healing potential and maintain that they are able to treat and cure all types of disease.

Around one-third of the traditional healers belong to one of the registered associations for *Dingaka* and the remaining group almost without exception expressed their interest in joining such an association.

The various skills mastered by the *Dingaka* have demanded comparatively long periods of training under the guidance of an older healer.

For the group of Faith Healers the questions on training are not relevant, as these healers consider their role merely one of conveying the healing power of *Modimo* to the patient.

From the utilisation survey it appears that more than half of the rural and approximately one-third of the urban population interviewed could be classified as illiterates.

The majority of the rural and about one-third of the urban population has remained faithful to the traditional Tswana religious beliefs, while the remaining group were members of either one of the European or one of the African Independent Churches.

In the rural population the majority of church members belonged to the latter type of religious societies while in the urban group the distribution between European and African Churches was 50–50. The membership of a certain type of church seems to have as much social as religious connotations.

The majority of both the rural and the urban population interviewed could be classified as socially underprivileged, although the urban group generally seemed to be somewhat better off than the rural.

The majority of both the rural and the urban population had utilised modern health care services – which means visited the nurse or doctor, been admitted to the Hospital and/or used drugs prescribed within the modern health sector – on one or more occasions during the twelve months preceding the interview.

Approximately one-third of all the interviewed women in the rural areas but only one-tenth of the women in the urban areas had delivered a child during the surveyed period. The majority of the mothers in the rural areas and more than one-fifth of the women in the urban areas chose to deliver their child at home, assisted by a Traditional Midwife.

The profile of symptoms and disease and other causes for seeking modern health care was examined and it appeared that approximately one-fifth of all visits to the clinic or hospital were made with complaints which could be classified as psychosomatic.

Symptoms which might indicate the presence of a communicable disease accounted for approximately one-tenth of all visits to the modern sector. Only a minor proportion of all visits were made for preventative reasons.

The above findings seem to characterise the modern health care sector as predominantly curatively oriented in its contacts with individual adult health-care utilisers.

More than two-thirds of the rural and approximately one-third of the urban population had utilised traditional health care services on one or more occasions during the preceding twelve months. The utilisation of traditional health care showed a decreasing tendency with increasing social status in terms of geographical localisation in the urban community, while in the rural communities the utilisation was equally high in all the surveyed communities.

Although a significant proportion of both the rural and the urban population had visited both the *Ngaka* and the *Moprofiti* the majority of the rural population with traditional health care visits preferred the former type of healer. In the urban population the two types of traditional healers were visited equally often.

A strong positive correlation was found between church affiliation and the choice of type of traditional health care. Among the participants who had remained faithful to the traditional Tswana religious beliefs, a marked preference for the services of the *Ngaka* was demonstrated, while among the members of one of the African Independent Churches the *Moprofiti* was chosen in the vast majority of cases.

The members of the European Churches demonstrated a significantly lower tendency to seek traditional health care than any of the other religious groupings.

Even within the traditional health care sector psychosomatic complaints were very prevalent. Approximately 15% of all the visits to the *Ngaka* or *Moprofiti* were made with such symptoms. In the rural population almost one-fifth of all symptoms causing utilisation of traditional health care might have implied the presence of a communicable disease.

A very high proportion of all visits to the traditional sector by both the rural and urban population were made in order to seek advice on health problems or for preventative reasons in the traditional sense of the word.

Thus, in contrast to the modern sector, the traditional health care system seems to a very high extent to be occupied with prevention of disease and ill-health, although the scientifically educated observer would probably label many of these preventative activities as 'irrational'.

Payment by the patient to the *Ngaka* is generally made in the event the treatment proves successful only and in the majority of cases does not exceed a total of P20 (US$ 18).

Payment is only exceptionally made to the *Moprofiti*, who generally would consider his healing part of his religious work and a service to the members of the church.

A substantial proportion of the population interviewed had utilised both modern and traditional health care services because of the same disease (symptom). The reason given for this double consumption in the majority of these cases was quite simply the fact that the first course of treatment was not followed by recovery from the actual disease.

In this survey it was found that men would be relatively more inclined to seek traditional health care in case of disease than women.

It was also found that with increasing age an increasing tendency to seek traditional health care could be demonstrated. With an increasing level of education in the interviewed population group the tendency to utilise traditional health care services was decreasing. A marked tendency to increasing utilisation of modern health care services with increasing socio-economic status was found in the survey.

A marked trend to an increasing preference for traditional over modern care by decreasing socio-economic resources was also demonstrated.

In conclusion it has thus been demonstrated that the traditional health care system still plays a very important role in the everyday life of the population in Botswana, both in the rural and the urban communities.

The religious character of traditional healing has been demonstrated through the correlation between the religious beliefs of the health care seekers and their preference for a specific type of healing.

The modern health care sector according to the Primary Health Care Strategy, which has been fully adopted by the Government, should be dedicated to preventive work, but more than 98% of all individual visits by adults to the clinic or hospital are made for purely curative reasons.

In contrast the traditional sector has maintained its profile as predominantly occupied with the prevention of disease and ill-health in the individual contact with its patients.

Communicable diseases – which from public health points of view ought to be subjected to modern medical treatment – are to a very considerable extent still treated by the *Ngaka* or *Moprofiti*, while psychosomatic diseases, which demand thorough understanding of personal and socio-cultural factors in the individual case, are very often treated in the clinic or hospital, where, at least in the present situation, the risk of 'medicalisation' in such cases is high.

That the modern health care system has achieved a profile which seems to attract the comparatively privileged groups in society and to some extent reject the underprivileged groups is considered an important finding in this survey.

No doubt the majority of health problems – of which again the majority presumably are preventable – are found in the socially underprivileged groups in the community, and to attain the alluring goal of Health for All the modern health care sector must carefully examine the question, why so large a proportion of its resources seems to be monopolised by those who, objectively, seem to need them least.

A study of the approach and activities of the traditional healer and co-operation with him might prove helpful as part of this necessary process.

It is emphasised that a study of the present nature – predominantly using the methods of descriptive epidemiology – reveals part of the truth about human behaviour only.

An in-depth investigation, using the methods of social sciences including longitudinal participant observation of the behavioural patterns in sampled groups of the population, will be added to the present study in order to give a comprehensive and valid picture of the preferences in terms of choice of health care alternatives by disease/illness and symptoms in the population of Botswana.

THE CHANGING ATTITUDES TOWARDS TRADITIONAL HEALERS

The existence of *Dingaka tsa Setswana* was hardly acknowledged by the Bechuanaland Protectorate Administration until the 1920s. In 1927, however, the Protectorate Administration decided to take action against *Dingaka* and passed the Witchcraft Proclamation, which is still in legal force in Botswana (see Appendix IV).

The stated aim of this proclamation was 'to suppress the imputations or practice of pretended witchcraft'.

Studying the laws passed by the Tswana Chiefs during the early part of the 20th century (Seeley 1973), and comparing those to the above proclamation made by the colonial administration, a striking contrast appears.

While the Tswana Chief acknowledged *bongaka* (which means the art of traditional medicine) as a tribal healing skill and merely wanted to bring the work of the *Dingaka* under his control the colonial administration was determined to eradicate *Dingaka* from Tswana society, considering them representatives of vicious, heathen beliefs.

The Witchcraft Proclamation was aimed directly at the 'witchdoctor', which means the Diviner, and his supernatural manipulations and mystical healing technique.

The Herbalists, in contrast, were accepted as 'honest persons, who mix medicines for the purpose of curing their fellows' (Bechuanaland Protectorate Administration, files 37/4 and 6/1).

During the 1960s the control over the *Dingaka* was transferred from the central to the local level. The District Councils were given authority to issue licences to *Dingaka*. No distinction was initially made between Herbalists and Diviners in this respect.

In 1966 Botswana achieved its independence from colonial rule. The time had come to reappraise certain of the social institutions of Tswana culture, which had been neglected or suppressed by the colonial administration.

However, the heritage of the Protectorate Administration can plainly be seen in the attitude adopted by the independent Government: the Diviner, associated with the supernatural, must be eliminated, whereas the herbalist, concerned only with physical forms of healing, is to be granted the stamp of legitimacy through the possession of a licence, issued by the District Council (Ministry of Local Government 1969; Dennis 1978).

In the early 1970s Dingaka associations were being formed in Botswana. This should be seen as a consequence of the legal and social persecution from which traditional practitioners, particularly the Diviners, were continuously suffering. The formation of 'professional associations' by the *Dingaka* themselves thus was a political move to achieve social acceptability in accordance with European criteria.

The associations which were formed (see Appendices I and II), however, never gained any real influence vis-à-vis the Government. They soon became subjected to personal cultism and factionism. They were not able to act collectively to represent the interests of *Dingaka tsa Setswana* towards the Government and some of the associations have shown recent signs of disintegration.

Even more seriously, the existing associations of traditional healers disregard the fact that one-third of all Tswana healers are *Baprofiti*, with whom none of the associations communicate. The *Baprofiti* are not organised, but represent approximately 160 different societies of churches (see Appendix III), which do not communicate with each other. Thus the group of traditional healers in Botswana do not yet have any common forum or body, which can promote their interests in dealings with the Government.

The important question at the present time is whether such a national body – similar to the Zimbabwe National Traditional Healers' Association (ZINATHA) – should be formed in Botswana in order to serve the interests of both the healers and the country?

The following section will examine this crucial question.

PROPOSALS FOR THE GUIDANCE OF FUTURE CO-OPERATION

The options for health care planners in developing countries regarding official attitudes towards traditional medicine could be systematically described as four [Kikhela et al 1981):

Option 1: Making traditional medicine illegal.
This line has in Africa been followed by Kenya and the Ivory Coast. In the colonial era this policy was implemented by the majority of colonial administrations in African countries.

Such a policy could perhaps best be characterised as a 'line of self-deception' in which the lack of understanding of African culture and religion is formally expressed in a number of proclamations in complete contradiction to the actual life style of the people.

Option 2: Informal recognition of traditional medicine.
This could be characterised as a *laissez-faire* policy, where the concern of the official authorities is focused on modern, Western health care and the existence and significance of the traditional sector is more or less ignored. This, rather like the first option, also seems to be leading to a state of self-deception in which the country deprives itself of the potential positive effects of co-operation with the traditional sector and deprives itself of important epidemiological information on the utilisation of health care in the traditional sector.

This option may even be dangerous, because it could become an incitement for traditional healers to adopt, successively, the conceptions and practices of the bio-mechanically oriented modern medicine, thereby defecting from their own holistic views and unique integration into the local cultural and social environment. This might contain serious negative implications for the future health care for the population.

Option 3: Simple legislation regulating traditional medicine.
Simply licensing traditional practitioners does not necessarily imply any regulation of traditional medicine, but has served purely fiscal purposes in many African countries, including Botswana. Simple legislation might

regulate certain negative effects of traditional practices but does not seem to imply any substantial improvement of the comprehensive health care system of the country.

Option 4: Co-operation with traditional healers.
In Botswana the official attitude towards traditional medicine could be described as a process of gradual development from Option 1 (during the colonial era) via Options 2 and 3, and now facing Option 4 as the desirable common denominator for future policy. This policy has been formulated by the Government in the most recent National Development Plan (1979–85) where section 13.28 reads as follows:

> There are a large number of traditional practitioners of various types who are frequently consulted on health and personal matters. The Ministry of Health will continue its policy of gradually strengthening links with traditional practitioners – both diviners/herbalists and faith healers. The emphasis will be put on improving mutual understanding, especially about the practices and techniques of the traditional practitioners.

A policy for co-operation between the modern and the traditional health care sector could in principle be formulated in three different ways:

One could choose an integration of the two systems, implying inter alia, an employment of the traditional healers by the Government in some form or the other.

The co-operation could also take the form of a *professionalisation* of the traditional healers, implying Governmental control of their activities by means of laws and regulations.

And finally *co-operation* could be developed between two independent sectors, not intending to control or regulate but to respect the unique character of each other.

An *integration* of traditional and modern medicine is seen by the author as a bad choice, as this integration is bound to be deleterious for the unique character of traditional medicine. To modern medicine an integration would imply short-term advantages, only to traditional medicine it would most probably act as a 'kiss of death'.

A professionalisation of traditional medicine, implying control and regulation of the activities of the traditional healers, is seen by the author as a bad choice for the co-operation policy for the following three reasons:

The traditional healer, as it has appeared in the preceding description of his social role and significance, occupies a unique position in the Tswana village. He is a socio-culturally integrated local community leader and through close co-operation with him the success of the primary health care strategy – based on local community participation in preventative health work – might be secured. Professionalisation implies an obvious risk of disrupting the healer's socio-cultural integration and must thus be avoided.

It has been stated that regulation and control of the activities of the traditional healers by the authorities is necessary to avoid a misuse of his power in the local community. This statement is not necessarily valid. The existing mechanisms for social control in the local community seem to be effective and act immediately to regulate and eliminate any excessive power of a particular member of the community immediately this power is used for purposes other than those beneficial to the community as a whole.

When and if a professionalisation of traditional medicine takes place and the traditional healer is thus removed from his socio-cultural integration in the local community control by the authorities of his activities will be necessary.

But if a professionalisation is avoided, the necessary control and regulation of his activities will be satisfactorily exercised by the intact traditional community.

From this rule of an effective social control in the indigenous Tswana village an important exception must be observed: the recently appearing group of alternative traditional practitioners – or neo-herbalists – represents no socio-cultural integration and they are often practising their healing skills on an ambulatory basis.

Thus official regulation of their activities is mandatory to avoid charlatanism and commercialism.

A professionalisation of traditional medicine implies a substantial risk of imposing some of the analytical, bio-mechanical concepts of modern medicine on the traditional healer and directing him towards those elements of traditional healing – like, for example, herbalism – which may be accommodated within the framework of modern medical thinking. Such a development might not necessarily be seen as a progress towards health for all Batswana. The value of traditional medicine to a large extent is defined in the field of its conceptions of illness and disease.

It is modern medicine which must widen its analytical views and conceptions and learn from the synthesising and holistic views of traditional medicine – not the other way round.

Preventative activities and preventative thinking dominate the field of traditional health care.

As part of a professionalisation of traditional medicine an obvious risk exists of imposing the curatively biassed way of thinking and working of the modern health care sector on the traditional one. Signs of such an influence have been noticed in Botswana, where a group of traditional healers are planning to build a 'herbalistic hospital'. Such a development most probably will not contribute significantly to the improvement of the health of Batswana.

Regarding the above considerations a suggestion is made that the future co-operation between modern and traditional medicine in Botswana should take place between two independent partners at all appropriate levels of community life and be characterised by mutual respect, open-mindedness and interest in learning and modifying conceptions and practices, when necessary.

The following proposals have been made to the Ministry of Health of Botswana, intended to form the basis of the discussions about the formulation of the future co-operation policy in Botswana.

It has been suggested, regarding organisational structure, that a departmental committee should be appointed in the near future, charged with initiating and drawing up guidelines for co-operation. On important issues the committee should consult existing organisations representing modern medicine, as well as nationwide organisations representing all main groups of traditional healers. Since the cult of personality and the forming of factions are characteristic features of traditional medicine in Botswana it is to be expected that all of the existing organisations of traditional healers will demand representation at consultations with the departmental committee.

So far four national *Dingaka* organisations have been registered in Botswana. The particulars regarding these Associations are found as Appendix I and their constitutions as Appendix II to this paper.

The question of the representation of the Independent Faith Healing Churches (see Appendix III) in the departmental committee has yet to be solved.

At the regional level, it has been suggested that regional committees be established on the initiative of the Public Health Team which should include all active representatives of organisations of traditional medicine in the region. These regional committees should act on central initiatives and be responsible for training courses and detailed planning of co-operation in each district in the region.

At the local level it is suggested that the Village Health Committees, which already exist in some areas (and which ensure local participation in primary health care initiatives and prevention in the broadest sense of the work), should elect the local traditional healer to a leading position in their organisation.

Questions concerning training are considered essential and should, as already mentioned, contain initiatives aimed at traditional healers as well as at scientifically educated health care workers. All health care personnel workers from so-called 'developed countries' who are sent to assist 'developing countries' should, before leaving home, be made familiar with the principles of traditional medicine and its treatment traditions in the host country in which they will work.

Research programmes are of prime importance and priority should be given to projects of an epidemiological nature, as well as projects within the fields of ethno-psychiatry, psychology, sociology and anthropology.

A comprehensive research programme has recently been initiated in Botswana. The programme aims at broadening and deepening the knowledge of traditional medicine in Botswana, acquired through the present survey and a number of other, minor, surveys.

Traditional conceptions of causes of disease and of taboos related to nutrition, pregnancy and delivery will be studied in some depth. The process of interaction between the traditional health workers and their patients will be studied.

The field of herbal medicine in Botswana will be described through an identification and detailed description of herbal drugs used by healers. On the basis of this screening – which has so far identified approximately 200 species of medicinal plants – it is hoped that phytochemical and pharmacognostic studies can be initiated.

Since the work of designing preventive programmes and securing the participation of the local population in primary preventive activities is considered essential, detailed plans have been drawn up for regional and central support for the work of the Village Health Committee.

No specific legislation to regulate the co-operation between traditional and modern medicine in Botswana has been considered advisable. On the contrary, it has been suggested that the existing legislation, which is of a decidedly colonial nature, showing little understanding for certain important features in Tswana culture, should be abolished.

SUMMARY

Two systematic responses to the call for health could be defined in the contemporary Tswana culture. One is the modern, bio-mechanically oriented health care system, brought to Botswana by the advent of Western civilisation. The other is the system of traditional health care, deeply rooted in the indigenous Tswana culture and serving vital functions of social, cultural and judicial control in the traditional society.

The traditional healer in the Tswana village – basing his conceptions of causes of disease and his preventative and curative practices on well-defined religious beliefs – has generally been rejected by representatives of the Western civilisation, who have defined him as a 'witch-doctor' and seen his conceptions and activities as exclusively harmful and a threat to progress, especially in the field of modern health care.

Recently, however, a re-evaluation of the role of traditional medicine in the Tswana villages has been made by some modern health workers. Through a number of studies it has become evident that traditional medicine still plays a very important role in the everyday life of the rural population of Botswana and that the traditional healers – both the *Dingaka* and the *Baprofiti* – are true local community leaders.

Traditional medicine in Tswana culture – being far more than merely an instrument for curative care – must be evaluated on its own premises and is not directly comparable to the system of modern medicine. An integration of the two systems might be deleterious to both, while an open minded co-operation – characterised by mutual respect and willingness to learn – might convey important values to both health care systems and facilitate the progress towards 'Health For All Batswana'.

Basing its policy on the above consideration the Ministry of Health of Botswana has formulated its strategy for the future co-operation between the traditional and the modern health care sector, to be implemented at the central, regional and local level. The results from comprehensive research activities currently undertaken in Botswana, will guide the detailed planning of this policy, aiming at recognising the potential values of traditional medicine in the Tswana villages and utilising these values for the benefit of the health of the population.

REFERENCES

Bechuanaland Protectorate Administration. Office Files 1908–1927, files numbered 37/4 and 6/1. Botswana National Archives.

Boshill, A., (1975), *Witchdoctor*. Johannesburg: The Museum of Man and Science.

Bø, O., (1972), *Folkmedicin og laerd medicin*. Oslo: Det Norske Samlaget.

Chavunduka, G., (1978), *Traditional Healers and the Shona Patient*. Gwelo: Mambo Press.

Dennis, C., (1978), 'The role of *Dingaka tsa Setswana* from the 19th Century to the Present', *Botswana Notes and Records*, 10, pp. 53–66.

Kikhela, N., *et al.*, (1981), 'Africa's two medical systems', *World Health Forum*, 2, 96–99.

Lalonde, M. A., (1975), *New Perspectives on the Health of Canadians*. Ottawa: Ministry of National Health and Welfare.

McKeown, T., (1972), *Population Studies*, 26, 11.

Makhurane, P. M., (1980), paper in Fako, T. T., (ed.), *Health, Illness and the Socio-cultural Setting* (Seminar Proceedings), Gaborone: N.I.R.

Mead, M., (1955), *Cultural Patterns and Technical Change*. New York: Mentor Books.

Ministry of Local Government and Lands (1969), Circular from the Permanent Secretary, Ref. no. LG/18(130).

Schapera, I., (1976), 1984 (rep.), *The Tswana*. London: International African Institute.

Seeley, C., (1973), *The Reaction of the Tswana to the Practice of Western Medicine* (Unpublished paper, University of London.) Botswana National Archives.

Staugard, F., (In press.) *Traditional Healthcare in Botswana*. Monograph.

Sundkler, B. G. M., (1970), *Bantu Prophets in South Africa*. London: Oxford University Press for the International African Institute.

Time Magazine (1982), 120, 52, p. 44.

WHO (1978), *The Promotion and Development of Traditional Medicine*. (WHO Technical Report Series 622.) Geneva: WHO.

APPENDIX I

Dingaka associations registered in Botswana by 31 December 1983

Total number of associations: 4

Name of association	*No. of members*	*Headquarters*	*Reg. date*
The *Dingaka* Society	225	P.O. Box 150, Gaborone	27/04/73
The Botswana *Dingaka* Association	31	P.O. Box 19, Ramotswa	/73
Kwame Traditional Association	1,629[1]	P.O. Box 49, Selebi-Pikwe	02/05/77
United Herbalists Association	56	P.O. Box 219, Mahalapye	02/03/79

[1] The author has only been able to find verification for a small fraction of the registered number of members of this Association.

APPENDIX II.1

THE BOTSWANA DINGAKA SOCIETY

Our Society will be governed by the regulations embodied in our constitution as shown below:

1. General membership meetings will be held annually to discuss the overall operations of the society.
2. We pledge ourselves to examine every patient or anything using our traditional apparati and treat all types of diseases wherever it is possible for us to do so.
3. We shall have a board of Tswana Traditional Medical Examiners to inspect all the Tswana traditional doctors so as to ensure that each one of them is doing his (or her) work competently, fairly and in accordance with the Tswana traditional healing practices. The Board will furthermore check and condemn all underground manipulations of witchcraft. It will have to see to it that there is coordination, cooperation and spirit of trust between the doctors and patient.
4. We shall establish institutions where Tswana traditional medical practices will be carried out.
5. We shall teach anybody who wants to be a Tswana traditional doctor and the fee charged for tuition will be P100.00 for a period of one year.
6. At the end of the year a trainee will be examined and if he or she passes he/she will be presented with an authentic certificate after having paid an examination fee of P4.00
7. Our aspiration is to consolidate our efforts in the spirit of oneness so as to be able to serve the Botswana nation faithfully and with the love of mankind.
8. Our society membership is open to anybody who is interested in it, and membership joining fee is P6.00.
9. Subscription fee will be P4.00 a year.

10. Any traditional doctor who wants to be examined by the society in order to qualify for a medical certificate will pay P6.00 after s/he has been given a test case in which s/he proved herself/himself a competent practitioner.
11. We shall open a savings account for money coming in as membership fees, subscription fees and testing fees.
12. The Society's account books will be audited after every three months by the society's auditors.
13. The employees of the Society will be paid out of the Society's funds.
14. The Society's constitution will be reviewed and amended from time to time when ever it is necessary to do so.
15. The General elections for office bearers will be held after every five years.
16. No Tswana traditional doctor who is a member of the society is allowed to indulge himself/herself in any cases of witchcraft manoeuvres.
17. The Society will try to encourage its members to specialise in various fields of medical practices.
18. The Botswana Dingaka Society will work in close relationship with the European doctors, and therefore all cases which the Society members are not able to treat will be referred to European doctors.

OFFICE BEARERS OF THE SOCIETY'S EXECUTIVE COMMITTEE

1. President
2. Vice-President
3. Chairman
4. Vice-Chairman
5. Secretary General
6. Recording Secretary
7. Treasurer
8. Two Auditors

FUNCTIONS OF THE OFFICE BEARERS

1. President
    (*a*) To formulate policies of the Society in consultation with his colleagues.
    (*b*) To see to it that the policies of the Society are effectively implemented.
    (*c*) To handle the overall administrative matters of the Society and to allocate functions to various members of the Society executive committee members.
    (*d*) To approve the appointment of the Society employees and look into their terms of service.
    (*e*) To represent the Botswana Dingaka Society at an international level where African Traditional Medical Practices or issues are discussed.
    (*f*) To preside at the annual general meetings for the elections of new office bearers of the executive committee of the Society members.
    (*g*) To determine the days on which the annual general meetings will be held and at which places.
    (*h*) To sign the certificates which are to be presented to those who qualify as Tswana Traditional Doctors.
    (*i*) To act as a liaison between the Society and the Government of Botswana and keep both of them informed about the other's views.
    (*j*) To make it a point that Society members reserve certain rights for him as president to exercise special powers on certain matters.
    (*k*) To delegate some of his powers to certain members of the Society.
    (*l*) To coopt certain individuals from the public to the Society with the approval of the executive committee.
    (*m*) To approve of the appointment of the Tswana Traditional Medical Supervisors in the various districts.
    (*n*) To guide and advise the Society members on policy and general administrative procedure.

(*o*) To call for emergency meetings on matters of urgency.
(*p*) To keep contact with other African Traditional Doctors outside Botswana.

2. Vice-President
(*a*) To deputise for the president on policy and overall administrative matters of the Society as laid down above.
(*b*) To refer all cases which are beyond his responsibility to the president for action.
(*c*) To keep the president informed of the current events of the Society.
(*d*) To keep a close watch or supervision on the operations of the executive committee.
(*e*) To collect all necessary information from the executive committee for presentation to the president.
(*f*) To advise the president on various matters related to the needs and running of the Society.
(*g*) To accept day-to-day instructions from the president as the need arises.

3. Chairman
(*a*) To preside at executive committee meetings to discuss whatever has been tabled for processing.
(*b*) To see to it that every executive member of the committee attends to his duties accordingly.
(*c*) To prepare agendas for the executive committee meetings.
(*d*) To see to it that the democratic committee procedure is followed at all the meetings, and to ensure that every member of the committee is well acquainted with that procedure.
(*e*) To make it a point that all members of the committee attend the meetings regularly.
(*f*) To disseminate all necessary information to the committee members and the Society as a whole.
(*g*) To make sure that matters discussed at committee meetings are productive and beneficial.
(*h*) To help the president and vice-president in the implementation of the society's policies.
(*i*) To create smooth working relations among the committees members.

4. Vice-Chairman
(*a*) To act on behalf of the chairman when the chairman is not available, but operating only within the framework as laid down before the chairman to work on.
(*b*) To advise the chairman on all matters of procedure, administration and policy.
(*c*) To accept day to day instructions from the chairman.
(*d*) To help the chairman in his overall responsibilities.

5. Secretary General
(*a*) To handle all correspondences with the external traditional and non-traditional medical agencies or societies.
(*b*) To compile both internal and external annual reports and distribute them to all members of the Society.
(*c*) To arrange external visits of the Society officials with the president, vice-president, chairman and vice-chairman.
(*d*) To help the recording secretary in discharging his normal duties i.e. keeping all the records of the Society up to date.
(*e*) To operate within the instructions given to him by the president, vice-president, chairman and vice-chairman.

(*f*) To help the president, vice-president, chairman and vice-chairman in implementing procedures and administrative policies.
(*g*) To promote and popularise the name of the society externally.

6. Recording Secretary
(*a*) To take minutes at all the meetings of the Society members.
(*b*) To handle all the correspondences of the Society within the country.
(*c*) To compile annual reports of the Society and distribute them to all members of the Society.
(*d*) To publish notices, promote and popularise the name of the Society inside the country.
(*e*) To notify the Society members three weeks in advance about meetings which are intended to be held on specified days and places, and also distribute copies of the agendas connected with those meetings.

7. Treasurer
(*a*) To handle and be answerable for all financial accounts of the Society.
(*b*) To make sure that the Society's money entrusted to him is saved at the bank in the name of the Society.
(*c*) To ensure that those who withdraw the Society's money from the bank are only those who are allowed by the constitution to sign for the Society's money.

8. Two Auditors
Both of them have to inspect the financial records of the society and submit their report to the members.

SIGNING FOR SOCIETY'S MONEY WHEN A WITHDRAWAL IS MADE AT THE BANK

There should always be two signatures appearing on the withdrawal slip when the society's money is to be taken out of the bank, and the treasurer's signature must at all times be one of the two. Apart from the signature of the treasurer one of the following can countersign the slip:

President
Chairman
Secretary General

APPENDIX II.2
CONSTITUTION OF THE BOTSWANA DINGAKA ASSOCIATION

1. The name of the Association shall be:
'THE BOTSWANA DINGAKA ASSOCIATION'.
2. The aims and objects of the Association are:
(*a*) To control the practice of Dingaka (Herbalists) in Botswana and to aid and help the practice of Herbalism in Botswana;
(*b*) To train herbalists in Botswana and to ensure that they have adequate training and to ensure that they render adequate services in the practice of Herbalism and to this end to set and supervise examination of would-be Herbalists;
(*c*) To hold meetings at which practising Dingaka can attend and at which discussions can be held for the mutual help for members and also to try and encourage others to join the profession and to become members of the Association;
(*d*) To discipline members who are unprofessional in their conduct and to this end to make laws to be obeyed by members;
3. At annual meetings to be held in each calendar year there will be elected a

Supervisor and his Helper, A General Secretary and an Assistant Secretary, District Chairmen and District Secretaries for outlying areas, a Treasury and Executive Committee consisting of SIX (6) members. At General Meetings the supervisor will be the Chairman.

4. The Supervisor will supervise generally the work of the Association, the Training of learners, the examination of would-be learners and shall issue certificates of proficiency. He will be assisted by his Helper. The Secretary shall keep in touch with all members of the Association and with the District Chairmen and will advise all members of the dates of General Meetings and will prepare lists of would-be members of the Association to undergo training and submit them to the Supervisor, to collect reports of breaches of discipline or unprofessional conduct of members of the Association and lay them before the Executive Committee. The Assistant Secretary will assist the Secretary and shall record the minutes of all meetings and Executive meetings and will prepare Agendas of matters to be considered by meetings. The Treasurer shall keep records of all monies received and shall open a Bank Account in the name of the Association wherein he will deposit all monies. The Financial Records of the Association will be laid before a General Meeting each year. The Executive Committee will carry out all Resolutions passed at General Meeting each year. The Executive Committee will carry out all Resolutions passed at General Meetings and shall meet whenever called to consider breaches of discipline and to impose the penalties therefor and generally to carry out the Executive side of the Association through the Secretary. The Executive Committee shall have full powers to punish members found guilty by the Committee of unprofessional conduct and may expel members from the Association in suitable cases.

APPENDIX II.3
THE KWAME TRADITIONAL ASSOCIATION OF BOTSWANA

1. NAME: The Association shall be known as:
   The Kwame (Legwame) Traditional Association of Botswana.
2. PREAMBLE
   In the midst of the Street of it, and on either side of the river was there the Tree of Life, which bare twelve manner of fruits, and yielded her fruit every month, and the leaves of the tree were for the healing of the nations.
   (Revelation 22:2)
3. AIMS AND OBJECTS
   (*a*) To unite the Botswana Herbalists and Dingaka.
   (*b*) To teach them the proper use of African Herbs.
   (*c*) To register members and to approve certificates issued by the association.
   (*d*) To guide members against any abuses and corruption.
   (*e*) To provide adequate apprenticeship facilities to all trainees under the tutorship and auspices of the Association.
   (*f*) To inculcate a Christian spirit among all members of the Association.
   (*g*) To create and encourage a spirit of neighbourly cooperation between the Association, Government and Local Authorities and any such other social Society along the boundaries and borders of the Republic of Botswana.
4. THE GENERAL MEETING
   There shall be a general meeting once a year at which the executive and other fitting committees shall be elected.
   (*a*) *Composition*. The general meeting shall consist of members elected from the

Net Net

various branches throughout the country at their respective meetings for this specific purpose.

Beginners

Trainees

1. Beginners of Herbs will be trained for three successive years before they are given full membership Certificate for the Association of the Kwame Traditionals.
2. They will be given some tests during this period. Successful ones will be issued with Temporary Certificates.
3. Herbalists who wish to further their knowledge of Herbs will be tested first to find out what their experience in Herbs is like.
4. They will only be examined at the annual conference. Those who pass will be issued with Association's full Certificate.
5. Traditional beginners in Lots casting and Herbs will be trained for six successive years before they are allowed to practise alone.
6. From time to time they will be taken out to the mountains for the practice of casting lots and other mountain Herbs and Roots barks. A practice of Traditional healing songs and dancing will be taught to these trainees. Temporary Certificates as Scholars will be issued to them and frequent tests will be given and practical work will be performed till the end of the sixth year.

(*b*) Any major issues such as misconduct of members, venue, finances of the Association, election of office-bearers may and are discussed at this meeting, and each branch shall meet expenses for its delegation to this General Meeting.

5. POWERS

The General Meeting shall have the powers to:

1. Examine closely all activities of the association for the current year;
2. Dissolve the Association by a two thirds majority of all delegates present, voting by either public or private ballot. After a dissolution, the assets and liabilities shall be divided on a pro-rata basis amongst the branches; the dissolution shall accordingly be reported to the Registrar and the Ministry of Health, Labour and Home Affairs;
3. Amend the Constitution;
4. Discuss any general matters under the heading 'General Business'. (Any business to be discussed at the General Meeting should be sent to the General Secretary of the Association in motion form a month in advance so that it can be circularised to all branches);
5. To elect office-bearers for the ensuing year of activity who shall be president, general secretary, treasurer, vice-president, recording secretary. Each district shall elect its own executive committee as above.

6. THE EXECUTIVE COMMITTEE AND ITS DUTIES

1. Make decisions and policies for the association in the interim of the General Meeting;
2. Fix a date for the next General Meeting;
3. Organise fund-raising campaigns, allocate and supervise projects for which these funds will be expended;
4. Operate a banking account in the name of the Association with any local bank or building society;
5. There shall be two signatories and that of the Treasurer to any cheque made out by the Association;
7. The treasurer shall present the budget at the General Meeting;

8. The Executive Committee shall hold office to the next General Meeting and any member qualifies for re-election.

7. OFFICE-BEARERS

All office-bearers are officers of the association and are answerable and responsible to the association.

A In addition to members of the executive committee, there shall be branch chairmen, branch secretaries or secretary-treasurers.

B Branch secretaries should forward the branches' activities to the general secretary two months in advance for inclusion in the Annual General Report.

8. DUTIES OF MEMBERS OF THE CENTRAL EXECUTIVE

(Members of the General Meeting)

1. *President*
   (*a*) Supervise the operations and activities of the entire Association;
   (*b*) Preside at all general or special meetings of the Associaton;
   (*c*) Supervise the training and apprenticeship of all student-herbalists and award certificates or diplomas;
   (*d*) Appoint three to five members of the executive committee to hear any complaints from or about any member of the Association.
2. *Vice-President*
   Shall substitute for the president in the former's absence, save on the Trial or Complaints committee.
3. *General Secretary*
   (*a*) Shall keep in contact with all branches of the Association;
   (*b*) Make known the work and activities of the association to the general public;
   (*c*) See to the enrolment of new members to the Association;
   (*d*) Convene the special or general meetings of the Association;
   (*e*) Keep a comprehensive record of general or special meetings, Trial Committee and all other matters of or about the association, its constitution or activities.
4. *The Recording/Assistant Secretary*
   As above in the former's absence.
5. *Treasurer*
   This officer shall, besides keeping and banking of all Associations funds, be the Accountant and Financial Secretary of the Association. He shall:
   (*a*) Present a detailed financial report at the general meeting;
   (*b*) With the President or Secretary, sign all cheques.

9. SPECIAL ARTICLES OF THE ASSOCIATION

1. No member of the Association shall run a business or any enterprise whatever of his own in the name and/or style of the Association.

2. Herbalists' shops shall comply with the trading laws of the Republic of Botswana as promulgated by Parliament from time to time.

3. All member herbalists shall be guided and controlled by the Medical, Dental and Pharmaceutical Laws.

4. The Association shall not hold itself responsible for wrongful activities or contraventions of the above laws or any law of the state by any member doing so on his own initiative.

5. The Association reserves the right to summarily expel any member who contravenes any item hereinunder mentioned.

6. The office of the Association shall be at Selebi-Phikwe, PO Box 49, telephone 411.

10. CONTROL OF DEFAULTERS
A board of seven or more members will be elected by the General Meeting. This board shall be known as Branch Inspectors, whose members will consist of a chairman, vice-chairman, secretary, vice-secretary and a treasurer. These members deal with defaulters and submit the reports to the General Secretary of the Association.
11. RESTRICTION
The Association is restricted to any members or any person who shall call himself/herself a Traditional Association Member. But practising of witchcraft and robbery, using human flesh, using poison bushes to kill, – by means of healing, giving thieves medicine to hide from the police, taking money from patients and going away with money and medicines, stealing livestock, using western medical injections is forbidden.

APPENDIX III.1

FAITH HEALING CHURCHES, REGISTERED IN BOTSWANA BY 29 FEBRUARY, 1984. TOTAL NUMBER OF CHURCHES: 158.

[Please observe that this is not a comprehensive list of churches and religious societies in Botswana. It includes Faith Healing Churches of Zionist origin, but excludes European (missionary) Churches (for example Anglican Church, Roman Catholic Church) and other religious denominations (for example Botswana Hindu Society, Botswana Islamic Society).]

Name of society	*No. of M'bers*	*Headquarters*	*Date of reg.*
Abanaesa Association Church	105	PO Box 68, Moshupa	16/09/82
Abraham Church of Botswana	210	PO Box 52, Lethiekeng (Molepolole)	04/06/82
Africa Born Full Gospel Church	550	PO Box 7, Moeng	28/05/79
African Gospel Church	N/A	Lobatse	18/01/74
African Evangelical United Church of Christ	N/A	Gaborone	15/08/73
Antioch Church of Botswana	265	PO Box 844, Gaborone	19/01/81
Apostolic Faith Church in Botswana	300	PO Box 24, Kasane	24/03/80
Apostolic Jerusalem Church	N/A	Morwa	07/12/74
Ascension Church	350	PO Box 114, Lobatse	06/01/75
Barongwa BA Morena	260	PO Box 10013 Francistown	03/09/81
Bethania Church of God	30	Radisele	20/06/75
Betheela Christian Church	105	PO Box 1410, Gaborone	20/07/79
Bethlehem City of Christ Church	N/A	Gaborone	25/04/73
Bethlehem City of Christ Church in Zion (BCCCZ)	2,000	PO Box 144, Tonota	13/08/76
Bethlehem Faith Mission	N/A	Kgagodi	18/06/73
Blessed Peace of Jesus Christ Church	347	PO Box 179, Serowe	01/12/81
Body Church of Jesus Christ	350	PO Box 57, Pitsane	05/08/81
Bontle Bethsada African Church	195	PO Box 39, Gaborone	20/04/82
Botshelo Apostolic Church	*ca.* 50	PO Box 480, S-Phikwe	13/08/82

Name of society	*No. of M'bers*	*Headquarters*	*Date of reg.*
Botswana Brightness Church of Zion	*ca.* 200	Tsetsebe	09/12/82
Botswana Crusaders Church	N/A	Francistown	25/02/75
Botswana Festival Church in Zion	250	PO Box 4, Tshesebe	08/10/78
Botswana Holiness Church of Christ	500	PO Box 336, Serowe	18/11/74
Botswana Independent Church	500	PO Box 15, Tsabong	06/03/79
Botswana New Apostolic Church	600	PO Box 1852, Gaborone	11/02/81
Botswana Spiritual Christian Church	150	PO Box 10263 Totitown (F-town)	02/07/75
Botswana Star Church in Zion	350	PO Box 89, Lobatse	22/05/81
Christ the Word of God	1,025	PO Box 003, Gaborone	16/07/75
Christian Apostolic Church in Zion of South Africa	N/A	Lobatse	01/11/74
Christian Apostolic Healing Church	1,200	PO Box 87, Gaborone	23/07/82
Christian Baatlhodi Apostolic	127	PO Box 71, Molepolole	18/04/80
Christian Holy Church in Zion of South Africa	N/A	Sikwane	15/11/74
Church of Botswana	150	Gaborone	15/04/80
Church of God in Christ	250	PO Box 397, Letlhakeng	27/04/73
Church of God Mission	N/A	Maun	25/04/73
Church of God of Prophecy	321	PO Box 79, Lobatse	16/04/73
Church of the Living God Apostolic	N/A	Serowe	05/05/79
Citizen Apostolic Prophet Church	N/A	Serowe	N/A
Dipesalema Church of Botswana	3,230	PO Box 20797, Gaborone	11/02/80
Diphapo Church	551	PO Box 29, Letlhakane	30/12/82
Ditiro Church of Botswana	250	PO Box 59, Mmadinare	06/07/79
East Foundation Apostolic Church of God	55	PO Box 30276, Tlokweng	08/12/82
Eleven Apostles Healing Church	N/A	Francistown	16/04/73
Elotha Apostolic Prophet Church in Africa	160	PO Box 20216, Gaborone	03/05/79
Emmanuel Holy Apostolic Church	260	PO Box 95, Kanye	05/01/76
Episcopal Apostolic Church in Zion in Africa	N/A	Kanye	30/01/76
Evangelical Religious Protestant Unity Church	N/A	Ghanzi	17/04/73
Evangelist Apostolic Prophet Church	30	PO Box 20246 Gaborone	22/04/83
Fair Heavens of New Bethlehem Apostolic Church	N/A	Letlhakane	29/04/75
Faith Gospel After Christ Church	1,460	Moeng	09/09/75
First Apostolic Church of St John in South Africa	24	PO Box 38, Thamaga	13/05/75
First Christ Apostolic Church	140	Mahalapye	02/08/82
First Kappondolian No. 2 Apostolic Jerusalem Church Zion of the Republic of Botswana	N/A	Mmathethe	18/05/72
Five Apostolic Church	115	PO Box 319, Mahalapye	22/08/75
Forward in Faith	N/A	Gaborone	17/10/74
Foundation of Truth Sanctuary	N/A	Lobatse	16/08/74

Name of society	*No. of M'bers*	*Headquarters*	*Date of reg.*
Four Gospel of the Lord Church	300	PO Box 2002, Gaborone	04/11/82
Free Church of Botswana	1,377	PO Box 138, Molepolole	17/04/75
Full Church of Africa	N/A	Francistown	18/11/74
Full Gospel Church of God	700	PO Box 187, Lobatse	17/10/73
Galatia Church in Zion	80	PO Box 142, Serowe	05/07/74
General Apostolic Church of Botswana	357	PO Box 488, Gaborone	14/10/74
Gospel Messengers Church	450	PO Box 713, Francistown	10/10/78
Gospel of God Church	6	PO Box 10104, Francistown	23/08/77
Great Christian Church of Botswana	100	PO Box 37, Palapye	13/03/79
Guta Ra Jehova Church	N/A	Tutume	22/08/75
Guta Ra Mwari (City of God)	N/A	Francistown	18/04/74
Hand of Lord Apostolic Church	N/A	Lobatse	09/10/79
Head Mountain of God Apostolic Church in Zion	850	PO Box 20954 Gaborone	08/08/74
Healing Church in Botswana	1,000	PO Box 413, Selebi-Philwe	17/10/74
Hermon Church	*ca.* 100	PO Box 16, S-Phikwe	26/04/79
Holy Apostolic Church in Zion	53	PO Box 20936	20/07/79
Holy Banner Mission Church of Africa (THABALA)	350	PO Box 13, Letlhakeng	21/05/79
Holy Bethsaida Apostolic Church of Botswana	780	PO Box 370, Serowe	08/12/80
Holy Bontle Apostolic Church in Zion	2,048	PO Box 39, Rakops	14/08/74
Holy Christian Church	235	PO Box 839, Serowe	08/10/75
Holy Free Corner Stone Apostolic Church	830	PO Box 104, Francistown	27/04/73
Holy Galileo Apostolic Church	85	PO Box 79, Francistown	12/02/75
Holy Sarda Apostolic Christian Church of South Africa	400	PO Box 39, Mmatsetse	27/04/73
Holy Zion Church of Botswana	851	PO Box 108, Molepolole	04/10/77
*Hosanna Religious Traditional Association	196	PO Box 27, Ramokwebane	16/04/81
Independent Church of Francistown	21	PO Box 478, Francistown	04/03/81
Jacob's Ladder Church	520	PO Box 509, Kanye	04/06/75
Jericho Church	479	PO Box 639, Francistown	23/08/74
Kanana Church of Botswana	250	PO Box 463, Kanye	28/01/82
Lefika Je Le Sakhuting	50	PO Box 10203, Tuti-Town, Francistown	30/12/82
Light of God Church	100	PO Box 28, Mmadinare	02/05/75
Light of Life Church in Botswana	N/A	Lobatse	02/12/75
Local Church of Botswana	N/A	Lobatse	19/04/74
Love of God Church	861	PO Box 104, Francistown	04/12/81
Memorial Apostolic Church	121	PO Box 31, Molepolole	01/04/75
Messiah Church of Ten Commandments MCC	182	PO Box 4, Ramokgwebane	23/01/79
Morian Episcopal Church	N/A	Mahalapye	27/09/74

Name of society	*No. of M'bers*	*Headquarters*	*Date of reg.*
Morning Star Apostolic Church of Christ	35	PO Box 26, Tutume	03/09/81
National Church of God in Christ in Botswana	155	PO Box 1500, Gaborone	28/05/82
Nazareth Church of Botswana	575	PO Box 7, Ramatswa	26/04/74
New Apostolic Church in Zion	319	PO Box 10, Tonota	08/07/74
New Apostolic Prophets Church	N/A	Radisele	13/08/74
New Convert Church of Christ Mission	410	PO Box 1543	31/12/82
New Foundation Apostolic Church of Christ in Jerusalem	150	PO Box 1203, Gaborone	03/01/80
New Jerusalem Apostolic Church in Zion	N/A	Francistown	15/11/74
New Zealand Board Church of Christ	300	PO Box 293, Francistown	23/09/82
Noah Church	257	PO Box 50, Letlhakeng	27/04/79
Nomere Church of Africa	50	PO Box 6, Moeng	27/07/81
Old Apostolic Church of Africa	3,000	PO Box 1, Lobatse	08/10/74
Original Apostolic Church	900	PO Box 180, Mahalapye	20/05/81
Peace Ever Church of Botswana	N/A	Tutume	10/03/81
Persia Church of Zion in Botswana	*ca.* 210	PO Box 480, Selebi-Phikwe	04/10/82
Phutego Ya Ga Keresete	555	PO Box 352, Gaborone	01/04/77
Revelation Blessed Peace Church of Botswana	N/A	Selebi-Phikwe	01/03/76
St Andrew's Society of Botswana	58	Private Bag 0030, Gaborone	25/04/73
St Anna's Church	986	Private Bag 34, Francistown	14/01/81
St Apostolic Church of Botswana	200	PO Box 86, Mahalapye	26/03/76
St Cana Apostolic Church in Zion	50	PO Box 839, Francistown	10/06/82
St David Apostolic Healing Church	N/A	Serowe	14/10/74
St Emmanuel Apostolic Church of South Africa	125	PO Box 377, Gaborone	06/03/79
St Engenas Zion Christian Church	7,950	PO Box 10024, Gaborone	17/09/74
St Ezekiel Church of Botswana	300	Private Bag 938, Matolwane	08/11/82
St Faith Holy Church	5,013	PO Box 168, Francistown	25/06/78
St Gallery Church	401	PO Box 1888, Gaborone	28/11/77
St Gethsemane Church of Christ in Botswana	505	PO Box 1293, Gaborone	16/01/75
St Jacob's Apostolic Church	N/A	Gaborone	20/11/79
St James Church	128	Private Bag 9, Lobatse	01/09/75
St Jerusalem Africa Church	108	PO Box 10, Maitengwe	20/05/81
St John Apostolic Faith Mission	7,400	PO Box 735, Gaborone	25/01/77
St Joseph Church	1,042	Private Bag 11, Palapye	03/06/75
St Joshua Christian Apostolic Church	140	PO Box 535, Francistown	14/12/82
St Lazarus Apostolic Faith Mission of Botswana	185	PO Box 605, Serowe	15/04/80

Name of society	*No. of M'bers*	*Headquarters*	*Date of reg.*
St Lewis Zion Church of Botswana	150	PO Box 1216, Gaborone	15/04/80
St Luka Faith Mission Church	52	PO Box 72, Oodi	30/11/79
St Luke's Gospel Church of Botswana	N/A	Gaborone	15/12/75
St Mark's Service Church	400	PO Box 1642, Gaborone	24/07/74
St Mary's Church	300	PO Box 454, Francistown	04/12/81
St Mathew's Apostolic Faith Church	800	Private Bag 03, Gaborone	27/04/73
St Michael's Apostolic Church	475	PO Box 1494, Gaborone	19/08/74
St Moses Church	300	PO Box 244, Serowe	07/09/81
St Patmos Faith Mission Apostolic Church in Christ	N/A	Palapye	14/02/75
St Paul's Apostolic Faith Mission Church of South Africa	340	PO Box 1058, Gaborone	23/10/74
St Paul Apostolic Faith Mission of Botswana	2,595	PO Box 5149, Mofatsana	27/04/73
St Peter's Apostolic Faith Mission	6,900	PO Box 321, Selebi-Phikwe	27/04/73
St Philip's Faith Healing Church	1,900	PO Box 17, Palapye	28/04/72
St Steven's Apostolic Mission Church	30	PO Box 118, Francistown	14/07/82
St Isaac's Church	65	PO Box 196, Mochudi	05/12/75
Sediba Sa Matshediso Church	20	Mmanyana	12/03/75
Seven Stars Church in Botswana	58	PO Box 50, Ramokgwebane	30/04/79
Spiritual Healing Church	570	PO Box 158, Gaborone	30/04/73
Sun Church of Botswana	79	PO Box 20116, Gaborone	27/12/79
Taupedi Apostolic Church of God	605	PO Box 34, Kanye	03/11/76
Tlolaganya Healing Church	130	PO Box 109, Lobatse	21/01/75
Tribunal Christian Church Keep Holy Sabbath	176	PO Box 91, Francistown	30/07/74
Twelve Apostles Church of Africa	900	PO Box 644, Gaborone	26/03/79
Twelve Prophesy Church	290	PO Box 641, Serowe	05/09/79
United Apostolic Faith Church	120	PO Box 302, Bobonong	08/08/79
United Evangelical Church of Christ in Africa	150	PO Box 20767 Gaborone	07/12/75
Zion Apostolic Church	*ca.* 100	PO Box 23, Silkwane	31/03/81
Zion Christian Church	10,700	PO Box 150, Mahalapye	22/12/75
Zion Christian Church of Botswana	N/A	Gaborone	22/12/69
Zion Congregational Church of South Africa	110	PO Box 24, Tshane	21/03/79

*It is disputable whether the Hosanna Religious Traditional Association should be included in this list of Faith Healing Churches of Zionist offshoots. The Hosanna Association – according to its constitution (see Appendix III.2) – is formed mainly to worship MWALI, the God of rains in the minority Bakalanga tribe in Botswana. However faith healing seances are conducted in the church.

APPENDIX III.2

CONSTITUTION OF THE HOSANNA RELIGIOUS TRADITIONAL ASSOCIATION

1. Establishment
   There is hereby established an Association to be known as the HOSANNA Traditional Association with the aims and objects stipulated hereunder.
2. Statement of Beliefs
   The HOSANNA Traditional Association is a religious Association dedicated to the worship of MWALI. It is intended for the preservation of the traditional worship. The worship of MWALI through the Traditional Ceremonies of Daka and Celebrations by HOSANNA and, all who believe in the existence of a Higher Spirit, through dancing and praying for rain is an important aspect of Black Culture and is a contribution to the cultural and moral fibre of a nation.
3. Aims
   The HOSANNA Traditional Association will have the following aims and objects:
   (*a*) The worship of MWALI in the traditional and customary manner.
   (*b*) The preservation of culture and the propagation of cultural worship by all HOSANNA and their followers.
   (*c*) The unification of all HOSANNA and encouragement of true and faithful worship of MWALI by all his followers in Botswana.
   (*d*) Spreading the Gospel of MWALI and the continuation of traditional ceremonies conducted in consultation with and active cooperation of the local communities.
   (*e*) The praying for rain at least once a year and as more often as may be necessary in any particular year.
   (*f*) The establishment of cooperation and active participation of any local community in the activities of HOSANNA.
4. Membership
   Membership of the Society shall be open to all known and admitted HOSANNA and to all people who believe in MWALI and dedicated to His worship. Applications for Membership to the Association shall be made to the Executive Committee of the Association in such manner as may be prescribed in the Regulations of the Association.
5. Organs of The Organisation
   (*a*) The Executive Committee
   (i) There shall be an Executive Committee of the Association whose membership shall be as follows:
   The President
   Vice President
   Secretary
   Treasurer
   Two Members of the Association
   (ii) The Executive shall be chosen every two years by the Annual General Meeting of the Association and members thereof shall be eligible for reelection.
   (*b*) (i) The Association shall hold an Annual General Meeting to which all members shall be invited to attend and speak on any matter affecting the Association.
   (ii) The Annual General Meeting shall be the main organ and policy

body of the Association, which shall give guidance to the Executive in the administration of the Association.

6. Functions of the Executive
   (i) The Executive Committee shall be the organ to carry out the administration and running of the Assocation. The Executive shall execute and implement decisions taken at the Annual General Meetings. It shall be the duty of the Executive to call the Annual General Meeting at such times and venues as it may decide from time to time.
   (ii) The President of the Executive shall also be the President of the Assocation. He shall preside at all meetings of the Annual General Meetings and of the Executive Committee and in his adsence the Vice-Chairman shall preside.
   (iii) The Secretary shall conduct all the correspondence of the Association and shall keep minutes and records of all meetings of the Executive and the Annual General Meetings. At the instruction of the Executive or the President, the Secretary shall issue notices calling Meetings.
   (iv) The Treasurer shall, subject to the directions of the Executive, be responsible for the finances of the Association. He shall keep proper financial records so as to show a true and accurate record of the state of the Association's finances.
7. Finance
   (*a*) The Association shall open such bank accounts as the Executive may decide from time to time. All monies collected on behalf of or received by the Association shall be used for the purposes of the Association. Collections shall be given to the Treasurer who shall issue a receipt and the money shall go into the Association's bank account.
   (*b*) The Association may employ and pay such officials, staff and others as may be necessary for the performance of this work.
8. Subscriptions
   Members of the Association will pay such subscriptions and/or joining fee as may be established from time to time by the Association at any Annual General Meeting or through the Executive Committee. The monies so collected shall form a general fund of the Association and may be used for any of its purposes.
9. Registration
   The Association shall become a registered or exempt Association in terms of the Association Act as soon as this Constitution has been approved by members which shall be presented to the Registrar of Societies with the necessary applications.
10. Alteration of the Constitution
   (*a*) This Constitution may be altered only by Annual General Meeting. (–) of intention to alter the Constitution shall be given in advance of the Annual General Meeting so as to give members opportunity to reflect upon the proposed alterations.
   (*b*) There shall be Rules and Regulations of the Society governing the detailed administration of the Association and such Rules and Regulations may be altered by the Executive and confirmed by the Annual General Meeting.

APPENDIX IV

PROCLAMATION
by
His Excellency the High Commissioner

No. 17 of 1927. – Promulgated 29 April 1927

Entitled 'The Bechuanaland Protectorate Witchcraft Proclamation, 1927'.

Whereas it is expedient to suppress the imputation or practice of prevented witchcraft in the Bechuanaland Protectorate:

Now, therefore, under and by virtue of the powers in me vested, I do hereby declare, proclaim and make known as follows:-

1. Any person who imputes to another the use of non-natural means in causing any disease in any person, animal or thing, or in causing injury to any person or property, or who shall name or indicate another as a wizard or witch, or who by means of pretended supernatural power indicates any one as being responsible for, or the cause of, any injury to any person, animal or thing shall be liable upon conviction to a fine not exceeding fifty pounds or in default of payment to imprisonment with or without hard labour for a period not exceeding three years.

2. Any person who having named or indicated another as a wizard or witch or having by means of pretended supernatural power indicated another as being responsible for, or the cause of, any injury to any person, animal or thing shall be proved to be by habit or repute a witch doctor or witch finder shall be liable on conviction to a fine not exceeding one hundred pounds or to imprisonment with or without hard labour for a period not exceeding five years.

3. Any person who employs or solicits any witch doctor or witch finder to name or indicate another as a wizard shall be liable upon conviction to a fine not exceeding ten pounds or in default of payment to imprisonment with or without hard labour for a period not exceeding three months.

4. Any person professing a knowledge of so-called witchcraft or the use of charms who shall advise any person applying to him how to bewitch or injure persons, animals or other property, or who shall supply any person with the pretended means of witchcraft, shall be liable on conviction to the punishments provided by section two.

5. Any person who on the advice of a witch doctor or of his pretended knowledge of so-called witchcraft shall with intent to injure, use or cause to be put into operation such means or processes as he believes to be calculated to injure any person or property shall be liable upon conviction to the punishments provided in section two.

6. Any person who for purposes of gain pretends to exercise or use any kind of supernatural power, witchcraft, sorcery, enchantment or conjuration, or undertakes to tell fortunes, or pretends from his skill or knowledge in any occult science to discover where or in what manner anything supposed to have been stolen or lost may be found shall be liable upon conviction to the punishments provided by section two.

7. This Proclamation may be cited as the Bechuanaland Protectorate Witchcraft Proclamation, 1927, and shall have force and take effect from the date of its publication in the Gazette.

3 I. A. J. Semali

ASSOCIATIONS AND HEALERS: ATTITUDES TOWARDS COLLABORATION IN TANZANIA

INTRODUCTION

WHO's appeal for the use of traditional healers and traditional birth attendants has resulted in widespread efforts to bring together modern health care and traditional medicine especially in the achievement of health for all by the year 2000. Incorporation of traditional healers and birth attendants in health projects in some parts of Africa has been observed to enhance the success of such projects (Chen 1979; Bayaun 1976; Laoye 1981). We may have to agree that the success recorded on the part of traditional medicine in such projects could be due to traditional healers and birth attendants being valued and trusted by their particular communities, and also their being conversant with the indigenous culture and traditions. Nchind (1976), observing the same, said that 'traditional medicine fulfils the four criterions of accessibility, acceptability, dependability and availability'.

In Tanzania there have been a number of efforts to promote traditional medicine. In 1908 Dr Weck, a staff surgeon in the German forces, wrote about traditional medicine practice in some localities of the then Tanganyika Colony. In his writing he observed a number of diseases being managed by the traditional healers in these communities.

In 1929 the colonial Government enacted the Witchcraft Ordinance. This ordinance was prompted by some complaints about witchdoctors: it declared witchcraft a crime and differentiated it from '*Uganga*' the traditional (indigenous) way of diagnosing and treating illness. Though the colonial Government appreciated then the existence of traditional medicine alongside their own, there was still not much effort to promote traditional medicine.

In 1969 the Chief Medical Officer of Tanzania directed Regional Medical Officers to investigate the practice of traditional medicine. In 1971 a National Union of Traditional Healers (UWATA) was established, but unfortunately for various reasons it could not live long; it started disintegrating just after its formation, and in 1974 it was officially banned.

In 1974 the Traditional Medicine Research Unit was established under the University of Dar es Salaam. In general it is charged with carrying out various investigations regarding traditional medical practice in Tanzania; this includes botanical, phytochemical, pharmacological and clinical evaluation.

The Unit is now directing some of its efforts towards such aspects as the role of traditional medicine in primary health care as well as collaboration with modern health care. Such aspects have prompted, for example, studies of the attitudes of allopathic health workers towards traditional medicine (which were found to be fairly positive), and the views of modern health workers in Tanzania on whether traditional medicine has any medical benefits (Semali 1982; 1983).

It can be gathered from this that Tanzanian officials are aware of the existence of traditional medicine in the country. Such co-existence of traditional medicine with modern health care should prompt one to look, first at how the two health care systems could complement each other, at least at primary health care level, and second, what efforts have been made to institutionalise traditional medicine.

COLLABORATION

As some modern health workers had already indicated, they accepted traditional healers' involvement in the delivery of primary health care (Semali 1982).

A study was therefore done to find out whether traditional healers would accept such collaboration with modern health workers and what should be the nature of this collaboration. An open-ended questionnaire was prepared in English, then translated into Swahili and back to English by different persons; when consistency and uniformity were established, the Swahili version was pre-tested and some amendments were made. The study took place from February to April 1983. Initially, some questionnaires were self-administered while others were administered by the author. In comparing the information elicited by the self-administered tests and those interviewed directly there was no difference; hence they were analysed together.

The study was done in Kinondoni District, one of the Urban Districts of Dar es Salaam City. The population of this district is 300,000 people (National Census 1981). This district has about 400 full-time traditional practitioners, of whom 320 (80%) were interviewed. 92% of the interviewed healers were males while 8% were females. About 70% of the healers were 41 years of age or above while 27% were 55 years old or above.

They were asked to mention how many clients they had seen the previous day to the interview. On average it was 20 patients per day, ranging from 10 to 35 patients; hence, on average, 8,000 people are seen by traditional healers every day in this district. At some places, 10–15 people were waiting their turn to see the traditional healer. The traditional healers were asked whether they would accept collaboration with modern health workers: 94% agreed and gave reasons for agreeing to collaborate with modern health workers as follows: 92 (28%) of them said that modern medicine is more advanced and traditional healers would benefit, while 95 (29%) said that they were treating the same people, so why should they not join forces? 80 (25%) said some diseases have no cure in modern medicine yet they could be cured by traditional medicine. The traditional healers who rejected collaboration with modern health workers claimed that traditional medicine and modern medicine are incompatible, while a few said they did not know the feelings of modern health workers.

They were then asked what should be the nature of such collaboration. 16% said that traditional healers and modern health workers should feel free to exchange patients. 112 (35%) said that traditional healers should submit their regimes for research and working out of dosages, while 80 (25%) said common treatment centres for traditional medicine and modern medicine should be established.

They were then asked whether they would accept training on some aspects in modern health care: 91% said yes. When they were asked why they wished to be trained, 195 (61%) traditional healers said they would be in a position to offer better services to their clients; 54 (17%) said they received many patients with various health problems at their treatment centres. Other reasons were mostly educational needs. Those who said no to training had the following reasons: they were too old to be trained; they did not have the standard basic education required for training in modern health care. Six traditional healers said that what they already knew was enough.

The traditional healers were also asked if they had ever referred a patient to modern health workers: 61% said no. The diseases of patients referred to modern health care included: tuberculosis, anaemia in pregnancy, failure of traditional medicine, diarrhoea, surgical problems and others.

Those who responded negatively to collaboration gave some reasons for doing so. For long, traditional healers have been abused, referred to as liars or witches, yet despite such discouragement people still resorted to traditional healers even when modern health care was immediately available. Even today, articles in the newspapers and other mass media refer to traditional healers as dangerous elements in society. Such reports make the traditional healers very bitter. It may be true that among them there are some bad elements but these should not be left to spoil the public face of traditional medicine. At present, traditional medicine also has its quacks, and this may make it difficult to pick out the genuine healers. Though it would be difficult to exercise strict professional control over the practice of traditional medicine, it may be necessary to institute measures to phase out or control quackery and misconduct. A national, strictly professional organisation of traditional healers could be initiated, but first a thorough *post mortem* should be made on the former organisation 'UWATA' to make sure the same problems do not arise again. In short, it seems that with some legal backing and a government directive on traditional medicine, traditional healers may be expected to make a special contribution to the betterment of human health.

ASSOCIATIONS AND COMPANIES

The establishment of an effective organisation or association of healers may be considered as one step towards the professionalisation of traditional healers (including traditional birth attendants). Such a step towards professionalisation should be in accord with the country's laws and society's norms. For, apparently, many traditional healers are busy forming healing groups, some of whose goals may not be in the interests of the nation, while others are highly individualistic. The situation becomes more complex when groups with diverse interests approach the Government for registration as a professional group, and the registrar then is unable to tell which group may be genuine. It is imperative under these circumstances for legislatures in Africa to consider legal aspects in governing the professionalisation of traditional medicine.

In Tanzania there is no law which prohibits or governs the practice of traditional medicine. However there are some laws which may affect the traditional healer from time to time, for example, the Societies Ordinance of 1954 under which societies/associations of traditional healers become registered, and the Witchcraft Ordinance which prohibits the practice of witchcraft.

Apart from UWATA, mentioned earlier, there are also a number of associations of traditional healers either with official Government registration or which have at one time been registered. There are two main types of associations of traditional healers. The first type is where the association is a collection of traditional healers who have come together to seek joint registration and enjoy full legal status.

In this category we have two sub-types: i. those registered as associations and answerable to the registrar of societies; ii. those registered as a company and answerable to the registrar of companies. In the second category are those who come together under a common, 'branded' ancestral spirit, and operate under the name of that spirit.

In the light of the above we can then discuss each type of association in terms of their activities and how much professionalisation could have been achieved under such conditions. In the first type we have in Tanzania the former UWATA (Umoja wa Waganga Tanzania or Traditional Healers' Union of Tanzania), the former Union of Tanzania Traditional Medical Research and the Association of Tanzanian Herbalists (Chama cha Waganga wa Mitishamba). Kilimanjaro Herbalist and Medication Services are now in the process of being registered; IPROMAC (International Petty Products Manufacturers Cooperative Society Ltd) and MAACO (Madawa ya Asili Company or Traditional Medications Company) are companies. UWATA stems from the earlier Traditional Herbs Association of Handeni district and immediately gained national popularity. UWATA started to operate in 1971 while in the process of being registered, and assumed the status of a fully fledged, functional society.

UWATA

The association (UWATA) had the following constitution (in summary):

i. To treat all types of diseases;
ii. To control all cultivation, harvesting and administration of all herbal materials;
iii. To market medicinal plants or the products;
iv. To promote the national culture, games and gymnastics;
v. To unite all traditional healers;
vi. To establish treatment centres all over the country.

The qualification for being a member was as follows: any citizen of Tanzania, provided he/she accepts the constitution; it was not stated in what circumstances one ceases to be a member, nor was a code of conduct spelled out explicitly. The society had a National Chairman with a number of assistant chairpersons, a secretary general, national council members and heads of various activities within the association.

The association attracted many traditional healers within the urban set-up, some of whom were not traditional healers but quacks, while others were opportunists. The leaders travelled to a number of towns soliciting membership. In some areas they managed to attract quite a good crowd. The soaring membership was very short-lived, when a number of problems started. Some of the problems were monetary.

All members of the association were supposed to hand in all or part of their financial proceeds to the central pool. The association headquarters had a bank account, but it was believed by the office-holders that an association without money was not really an association; in consequence, many of the office-holders wanted to be signatories for the account at the bank. At the same time, the association had appointed neither a financial controller nor an auditor for their finances, yet the association was handling money earned by its members. Furthermore, it seems many members were concerned lest the office-holders were embezzling their money. It seems, in brief, that financially and constitutionally the Association (UWATA) was functioning as a profit-making, commercial body, and as such every member was a share-holder and had the right to be concerned about the management of his shares and to fight for control with other share-holders.

As a professional body, UWATA managed to open a number of treatment centres in the country. Its members were always coming forward to display their talents to cure, and they organised several treatment sessions in a number of areas throughout the country. At one session they tried to treat a tumour of the eye, but failed, and later the patient had to undergo enucleation. At another they organised uvulectomies with some fatal results. As a consequence of these deaths, tension within the Association ran very high and it was feared that it would lead to physical assaults or confrontation.

Leadership in the society was very much an individualised affair as indicated by one of the members during a council meeting; 'some healers think they can make the association their property'. This member was attacking some of the office-holders who seemed to be above the Association's constitution; at the same meeting it was a concern of another member that many traditional healers were competing for the post of Association secretary, yet they did not know how to read or write. On another occasion, a post already held by one person was allocated to another; the new appointment caused much confusion within the Association, and divided the membership. The meeting then apparently agreed that all office-holders should resign, and a secret ballot should be held to elect new office-holders. But the traditional healers failed to reach a consensus and had to consider asking the Government to intervene.

Until this time the Association had managed to unite several traditional healers which was one of their objectives. However, they failed in a number of areas – for example, in sustaining an elected leadership because of power struggles, or in having no code of conduct; and furthermore they were also functioning as a trading company. For these reasons and because of the tensions within the society, the Government agreed to serve UWATA with a notice of de-registration.

OTHER ASSOCIATIONS

Another association is the 'Association of Tanzania Herbalists and Ayurvedic Medicine' registered in 1980. It charges entry and monthly fees from its members; its objectives, briefly, are to collect herbs from various traditional healers for research purposes, to promote traditional medicine in the country and to educate its members on various methods of healing.

COMPANIES

Others have been registered as companies. MAACO and IMPROMAC are still maintaining their registration titles, though with some problems which seem common to all.

Apparently these companies took off after the Government had banned UWATA, as the company directors seem to have come from the divided, ex-UWATA leadership. As a result, each group decided to form its own company. The two companies are believed to be at loggerheads with each other. Members do not trust each other, frequent quarrels occur between share-holders and officials, and this has led to steadily diminishing membership. One managing director now owns some businesses and farms, and has little to do with the company or with traditional healing. A member of one of the companies was quoted as saying 'that the managing director is not working, but wants all the money I have made to be the company's property, and so I've decided to quit the company'. The companies managed to acquire offices and farms for medicinal plants, yet the offices have the barest minimum of office equipment – only a chair and a table – while the farms, which could be considered one of the important assets of the company, have hardly been given the expertise required to manage them. Another business involvement of these companies included the timber for which the companies were officially registered in addition to their traditional healing practice. As timber trading is a fairly lucrative business in Tanzania, it is believed that some of the companies made a lot of money out of timber, and thereafter some of the directors, having made their fortunes, decided to quit.

ASSOCIATIONS AS CULTS

The second type of association seems to be more common along the coastline and in the coastal hinterland. Here the traditional healers associate or behave as associates, under an ancestral spirit. One association, called 'MSEKWA' (the name of the spirit), has more than thirty members and three treatments centres. Their fees are very moderate, and refundable if the cure is not successful; and they keep records in which the patient signs if the cure is a success or failure.

There are two ways of becoming a member, one by being of the familial lineage and the other by being a previous patient – that is, by having consulted the clinic and had one's sufferings diagnosed as due to one having ignored the healing skills or therapeutic paraphernalia of one's dead grandparents. The patient is then sent to search for the paraphernalia and join the clinic as a healer. Attachment to the clinic is justified by the fact that if it was not for the 'MSEKWA' spirit one would not know to remember that one's grandparents were healers and that one is supposed to take over their expertise; it was the failure to take over their healing skills and equipment that made one ill. After taking on the healing role one is accepted by the spirit as one of its descendants and in the course of healing one will be identified as such.

78% of these traditional healers agreed to having common treatment centres; they gave reasons for the need of having common treatment centres as: i. traditional healers will have the opportunity to learn from each other and consult each other in the course of treatment; ii. patients will be able to identify without problem a place of treatment. Those who rejected such centres gave the following reasons: i. each traditional healer has his/her own ways of treatment which may be incompatible; ii. some traditional healers are witches.

It seems then from the above discussion and observations that traditional healers are very much in favour of association. What discourages associations are personal ambitions and perhaps lack of proper guidance and the limitations of leadership. In contrast, self-selected groups seem to run smoothly, yet, if we only encourage self-selected groups we can hardly achieve professionalisation as a national objective. Associations should be encouraged to focus more on their profession, to promote it and guide its growth, and less on its potential for financial gain and power. Traditional healers are clearly trying to keep abreast with the developing world, but these efforts could be more effective if they united as a professional group.

TRADITIONAL HEALERS AND WESTERN MEDICINE

As observed by Oyebola (1979), traditional healers in Africa have been trying to improve their practice by copying some of the modern techniques, such as making capsules or testing urine. In Tanzania some traditional healers use stethoscopes and thermometers to examine their patients, while others have wards for patients and full-time students learning traditional practice. It is thus evident just how eager those traditional healers are to learn or copy from modern health workers. Though traditional healers see such copying as a way to move forward, there is a danger too, as traditional medicine may be forced to change its cultural orientation, and as a result it will try to function and present itself as modern medicine.

85% of the respondents agreed to accept instruction in modern medicine. It seems, from the reasons given by traditional healers, that they are not seeking a common platform with modern health workers but they accept the superiority of modern health workers. However they may not have any other alternative since they know that the practice of modern health care is fully backed by the Government. It is, then, only through the Government machinery that the terms on which to collaborate can be established. It is one's hope that collaboration could start in areas where there will be the least infringement on each other's clinical territory. As in Ghana and Nigeria, traditional healers and birth attendants could be exposed to some modern health care projects, and then be provided with modern facilities; but a careful watch is needed as such facilities may be used as a means of exploiting their clients. These traditional healers must also be armed with the necessary knowledge to handle such facilities with maximum safety to human beings. Those who patronise traditional medicine also have a part to play in deciding if, or how, to professionalise traditional medicine; for it is they, by their continuing to use traditional medicine, who are judges of its effectiveness.

Many people (Tessema 1980; Howard 1978; Mshiu 1982) have urged the incorporation or collaboration of traditional medicine with modern health care. While it is important to implement such suggestions the problem remains that traditional medicine in Africa is not institutionalised in the way it is in India and China; healers are affiliated more to small localities and their practice is not uniform. Given such non-uniformity, it seems difficult to establish an immediate professional homogeneity. As the traditional healers have indicated their willingness to collaborate and learn from modern health workers, we may then utilise their position in the society to promote health. This suggestion may also be supported by the findings of Heggenhougen (1981) in Hanang District (Tanzania), that the success and co-operation extended to village health workers was a function of their social status in the society. Then within primary health care we can expect the traditional healer or birth attendant to be involved in educating the villagers, to bring about behaviour changes in respect of prevailing health problems, their prevention and control. They will also be expected to influence culturally-related nutritional problems as well as promoting food supply, preparation and distribution within the family. The traditional healers can also mobilise people in self-help projects, such as digging trenches and wells and the utilisation of such facilities, while traditional birth attendants attend to pregnancy problems and the new-born and, given the success reported from other areas (Sene 1983), they could be encouraged to identify and refer serious cases as well as implement vaccination programmes. While traditional healers are keen to use and learn modern techniques they could also be provided with first aid kits to care for minor ailments and injury. The importance of referring patients should be made clear to traditional healers while the village authority will be charged with procurement of the drugs. But first we should also establish educational facilities for traditional healers and traditional birth attendants, as suggested by Heggenhougen and Mkumbwa (1982).

While the health planners are planning to incorporate traditional healers into the primary health care, not much consideration has been given to traditional healers as a professional group, how best to foster their profession. In general, traditional healers have been eager to form associations but are faced with leadership problems. It seems governments should come forward and give guidance to traditional healers on professional associations. Members should be educated on the role of leadership and representing the interest of the members; and their activities should be strictly professional. Also the Government should help monitor issues which may be considered sensitive. Indeed, one post, for example the Secretary-General, might have to be a government appointee.

REFERENCES

Bayaun, A., (1976), 'The training and activities of village midwives in Sudan', *Tropical Doctor*, 6, 3 (July).

Chen, P. C., (1977), 'Incorporating the traditional birth attendant into the health team, Malaysian example', *Journal of Tropical and Geographical Medicine*, 29, (June).

Dhadphale, M., (1979), 'Attitudes of Zambian female in spirit possession (Ngulu)', 59, 9, *East African Medical Journal*.

Heggenhougen, H. K., (1981), *Village Health Workers Providing Primary Health Care in Hanang, Tanzania. Report on a Pilot Survey*.

Howard, G. R., (1978), 'Social Economic Factors affecting utilization of a rural Indian hospital', *Tropical Doctor*, 8, 4 (October).

Jeliffe, D. D. and Jeliffe, E. F. P., (1977), 'Cultural cul-de-sac of Western Medicine', *Transactions of the Royal Society of Tropical Medicine and Hygiene*, 71, 4.

Laoye, A. J., (1981), 'Selling health in the market place', *WHO Forum*, 2, 3.

Mbilu, M. J., Mandara, M.P. and Arkutu, A., (1981), 'Traditional birth attendants in Miono Division, Bagamoyo District', *Dar Med. Journ.*, 8, 2.

Mkumbwa, E. and Heggenhougen, H. K., (1982), 'Village health workers for primary health care in Tanzania', *Nordisk Medicin*, 97.

Mshiu, E. N. and Chhabra, S. C., (1982), 'Traditional healers and health care delivery in Tanzania', *Tropical Doctor*, 12.

Nchind, T. C., (1976), 'Traditional and Eastern medicine in Africa', *Tropical Doctor*, 6, 3.

Oyebola, D. D. O., (1979), 'Some aspects of traditional medicine as practised by the Yoruba', *East African Medical Journal*, 56, 1.

Press, I., (1978), 'Urban folk medicine: a functional review', *Ann. Anth.*, 80, 1.

Semali, I. A. J. (1982), 'The opinion of allopathic health workers on traditional medicine/healers and degree of contact with the two.' Submitted to the University of Dar es Salaam for the partial fulfilment for the award of DPH.

Semali, I. A. J., (unpublished), 'Has traditional medicine any curative benefit?, Modern health workers' views'.

Sene, Pape Marcel (1983), 'TBAs in Senegal', *WHO Magazine*, June.

Swantz, J. C., (1974), 'The role of the medicine man among the Zaramo of Dar es Salaam.' Thesis submitted for the degree of Doctor of Philosophy, University of Dar es Salaam.

Tanzanian National Census 1980, *Report*.

Tessema, S. S., (1980), 'Traditional medicine: past growth and future development in East Africa', *East African Medical Journal*, 57, 1.

Weck, Dr, (1969), 'Hehe medicine (1908)', *Tanzanian Notes and Records*, 70.
WHO (1978), *The Promotion and Development of Traditional Medicine*. (WHO Technical Report Series 622, Geneva: WHO.)

GOVERNMENT, ASSOCIATIONS AND THE UNIVERSITY: LIAISON IN MALAŴI

Malaŵi is signatory to the 1978 Alma Alta resolution of 'Health for All by the Year 2000'. Malaŵi cannot manage to achieve this goal if she depends on the present hospitals and medical officers as they are too few and localised in the urban centres. The Malaŵi Government is therefore incorporating traditional medicine in its programme of Primary Health Care (PHC).

We now know that traditional healers have claimed success in the treatment of several diseases and disorders such as cancer, diabetes, impotence in the male, infertility in the female, malaria, madness, bilharzia, asthma, epilepsy and venereal diseases. Some practise as dentists and deliver babies. It will be rewarding, therefore, if we scientifically improve upon the herbalists' methods and techniques.

GOVERNMENT

Traditional medicine is practised by two types of herbalists in Malaŵi: the Traditional Birth Attendant (TBA), and the Traditional Healer (TH). About 85% of the six million people in Malaŵi live in the rural areas where there is no access to facilities offered by modern therapy. Furthermore, about 60% of the children born in Malaŵi are delivered by TBAs (Msonthi 1982; Msonthi 1983). The Government of Malaŵi Ministry of Health is undertaking training programmes for the TBAs in all the twenty-four districts of the country and conducts frequent seminars in order to promote Primary Health Care (PHC) to the whole population through Primary Health Delivery Systems (PHDS). The TBA is not only a

midwife: but she is also a social worker because she continues to educate and advise the nursing mother in all aspects of good health care. She is also a practising herbalist because she gives prescriptions to the barren women, expectant women before and after delivery. She is specialised in diseases of women and children.

One way in which traditional medicine in Malaŵi can contribute to achieve the goal of 'Health for All by the Year 2000' is to incorporate THs and TBAs into the existing hospitals. A selected number of THs and TBAs who are authorities in any *one* disease could be given a patient at the hospital. The TH and TBA resident at the hospital concerned should treat his patient under the supervision of a medical practitioner. After the successful treatment of this patient, the TH and TBA could then be released to their village and be initially equipped with basic TBA kit, purified castor oil, Epsom salt and perhaps some outpatient tickets with the name of the TH/TBA clearly written at the back of the ticket. This means then that the TH/TBA can refer cases such as injuries, burns, abnormal maternity cases quickly to the hospital and only deal with such cases as he is qualified to treat. Moreover, several THs/TBAs in a given area could work as a team, each specialising in his own disease. In this way, there would be fewer cases going to hospitals particularly for these other cases such as mental diseases, venereal diseases, impotence in men and barrenness in women.

At the same time, retired medical assistants could play a part by opening up Government-assisted dispensaries in rural areas. These people could be furnished with the basic drugs. At a later date, when the THs/TBAs' work has been assessed, they can also be furnished with the basic drugs, although fewer and of selected type, as in the case of the retired medical assistants. This arrangement will not only achieve primary health care to reach the rural area but it will eradicate the feeling of competition among the herbalists and of working in isolation from one another. The Ministry of Health under the auspices of WHO are soon calling for a joint meeting of the medical officers and TH/TBAs together with research scientists to draw up a programme for future action.

ASSOCIATIONS

The herbalists of Malaŵi together with the TBAs have formed what is called 'The Herbalists Association of Malaŵi' (HAM) which has close collaboration with the Chemistry Department at the University of Malaŵi. The Herbalists' Association of Malaŵi (HAM) was originally called the Traditional Mediciners of Central Africa, Ochiritsa and was established in 1963, Registration number 1730 of Box 5119, Limbe, Malaŵi (see Illustration 4). The founder member is Mr. B. Simon Nkhoma who has had a stroke and is recovering slowly at his home in Chipande, Chiradzulu district. The Assistant Founder is Mrs. Agnes Chipatala who is also head of the Traditional Birth Attendants (TBAs) within HAM. The current chairman is Chief W. C. Mbatata, the Treasurer, Mr. L. Mussa and the General Secretary, Mr. J. G. Mmezalumo (see Appendix I). The committee members are Messrs Ndau, Asiki, Kafukule, Chibade and Saka. HAM has by far the largest registered membership some of whose members appear in Appendix I. HAM works hand in hand with the University and the Ministry of Health officials, so that HAM members are given qualifying certificates (see Appendix II) by the University after plant samples from those members have proved biologically active. The same members (TBAs) are given forms to complete as part of an exercise by the Ministry of Health to compile data on village health activities. HAM has a list of certified charges to their patients (see Appendix III) to ensure uniform charges to their patients by their registered practitioners.

Another rival association, of limited membership, is called 'The African Herbal Association', registration number 0445 whose authority was granted by the then Headquarters, Zomba. This association is under the chairmanship of Dr. James Willard (see Illustration 5). Their offices are in Balaka as shown in Appendix IV, where formal charges to patients are listed.

Recently there was yet another Traditional Doctors Association of Malaŵi led by Dr. Chipangula, a breakaway of HAM. Dr. Chipangula was very popular on the radio where among other things he tried to establish 'medical schools' on traditional medicine in Lilongwe and Blantyre. He was charging the interested students the sum of 180 kwacha for a six-month course. Unfortunately Dr. Chipangula did not have formal consultation and clearance.

Lately, I received a copy of a letter from the 'Traditional Doctors' Association of Malaŵi' (see Appendix V) from the executive chairman-designate, Dr. D. M. P. Ntikunthile, of Box 20, Kasangu, where the association is trying to seek recognition by the Government so that they could participate in the promotion of health care delivery in the country. This new association, if recognised by the Government, would

1 affiliate itself with the ruling Malaŵi Congress Party;

2 discourage corruption and cheating among its members by overcharging their patients, the maximum fee being ten kwacha per consultation;

3 encourage good behaviour to patients particularly to be moral to lady patients with reproduction problems;

4 stop the spiritual media from immoral aspects of healing practices;

5 discourage future tellers from unfounded predictions;

6 discourage the practitioners from dispensing poisons, arbortifacients;

7 discourage practitioners from dispensing fortifiers, these being medicines given to married men or women which can cause serious bodily harm if that person acts disloyally to his or her marital partner;

8 discourage the members from dispensing medicines that absolve or can acquit convicted criminals;

9 encourage its members to advance their research on the science of night-flight aeroplanes and fuel-less motor cars;

10 identify traditional dentists who use pieces of grass as their sole equipment for all dental practices;

11 encourage all its members to send their plant samples to the University laboratories for proper identification and extraction in the hope of producing drugs locally;

12 appeal to members to refer cases outside their knowhow to the hospitals in a reciprocal manner;

13 encourage close cooperation with the District Councillors on all projects on national development;

14 contribute forty percent of each member's income to his/her respective District Council School Fees Fund for needy children.

THE UNIVERSITY

The University has direct links with both HAM and the Government. Government and Party officials have always been invited to meetings between the University and the herbalists, and the Ministry of Health has always invited the University to their meetings with them.

The Department of Chemistry at the University of Malaŵi, in conjunction with other workers (Msonthi 1981a), is carrying out phytochemical research into the medicinal plants of Malaŵi, with the aim of producing a pharmacopoeia of the medicinal plants of Malaŵi as a starting-point (Msonthi 1981b). This investigation started in 1975 and is being supported by the International Foundation for Science, Sweden, but this research is very much in the infancy stage compared to other countries, such as those in West Africa for example. The major problem is lack of equipment (we have an UV, IR and an A30 HNMR spectrometers only), so that we have to rely on chemical and spectroscopic analysis by sending isolated materials or receiving chemical data by post. Otherwise, Malaŵi offers a vast flora, which is abundantly heterogeneous and some of whose species are rare. Our phytochemical results are promising and have been published elsewhere.

Most drugs are used indifferently in the fresh or in the dry state, i.e. in a state which allows their utilisation throughout the year. The plants are either usually stored whole or they are cut into small pieces and tied in a small bundle as a fine powder. Generally, artisan means are employed such as aluminium and earthenware pots or bottles, wooden pestle and mortar and filtering cloths. The most widely used preparations are the decoctions, the infusions, the gruel and the poultice.

The decoctions are made by boiling the plant part (root bark, stem bark, leaves, flowers or fruit etc), cut in small pieces and tied in a small bundle, heated on a moderate flame, and filtering while hot through a cloth. The infusions are prepared by soaking the plant part in water for half an hour.

The infusion is filtered and then drunk. The gruel is made by using the filtrate of the infusion to prepare a very light porridge, using maize or millet flour. The poultice is prepared by squeezing the juice from a macerated part of a fresh plant.

Sometimes, the whole plant is boiled strongly in water in a small pot. The patient inhales the vapours while covered with a blanket. The infusion may be used to bathe the whole body, say for colds and headache, or as a massage for polio appropriately. The whole plant may be carbonised and ground to a fine powder. Incisions are made near or at sites of infection and the charcoal powder is rubbed into them.

In conclusion, the THs and TBAs in Malaŵi are doing quite a good job in promoting primary health care to the rural population as 'bare-foot doctors'. It is hoped that the gap between traditional and western medicine will close soon in Malaŵi through the continued interest of the Malaŵi Government and the Malaŵi Congress Party. In this way we can be sure of achieving 'Health for all by the Year 2000' in Malaŵi.

ACKNOWLEDGEMENTS

We thank the International Foundation for Science, IFS, Sweden for financial support.

REFERENCES

Msonthi, J. D., (1981a) 'A survey of traditional medicinal plants of Malaŵi' Commonwealth Science Council, Natural Products Project Meeting, Mauritius (November), *Proceedings CSC ('81) ANC*, 3, pp. 129–46.

Msonthi, J. D., (1981b), 'Natural products research in Malaŵi', *Proceedings CSC (81) ANC*, 3, pp. 269–71.

Msonthi, J. D., (1982a), 'Traditional phytotherapy in Malaŵi', Catholic University, Rome (20 December).

Msonthi, J. D., (1982b), 'Traditional medical activities and primary health care'. International Social Science Research Conference, Zomba.

Msonthi, J. D., (1983a), 'Traditional birth attendants in Malaŵi: their role in primary health care', *J. Soc. Malawi*, 36, 1, pp. 40–4.

Msonthi, J. D., (1983b), 'Traditional medicinal plants research: an approach towards primary health care in Malaŵi', The University of Lausanne, Switzerland (19 July).

APPENDIX I

OCHIRITSA

Reg. No. 1730, 1963

Box 51119, Limbe

1. Founder – Bambo B. S. Nkhoma
2. Assistant Founder – Mai A. Chipatala
3. Chairman – Bambo W. C. Mbatata
4. Msungichuma – Bambo L. Mussa
5. Mulembi – Bambo J. G. Mezalumo

Members (Committee)

6. Mai Ndau
7. Mai Asiki
8. Mai Kafukule
9. Mai Chibade
10. Mai Saka

	Dzina	*Village*	*Mfumu*
11.	Miles Muli	Chikubeni	Chikowi
12.	Jester Namkwenya	Namkwenya	Chikowi
13.	Kasimu Namkwenya	Namkwenya	Chikowi
14.	Awalu Bonomali	Makanjira	Chikowi
15.	Nicks Sani	Chikumbeni	Chikowi
16.	Efelemu Sanawe		Mwambo
17.	Juma Nakutepa	Machilika	Kumtumanje
18.	Manyenje Chitupe	Kwezaziya	
19.	Ali Jauma	Mkwate	Malemia
20.	Gray Chihango	Namasalima	
21.	Afiki Maluwa	Naphwita	
22.	Sikweya Mussa	Mbatata	
23.	Ayesi Maulana	Machilika	Kumtumanje
24.	Wine Samu	Masambuka	Malemia
25.	Atabiya Adamu	Machilika	Kumtumanje
26.	Musilamu Malitata	Masaulo	Kumtumanje
27.	Margaret Mamakoka	Machilika	Kumtumanje
28.	Agnes Singano	Kalinde	Kumtumanje
29.	Edesi Mponda	Lipholo	Kumtumanje
30.	Catherine Chiwelengo	Luwambe	Kumtumanje
31.	Wiladi Salimu	Namadingo	Kumtumanje
32.	Henderson Kazembe	Chilamwela	Kalembo
33.	Gideon Ntalika	Khomoli	
34.	Afiki Adoni	Mtwiche	Malemia
35.	Abalileni Asima	Mtonda	Kumtumanje
36.	James Chambo	Kumilona	Kumtumanje
37.	Sande Mulu	Namadingo	Kumtumanje

	Dzina	*Village*	*Mfumu*
38.	Ajaba Makuluni	Namadingo	Kumtumanje
39.	Angasamaleje Alabi	Kwezaziya	Kumtumanje
40.	Chinawa Nyenje	Chinawa	Mwambo
41.	Sidileki Lomoliwa	Mwahumu	Chikowi
42.	Jamiya Theke	Theke	Kumtumanje
43.	Asumale Chachiwa	Theke	Kumtumanje
44.	Tamba Matola	Pongwe	Chikowi
45.	Baimani Saidi	John Table	Mwambo
46.	Dewa Kalidwelo	Somba	Mwambo
47.	Joseph Mamu	Mussa	Mwambo
48.	Aliki Makunganya	Nambesa	Mwambo
49.	Catherine Chinga	Nazombe	Kumtumanje
50.	Maswelo Magwera	Pinga	Kawinga
51.	Sailesi Kamwendo	Lambala	Kumtumanje
52.	John Bonomali	Nambesa	Mwambo
53.	Rashidi Nasuwadi	Ngongodo	Liwonde
54.	James Ayami	Ntaja	Chikowi
55.	Awema Nacheya	Chilima	Chikowi
56.	Aubi Somela	Mussa	Mwambo
57.	Asidi Abiti Saizi	Msepula	Mlumbe
58.	Ntaila Mussa	Ntamba	Mlumbe
59.	Matilda Galasiano	Gwaza	Mlumbe
60.	Amele Mpakati	Kosmoli	Mlumbe
61.	Kalikokha	Kaunde	Mlumbe
62.	Efelo Namuti	Nkhokwe	Mlumbe
63.	Wina Mitawa	Chibwana	Mlumbe
64.	Sigele Musa	Makalo	Chikwewu
65.	Jose Sesani	Waliyala	Mlumbe
66.	Lakisoni Sakwata	Chibwana	Mlumbe
67.	Kamyoza James	Chibwana	Mlumbe
68.	Gelezamu Nkhalala	Sawa	Mlumbe
69.	Medi Tawakali	Mbeti	Mlumbe
70.	Chimangeni Davite	Nkamwa	Mlumbe
71.	James John	Mwagala	Mlumbe
72.	Joseni Chitali	Ntaka	Mlumbe
73.	Dickison Malikebu	Mbeti	Mlumbe
74.	Sudi Ndala	Kapalala	Mlumbe
75.	Eleki Jackson	Kalimbi	Mlumbe
76.	Aidi Winga	Chikonde	Mlumbe
77.	Asani Wasayo	Kapalasa	Mlumbe
78.	Augustin Black	Chiomba No. 2	Mlumba
79.	Daniel Namakhwa	Mwandama	Mlumbe
80.	V. H. Sifa Songola	Sifa	Mlumbe
81.	Whiti Ndalali	Balamanja	Mlumbe
82.	Mikayeli Kalalichi	Kalalika	Mlumbe
83.	Issa Mbamba	Tung'ande	Mlumbe
84.	Kafumbi Magwele	Sangala	Mlumbe
85.	S. Nasolo Tapasya	Sangala	Mlumbe

Dzina	*Village*	*Mfumu*
86. Black Sasula	Chisweye	Mlumbe
87. Adisoni Muliwa	Balanga	Mlumbe
88. Wochi Makwinja	Chisweye	Mlumbe
89. Sayama Kabwila	Mathaphwa	Mlumbe
90. Yolamu Jenesi	Balamanja	Mlumbe
91. Robert Daimoni	Chikwenga	Mlumbe
92. Mkubila Milowe	Chisutu	Mlumbe
93. Ojesi Bwana	Mathanda	Mlumbe
94. Molesi Misisi	Mulozi	Mlumbe
95. Nonesi Peteye	Mbepula	Mlumbe
96. Sigele Kawanga	Chinganga	Mlumbe
97. Beatrice Nthephela	Mathipa	Mlumbe
98. Bazile James	Chombe 2	Mlumbe
99. Wailadi Madi	Chibwana	Mlumbe
100. Ababi Ngwangwa	Nkawa	Mlumbe
101. Akimu Nhkwanda	Chisitu	Mlumbe
102. Labisoni Ndalama	Bemtoto	Mlumbe
103. Adaki Mwachumu	Mwachumu	Mlumbe
104. Ndala Kamuyanje	Kamuyanje	Mlumbe
105. Maki Jawadu	Kaunde	Mlumbe
106. Golden Enock	Kagaso	Chikowi
107. Mbata Nyambi	Sikamu	Mlumbe
108. Febye Mendulo	Eliyati	Mwambo
109. Biba Somati	Chiwaula	Mwambo
110. Uladi Somati	Chiwaula	Mwambo
111. Benisoni Mkwezalamba	Mulotho	Mwambo
112. Kasonda Bwana	Mandot	Mwambo
113. Friday Chigawo	Mpakwa	Mwambo
114. Baulose Bulaye	Chidule	Mtumaje
115. Nena Malala	Mbela	Ntemaje
116. Ali Mtila	Makunganya	Mlumbe
117. Lilesi Meja	Binali	Mwambo
118. Matola Wali	Sumaili	Mlumbe
119. Sikuwandi Saidi	Kagula	Mtumanje
120. Mukanjili Ndenge	Masakula	Mpama
121. Matiki Kilisimesi	Magombo	Chikowi
122. Ayana Ndini	Chindamba	Chikowi
123. Amai Jine Saka	Makumbanjila	Mwambo
124. Wiski Tamani	Chipengule	Kumtumanje
125. Naphutu Mwamadi	Ngwalangwala	Kumtumanje
126. Lifa Misakwe	Ngwalangwela	Kumtumanje
127. Gelena Chilala	Mbatata	Mwambo
128. Belita John	Mbatata	Mwambo
129. Unena Chibade	Chibade	Chikowi
130. Ali Mwamadi	Likulumu	Mlumbe
131. Osteni Usamani	Mpindimuli	Mlumbe
132. Issa Amissa	Makanjila	Mlumbe
133. Simoni Sitima	Mulipa	Kadewele

	Dzina	*Village*	*Mfumu*
134.	Male Mikulumu	Mikulumu	Mlumbe
135.	Alina Kasanga	Makunganya	Mlumbe
136.	Mustafa Lajabu	Mikulumu	Mlumbe
137.	Gasteni R. Tamani	Mphatama	Kumtumanje
138.	Rashidi Hasoward	Mussa	Mwambo
139.	Jeladi Kachala	Maunda	Kuntumanje
140.	Alabi Malilo	Ntonda	Kumtumanje
141.	Daimoni Saidi	John Table	Mwambo
142.	Nepheye Chiwelenga	Luwabwe	Kumtumanje
143.	V. H. Lipholo	Lipholo	Kumtumanje
144.	Samuel K. Makawa	Salimu	Chikowi
145.	Makodi Umali	Mwalelo	Kalembo
146.	Loneye Machinga	Maphila	Mwambo
147.	Samson James	Madyelo	Mwambo
148.	Wilson Gama	Kumilinje	Mwambo
149.	Modesita Mulambe	Mulasola	Mwambo
150.	J. L. Bulaimana	Bulaimana	Chikowi
151.	Kapato Eliya	Ngundende	Malemia
152.	Daina Sudi	Tulisya	Mwambo
153.	Florence Mataka	Chilomelo	Chikowi
154.	James Mkhali	Chinangwa	Mwambo
155.	Nasasala Wiski	Nasasala	Mwambo
156.	Singatiya Saidi	Nasasala	Mwambo
157.	Wilson Sapala	Mapila	Mwambo
158.	Eleni Ezeki	Matache	Mlumbe
159.	Chiwajika Lomwe	Mpindinule	Mlumbe
160.	Estele Filipo	Manolo	Chikowi
161.	Elise Chanunkha	William	Chikowi
162.	Chepale Sadiki	Maulana	Chikowi
163.	Kinaya Salimu	Chibibi	Chikowi
164.	Cheyama Dini	Chindani	Chikowi
165.	Lusiya Kamwando	Majawa	Chikowi
166.	Tetete Mulangafiti	Kabola	Kanda
167.	Sinakweli Kagwili	Sitima Ntenda	Chikowi
168.	Chiukala Likaso	Chibibi	Chikowi
169.	Issa Amasi	Makanjila	Mlumbe
170.	Mageleta Muhome	Balakasi	Chikowi
171.	Jife Kasimu	Jife	Chikowi
172.	James Wasili	Chilombo	Chikowi
173.	John Midi	Mwamadi	Chikowi
174.	Amisi Akimu	Mkwanda	Chikowi
175.	Napheswa Mingale	Matache	Chikowi
176.	Chikumba Nkhunda	Kausa	Chikowi
177.	Saladi Ajaswai	Kausa	Chikowi
178.	Alfred Ali	Malajila	Chikowi
179.	Maurice Ali	Makanjila	Chikowi
180.	Awalu Bonomali	Makanjila	Chikowi
181.	Makisimosi Ndagonja	Sonkho	Chikowi

Dzina	*Village*	*Mfumu*
182. Kasimu Kanga	Namkwenya	Chikowi
183. Chidelanji Bamusi	Chibwana	Mlumbe
184. Chimangeni Ndapete	Chibwana	Mlumbe
185. Elise Mkwapatila	Nyeliwa	Mwambo
186. Achibibi	Ntweye Usigele	Chikowi
187. Abani Chisuse	Chibwana	Mlumbe
188. Ntela Khela	Mponda	Nkhokwe
189. Aliyasi Nkhokwe	Nkhokwe	Nkokwe
190. G. V. H. Ndinji	Ndinji	Nkhokwe
191. Thomas Tamani	Nkhokwe	Nkhokwe
192. David Nachidwe	Kumisuku	Mwambo
193. Thendo Makwinja	Mulasola	Mwambo
194. Ameme Chakwana	Mgomo	Chikowi
195. Mrs P. O. Chisale	Ntiya	Mlumbe
196. Medisoni Kaulesi		
197. Mr Chiphatala	Tawakali	Chikowi
198. Eunice Chibade	Chibade	Chikowi
199. Welasi Gunda	Mindano	Mwambo
Lyness Nyirenda	Zanyata	Mzikuwola, Mzimba Boma
Faine Mbale	Engalaweni	Inkosi yamakosi, Mzimba Boma
Faine Tembo	Mvakule	Inkosi yamakosi, Mzimba Boma
Akimu Nyirenda	Mterera	Inkosi yamakosi, Mzimba Boma
Zawanda Zimba	Chibeku	Inkosi yamakosi, Mzimba Boma
Fani Chimalilo	Devete Mumba	Mtwalo, Mzimba Boma
Mukunku Banda	Charwani	Mzimba Boma
Andileya Phiri	Tawn Sappors	
Lucy Phiri	Engalaweni	Mtwalo, Mzimba Boma
Esamunjhonalanga Katete	Eliyakimu	Mzukuzuku, Mzimba Boma
Esineti Ndhlovu	Mapupu	Mzukuzuku, Mzimba Boma
Evesi Mahove	Danyere Gausi	Mzukuzuku, Mzimba Boma
Kanyasko	Danyere Gausi	Mzukuzuku, Mzimba Boma
Fidesi Nyalanga	Munkhosana	Mzukuzuku, Mzimba Boma
Dalines Mvuma	Mabaleka	Inkosi yamakosi, Mzimba Boma
Abraham Ndhlovu	Munkhuze Jere	Inkosi yamakosi, Mzimba Boma
Tamala Jere	Thaza Nyirongo	Mzukuzuku, Mzimba Boma
Basikolo Nkoma	Vulakayini Ngwenya	Inkosi Yamakosi, Mzimba Boma
Fulakisoni Longwe	William Longwe	Inkosi yamakosi, Mzimba Boma
Alanesi Phiri	Chimutu Hala	Inkosi yamakosi, Mzimba Boma

Dzina	*Village*	*Mfumu*
Lavinesi Hala	Engalaweni	Inkosi yamakosi, Mzimba Boma
Viki Ruhana	Emphangwe	Mzukuzuku, Mzimba Boma
Goodness Ngwira	Mvakule	Inkosi yamakosi, Mzimba Boma
Nkongono Shaba		
Timuwele Soko		
Edward Nyirenda		
Kete Mtonga		
Danaliya Mbeye	Amoni Moyo	Mzikuwola, Mzimba Boma
Faidase Chilwa	Pitalndabanda	Mbelwa, Mzimba Boma
Vainase Gausi	Pitalndabanda	Mbelwa, Mzimba Boma
Washington Gausi	Danyere Gausi	Mzikuwola, Mzimba Boma
Mrs Nyakanyasko Gausi	Danyare Gausi	Mzikubola
Henderson Mabaso	Yeremiya Mabaso	M'mbelwa
Muliko Mweuka	Kamphete	Mtwalo
Elivigi Chirwa	Chikondawanga	Mzikubola
Matiresi NyaZimba	Engalawendi	M'mbelwa
Elivase Nyamachamo	Njhokora Nzima	Chindi
Laviness Chirwa	Dakalimare	Mzikubola
Kefulina Muhalule	Chibisa	M'mbelwa
Tenson Mzimu	Kenani Chavula	M'mbelwa
Daison Tisole Banda	Chilupulu Mtonga	M'mbelwa
Abiyana Chipeta	William Ngwenya	
Winston Nyirenda	Kaziwarwe	M'mbelwa
Eliya Chavula	Emanyaleni	Mtwalo
Egeness Chipeta	Kasoti	M'mbelwa
Aless gogo Sakala	Chiwelewele Msiska	Kachulu
Veronica Ngomezulu	Chimbayo	Chilowoka
Tamaliyapo Lazalo		
Mugwede Koma	Zebedia Nyirenda	M'mbelwa
Disease P. Luganga	Mopho Jere	Mtwalo
Sapulay Mtonga	Msuku	M'mbelwa
Luka Kubakufwa	Chilenje	M'mbelwa

APPENDIX II

Certificate (and letter of identification) given to those involved in the research into traditional medicine.

University of Malawi

CHANCELLOR COLLEGE
P.O. Box 280, Zomba, MALAWI

Date ....

Tagwira ntchito ndi a..
ndi ena posonkhanitsa ndi kulongosola zomera ndikuzichita mankhwala a makolo. Tiyamikira ali yense amene annathandize zofunika zake zaiye. Tiyamikira kulitu-rutsa bukhu la mankhwala a makolo a m'Malawi ndi kuthandiza maziko a mphichi zotsimikizira mankhwala ochiritsa.

Dr Jerome D. Msonthi
Senior Lecturer in Chemistry

B. S. Nkhoma
Head, Traditional Herbalists Association

W. Chakwana Mbatata
District Chairman, Traditional Herbalists Association

('We have worked with . . . . and others in collecting plants for traditional medicine. We thank all those who helped in any way. We are grateful for [help in] bringing out a book on traditional medicines in Malawi, which will be a fundamental contribution to establishing those medicines that heal.')

APPENDIX III

Herbalists Association of Malawi (OCHIRITSA)
P.O. Box 51119, Limbe (Reg. No. 1730, 1963)

Mitengo ya Mankhwala (Prices of medicines)

Maula ndi 50t (divination: 50t)

		Chipondan-thengo (deposit)	*Akachira* (full price)
1. Kusula	(to restore fertility)	K.4.50	K.15.75t
2. Misala	(mental illnesses)	K.6.50	K.20
3. Mtima	(heart diseases)	K.3	K.6.50
4. Zirengo	(physical disorders of the leg)	K.3.50	K.8.50

		Chipondan-thengo (deposit)	*Akachira* (full price)
5. Likango	(venereal disease used to punish adultery with one's wife)	K.1.75	K.6.75
6. Ntchofu	(bile; colic)	K.3	K.6.50
7. Ziwengo	(skin disease)	K.1.90	K.6.75
8. Mutu Waukulu	(severe headache)	K.3.50	K.5.75
9. Poliyo	(polio)	K.7.75	K.20.50
10. Msana	(back ache)	K.2	K.4.50
11. Khosi	(bad body smell caused by black magic)	K.1.50	K.3.50
12. Chitupila	(swollen body)	K.1.75	K.5
13. Mphumu	(asthma)	K.5.75	K.12
14. Tibi	(tuberculosis)	K.3.50	K.10.50
15. Kulumpha Mwana	(baby's illness caused by mother sleeping with other men)	K.3.50	K.5.50
16. Chibayo	(convulsions)	K.1.75	K.6.50
17. Chikuku	(measles)	K.1.75	K.4.50
18. Mphunzi	(worms in the stomach)	K.2.50	K.6.50
19. Khate	(leprosy)	K.4.50	K.10.50
20. Mbulu	(swollen stomach)	K.4.75	K.10.50
21. Njirinjiri	(epilepsy)	K.7.75	K.20.50
22. Chammimba	(stomach troubles)	K.3.50	K.5.50
23. Likodzo	(bilharzia)	K.1.75	K.5
24. Kutsilika nyumba	(to protect home against harmful black magic)	NO DEP.	K.25/ K.30.50
25. Chindoko	(venereal disease; syphilis)	NO DEP.	K.9
26. Chinzonono	(venereal disease; gonorrhea)	NO DEP.	K.10.50
27. Ntayo	(sleeping with woman who has just aborted)	NO DEP.	K.12.50
28. Mabomu	(v.d.; lymphogranuloma venereum)	NO DEP.	K.9.50
29. Kuchotsa ufiti	(to cleanse witchcraft)	NO DEP.	K.10.50
30. Kubereketsa azimai	(to restore fertility)	NO DEP.	K.5
31. Kutsirika Thupi	(to protect self against witchcraft)	NO DEP.	K.12.50, K.15, K.25

Ndi zina zomwe inu asing'anga mutha kuwona nokha, monga za mwai ndi zina zofuna munthu izo ndi zogwirizana awiri, koma ngati sing'anga awona kuti nthendayi sinditha kuli bwino kutumiza ku chipatala kapena kwina kwa yemwe amatha matendawo, kuti munthuyo achiritsidwe m'malo monchedwetsa.

(There are other health problems, but healers can always examine to see what the patient suffers from and discuss with the patient how the problem can be solved; but if the healer sees that he cannot cure the illness, then it is better for him to refer the patient to the hospital or to some other healer who is capable of curing the disease, so that the patient can be treated in good time.)

Note: 100 tambala = 1 Kwacha; K.2 = £1.

APPENDIX IV

African Herbalists Association
P.O. Box 142, Balaka
Tel. 581351

Mitengo (prices)

		Chiponda Mthengo (deposit)	*Akachila* (full price)
Kusula	(to restore fertility)	K.2	K.6
Misala	(mental illness)	K.2	K.5
Amtima	(heart diseases)	K.1	K.3.50
Zolenga	(evil spirit powers)	K.1.30	K.4.70
Likango	(venereal disease used to punish adultery with one's wife)	K.O.90	K.5
Ntchofu	(bile; colic)	K.0.80	K.3.20
Ziwengo	(skin disease)	K.0.70	K.2.50
Zotcheledwa	(?)	K.2	K.6.40
Amutu Waukulu	(severe heachache)	K.1	K.3.80
Poliyo	(polio)	K.2	K.7.30
Otema Mutu	(incisions on head)	K.0.95	K.4
Amsana	(back ache)	K.0.65	K.2.45
Khosi	(bad body smell caused by black magic)	K.0.57	K.2.55
Fundo	(boils)	K.0.80	K.3.35
Mphumu	(asthma)	K.0.78	K.4.70
Tibi	(tuberculosis)	K.0.79	K.7.40
Kulumpha Mwana	(baby's illness caused by mother's sleeping with other men)	K.2	K.3.60
Chifuwa	(stabbing pain in chest)	K.0.56	K.2.60
Chibayo	(convulsions)	K.0.68	K.2.80
Chikuku	(measles)	K.0.60	K.2
Phunzi	(worms in the stomach)	K.0.95	K.3.07
Makate	(leprosy)	K.2	K.5.50
Mbulu	(swollen stomach)	K.2.50	K.6.40
Zotupa	(swellings)	K.0.80	K.3.30
Njilinjili	(epilepsy)	K.0.90	K.5
Kutsirika Nyumba	(to protect home against harmful black magic)	K.7	
Chindoko	(venereal disease; syphilis)	K.0.85	K.4
Chinzonono	(venereal disease; gonorrhea)	K.0.80	K.4
Bizinesi	(business)	K.5	
Likodzo	(bilharzia)	K.0.75	K.3.50
Chisomo pa Ntchito	(popularity at work)	K.4	
Wotembenuza Mbeleko	(sterility; inverted uterus)	K.1	K.7
Ntayo	(sleeping with woman who has just aborted)	K.1.50	K.6.50

[on reverse of African Herbalists Association price list]

MANKHWALA OLETSEDWA NDI AWA OSAPEREKA MANKHWALA OIPA	(prohibited medicines and bad medicines not to be given)
Akupha Munto	(to kill someone)
Otaitsa Mimba	(abortifacient)
Osatchera Azimayi Ku Mwezi	(make woman cease menstruating)
Osasandutsa Mikango	(stop person changing into lion)
Ndulu Ya Ng'ona	(crocodile spleen)
OSAKWEZA KAPENA KUTSITSA MITENGO	(do not raise or lower prices)

[list printed in 1979]

APPENDIX V

Traditional Doctors Association of Malaŵi
M.C.P. Office
PO Box 20
KASUNGU
14th December, 1983

UKUMBUTSA ZA KALATA YOMWE TIDALEMBRA PA MIYEZI YAPITAYO

cc: The Administration Secretary,
Malawi Congress National Headquarters
PO Box 3880
Lilongwe
(copies to District Commissioner, Kasungu)
cc: Lecturer in Biology
Chancellor College
PO Box 280
Zomba
cc: The Secretary for Health
Ministry for Health
Capital City
Lilongwe 3
(copies to o/c Malawi Police, Kasunagu)
cc: The Secretary for Local Government
Ministry of Local Government
PO Box 30312
Lilongwe 3
cc: The District Chairman
Malawi Congress Party Office

PO Box 20
Kasungu (New first copy)
cc: The Regional Chairman
Malawi Congress Party Regional Headquarters
Lilongwe (New first copy)
cc: Malawi Police Divisional Headquarters for Central Region
Through: The Officer in Charge
Lilongwe Police Station
Lilongwe (New first copy)

Bwana

Ine mmalo mwa asing'anga anzanga ochuluka muno m'Malawi tipempha boma podzela mwa inu kuti litilole tikhale ndi bungwe lathulathu la asing'anga lotchedwa TRADITIONAL DOCTORS ASSOCIATION OF MALAWI.

CHOLINGA chokhazikitsila bungweli nkufuna kuthokoza pa Utsogoleri wanzeru wa Ngwa i yathu ya muyaya DR. H. KAMUZU BANDA polola kuti ife asing'anga tipitilize ntchito yathu yochilitsa monga momwe amachitila makolo athu. Kuthokoza kwathu kukhala kotere: Bungweli lidzagwapo pa chitukuko cha dziko lino pogawa ndarama za Umembership pa chaka chilihonse chonse ndi 40% ya sing'anga aliyense kupeleka ku District Council ya boma limene sing'angayo akugwilira ntchito, kuti zithandize ana amasiye, powalipilira succulu, ndi kuthandizapo pa chitukuko cha dziko lino.

2. Bungweli lifuna likhale member body ya Malawi Congress Party: Mdziko muno.
3. Bungweli lifuna kuthetsa umbabva wa asing'anga ochuluka amene amakweza mitengo kwa odwala awo, popeza mizu ndi mitengo imene agwiritsila ntchito mdziko muno sagula, kapena kuwods ayi, choncho sing'anga aliyense asapyoletse K10.00. Polipilitsa odwala amene amabwela ku chipatala chake.
4. Kuchenjeza asing'anga kuti azikhala ndi ulemu pa mabanja a weni wake, asamapezelapo njira yochitira dama ndi akazi amene afika ndi cholinga chodzasula (kufuna kubeleka) pa chipala chawo.
5. Kuchenjeza asing'anga amizimu kuti asamagwirira ntchito yawo pagulu, pakati pa anthu, chifukwa zinena zawo zina zimachotsa ulemu muninu. Monga kumabvulitsa neepato, lamba, duku kumutu, ndi kunena zolaula pakati pa gulu, kumuchititsa manyazi munthuyo.
6. Kuletsa zowombeza zonama, popeza zimapeleka udani kumidzi, ndi ndi kupasula midzi, ya eni ake chifukwa cha zonena zawo zina za bodza powombeza maula. Kuti ayanjane ndi atsogoleri amipingo. Popeza sakawalora akhristu awo kupita kwa asing'anga chifukwa cha bodzalo.
7. Kuletsa asing'anga kupereka mankhwala oipa monga:-
   (*a*) Mankhwala ophera munthu.
   (*b*) Mankhwala ochotsela mimba.
   (*c*) Kuika chambu kwa akazi kapena kuti kutsirika akazi.
   (*d*) Kauta kwa akazi amene amatsilika amuna awo.
   (*e*) Asamapereke mankhwala a ntherele pa mlandu, popeza zimalimbikitsa umbabya.
8. Bungweli lidzafufuzanso ngati pali sayansi. Popeza timamva kuti pali ndege zouluka usiku, magalimoto oyenda opanda mafuta, mafuta ake ndi mdima. Paliso ena ochotsa mano ndi tsekerea ndi zina zomwe zingakhale zopindulitsa m'dziko muno.
9. Bungweli lidzagwiranso ntchito yotengako mizu kwa asing'anga odziwika

pa zochiritsa kuwatumiza ku University of Malawi kuti akawayese ku Labotale ngati angadzatheke kupunga mankhwala achizungu kuchokera ku mizu yathuyi.

10. Kulangiza asing'anga kuti asamalekerere matenda odwalitsa kwambiri pachipatala chawo, komo kuwatumiza ku zipatala za boma zimene zili pafupi ndi iwo. Popeza sing'anga alibe zipangizo zothilira magazi m'thupi la munthu.
11. Bungweli lizigwira ntchito pamodzi ndi makhansalala a district council pofuna kupeza thandizo lothandizira chitukuko cha m'makhonsolo, Pong-wapo pachitukuko cha dziko lino.

Tiyembekezera chifunndo cha boma kulibvomereza bungweli.

Ine wan m'malo mwa asing'anga anzanga,

D. M. P. Ntikunthile
EXECUTIVE CHAIRMAN FOR THE HERBALISTS DESIGNATE

(for English summary, see pp. 101–2)

5 Patrick A. Twumasi and Dennis Michael Warren

THE PROFESSIONALISATION OF INDIGENOUS MEDICINE: A COMPARATIVE STUDY OF GHANA AND ZAMBIA

INTRODUCTION

In many parts of Africa, health care facilities are unequally distributed. The statistics show that health care facilities are mainly located in the cities and larger towns where the minority of the African population lives. Health statistics also reveal that modern health professionals prefer to work in the urban areas where supporting services and health logistics systems exist.

It is, however, in the rural areas of Africa that health hazards are more prevalent. Mortality and morbidity rates are far higher in rural than in the urban areas. Maternal and child care problems are extensive, and preventive health care facilities are virtually non-existent.

Numerous indigenous healers and birth attendants live in these rural communities where modern health care facilities and personnel are lacking. The logical question in this era of primary health care is why the orthodox medical system is reluctant to open a dialogue with the indigenous healers in order to improve health care in rural Africa.

Before national governments in the African region can legitimately incorporate the services of indigenous healers in orthodox national health systems there is the need to understand better these healers and determine whether they are interested and willing to submit to standardisation and regulation by national health institutions. It is also necessary to determine the processes and issues which can emerge in these cases where indigenous healers are seeking to achieve official national recognition.

Pertinent research questions include (1) what are the processes involved for an emerging occupation to attain a legitimate professional status? and (2) to what extent are indigenous healers willing or being compelled to organise themselves into a modern profession?

METHODOLOGY

The material for this paper is derived from fieldwork studies and consultancies which were undertaken by the authors in Ghanaian and Zambian communities. Studies were conducted on Ghanaian projects such as the USAID-funded Danfa Health Project, the WHO-funded Brong-Ahafo Rural Integrated Development Programme (BARIDEP), and the Primary Health Training for Indigenous Healers Programme (PRHETIH). Research work was also conducted in Zambia with support from IDRC/ Ottawa.

In the first part of this paper, there is a discussion of the Ghanaian situation; the second part looks at the Zambian situation; and the last section is an analytical part in which the main trends and issues involved in professionalisation are discussed.

DEFINITION

According to the World Health Organisation, indigenous healers are a

> group of persons recognised by the community in which they live as being competent to provide health by using vegetable, animal and mineral substances and other methods based on the social, cultural and religious backgrounds as well as on the knowledge, attitudes and beliefs that are prevalent in the community regarding physical, mental and social well-being and the causation of disease and disability (WHO 1978, p. 41).

As an acceptable definition, we can group Ghanaian and Zambian healers into four main types of specialities: traditional birth attendants; faith healers; herbalists; and spiritualists/diviners.

In terms of speciality area, traditional birth attendants focus on life crises. They have a special role to play at birth and at puberty ceremonies. In child birth, they are the midwives and they are also recognised as godmothers to young children. Throughout Ghana, especially in the rural areas, they are known as specialists in obstetrics. Their range of activities extends into the field of sex education and contraceptive counselling.

Faith healers are representatives or healers of religious movements such as the syncretic churches. Common among the faith healers are leaders of sectarian-based religious movements, the millennial and thaumaturgical churches. These churches are therapeutic centres.

Spiritualists include indigenous priests and priestesses, ritual and cult leaders and others who are specialists in divination. States of spiritual possession are a common feature. At times it is very difficult to make a clear-cut distinction between faith healers and spiritual healers. For analytical purposes, however, faith healers operate from their own religious movements and spiritualists are priests and priestesses of particular shrines.

Herbalists approach healing through the use and application of herbs. Their methods of treatment and operational procedures are often similar to the nosology of modern medicine. Nevertheless there are many subspecialities in herbalism (Warren 1982, p. 1873).

REVIEW OF LITERATURE

Theorists of the professions argue that professionalisation is a historical process whereby people who occupy certain role-positions within the societal division of labour (occupational group) tend to struggle to achieve a certain degree of autonomy and continually struggle to maintain that power. They organise their work activities, cultivate a distinct body of knowledge, develop norms of practice and codes of conduct for the training and socialisation of members of the group. They also establish rules of conduct between themselves and the larger society.

Paul Bennel (1982) has noted that research work in the area of professionalisation in the African continent has been neglected by many social scientists. This is true partly because of lack of written material outlining the stages of historical growth and development through which an emerging occupation struggles to achieve power and control over its own resources. In tracing the specific processes through which an occupational group attempts to reach professional status one needs to rely basically on oral traditions, and sketchy information from colonial reports. It is within this methodological frame of reference that the present authors are attempting to analyse indigenous healing in Ghana and in Zambia as an emerging profession.

In addition to Bennel's work, Terence Johnson (1972) has developed guidelines for understanding professional occupations in former British colonies. He feels that the British model of professions was transplanted into the former colonies, and that a profession is not an occupation but a means of controlling an occupation. Despite the impact of colonialism, one should not ignore the fact that before colonisation there were indigenous professional bodies which exhibited what are now known as universal professional traits.

Taking medicine and law as examples, the indigenous African professions have developed specific skills and techniques guiding their practice. It is also because of specialised professional knowledge that societal legitimation and professional integrity have developed. Professional traits were acquired by practitioners through long periods of training in systematic theory and in formal work discipline. Professional education was basically oriented to community service. Because of the important services which professionals gave to society they were usually protected by law in order to organise their schools and work procedures and in the training of the young. Professional bodies were and are communities within larger communities.

Oyebola (1981) provides insights into the stages of professional growth, development, and proliferation of Yoruba herbalist associations in Nigeria. The Yoruba healers' associations serve as meeting points for professional consultations, sharing knowledge and application of sanctions. Oyebola also found the existence of formal ethical rules for conduct in the charter of the Yoruba healers' associations. Disciplinary committees were established by members to deal with deviant behaviour and actual offending members. What is equally of interest to students of professional growth and development is the view presented by Oyebola that healers find it difficult to form a single national professional body because they are of so many different types, each with specialised techniques and knowledge.

Bannerman *et al.* (1981) in an interesting discussion of Oyebola's paper agreed that there is a growing interest in the study of indigenous medicine as an emerging profession, and that scholars must pay more attention to this area.

As argued by Bannerman *et al.* there were several reasons for the difficulty in organising national healers' associations in most African countries: (1) in pre-colonial times there were no national states as we know today but ethnic entities, and indigenous healers therefore grouped themselves along ethnic geographical lines, into district and local level associations; (2) there were various healing sub-systems, each one forming one occupational group; (3) language difficulties did not argue well for an umbrella national organisation; (4) distance was another factor which made it difficult for indigenous healers to form one body, and thus only those healers within a certain geographical ethnic area were able to form occupation groupings.

Sociological characteristics of indigenous healers' associations rested on the following factors: (1) they were rooted in a geographical area, or in a particular form of healing practice; (2) they were highly personalised and the leadership position was assumed by a charismatic and a prosperous healer of a great reputation.

Indigenous healers had the following characteristics: (1) a distinct body of knowledge which was supported by a theoretical paradigm, the knowledge of the healers being acquired through a long period of training; (2) the knowledge so acquired gave the healers an authority which was exercised and observed during their interaction with their clients; (3) a code of ethics which guided the practice of indigenous healing; (4) a community interest because of their services – they were given the freedom to work; and (5) the healers had a way of life, a professional culture in terms of their outlook, mannerisms, symbols and technological tools.

PART I: CASE STUDY FROM GHANA

Ghana has a population of about 12 million (Ghana 1980). Of this population, 71% live in rural areas. It is in these rural settlements that modern health care facilities are lacking, and indigenous healers of all persuasions loom large in rural society.

According to 1975–76 Ghana Government budget estimates, it is only 29% of the population that is served by modern health care services. Another indication of the unequal distribution of modern health resources is that in 1980 there were 900 physicians in Ghana of whom 80% worked in the public services located in the principal towns and cities. The average national doctor/patient ratio was 1:10,000. But in most rural areas, especially in the two northern most regions, the doctor/patient ratio was estimated as 1:40,000.

Ghana's National Health Planning Unit has noted also that at least 71% of the Ghanaian population is without easy access to the modern health care system despite the large public expenditure on health. The Unit has therefore recommended the recruitment and training of community health workers. It is on this basis that indigenous workers are being gradually encouraged to train for co-operation with the modern health service in order to improve and extend improved health care services to a broader public.

It must be noted, as we shall make clear, that in the 1960s (after Ghana's independence, in March 1957) all governments were taking an interest in indigenous medicine.

A HISTORICAL ACCOUNT

Before the advent of colonial contact in Ghana, indigenous health practitioners were the sole practitioners of medicine in the country. They treated ills, had consultations with a wider public and gave protective charms to people who asked for their services. Theirs was an ongoing legitimate activity. Experienced healers instituted training programmes, based on the apprentice model, to train young persons. They had consultations, referred patients and had developed a medical culture.

With the advent of colonial rule a new medical system was instituted in the country. The justification for the introduction of the new system was that the explorers and the entire colonial administration found the country beset with many preventable and communicable diseases. Western medical practitioners were posted to the then Gold Coast (now Ghana) to cure and treat ills (Twumasi 1981).

The practitioners of the modern system of healing were trained in formal Western schools of medicine with a distinct professional culture. They used highly sophisticated Western technological appliances in delivering health care. In essence the practitioners of the new system of healing were organised under an umbrella system, the medical profession.

Coming into contact with indigenous healing practices there was a conflict of interest, of operational style, in theoretical orientation and in organisational methods. The colonial Government encouraged the institutionalisation of the new system, modern medicine, by providing it with a legislative instrument. This was done in 1878 to support the establishment of the new system. The aim of the colonial Government was to liquidate "native practice of traditional medicine". The healers were thought "to be insincere, to be quacks who lived on the neuroses of their illiterate folks" (Twumasi 1981, p. 1381). The missionaries also added their voice to downgrade the practice of indigenous medicine. Due to ritual practices inherent in some healing practices, these healers were looked down upon by the Christians. Indigenous healing lost its prestige and was stigmatised. The colonial Government denied indigenous healers any official mandate. Since they did not have any legal backing and their practice was not officially recognised as a legitimate activity, the healers were forced to practise in secrecy.

It was not until Ghana's independence that there was a new awareness in Ghanaian culture created by the nationalist Government. It led the late President Kwame Nkrumah to look into the past and to revive African arts, culture and medicine. There was a conscious quest for an African way of doing things to distinguish the African from the European. It was within this frame of reference that Nkrumah's government in 1963 appointed Mensah Dapaah, who had returned to Ghana with an MSc from McGill University, 'to study and organise traditional healers to form Associations for the advancement of their art and techniques in the delivery of health care'. This led to the formation of Ghana's Psychic and Traditional Healing Association in 1963. It must be noted that spiritual and faith healers were grouped under the psychic wing and that traditional herbalists and traditional birth attendants were grouped under the traditional herbalist wing of the Association.

Mensah Dapaah had previously undertaken research work at the Akonnede Shrine, a psychic healing cult, at Larteh-Akwapim, in the Eastern Region of Ghana (Mensah Depaah 1968). He worked with Nana Oparebea, the priestess in charge of the shrine, who later became the newly formed Association's President. After his research work, Mensah Dapaah brought to the notice of the Government that 'to understand the practice of traditional healing, one must be prepared not to use the scientific method. The herbs can be studied from the scientific point of view but the total therapeutic process was hard to understand in a normal scientific way' (Mensah Dapaah 1968, p. 16). If we were to understand the therapeutic methods and treatment potential of indigenous healers the scientific method was not the only appropriate method. He also drew attention to the therapeutic skills of Ghanaian healers in treating ills, especially social and psychological illnesses.

The campaign which was embarked upon by the nationalist Government to promote cultural identity was reflected in post-independence national attitudes. It surfaced during the early 1960s immediately after Ghana was declared a republic within the British Commonwealth of Nations. The political climate was favourable. It buttressed the confidence of indigenous healers as a way to improve their public image and their practice. The position of the healers in regard to the law was still ambiguous. They were not given official recognition. It was an offence to practise indigenous healing or for people to use the services of Ghanaian healers. It was only when a healer used medicine to kill a person that the case would be brought to the law courts.

Mensah Dapaah at this point was asked to draw up a national charter to organise indigenous healers in the country. Faced with an enormous problem in the speciality areas of the healers, he categorised them as herbalists, faith healers, spiritualist-diviners and traditional midwives. He was able to classify them on the basis of their sources of power and actual knowledge and skills in operation.

The foundation for the development of the national association of traditional healers was established when, as secretary, Mensah Dapaah drew up the following objectives: (1) to uphold, protect and promote the best in psychic and traditional healing in Ghana; (2) to encourage the establishment of advanced training programmes in traditional healing; (3) to help to introduce and train medical students to appreciate the work of traditional healing; (4) to encourage research work into traditional medicine; (5) to establish clinics in remote places and to educate traditional healers in the districts in order to improve upon their practices (Brew-Graves 1977, p. 26).

After the fall of Nkrumah, the organisational structure of the Ghana Psychic and Traditional Healing Association drawn up by Mensah Dapaah fell to pieces. The destruction was part of an attempt by the military National Liberation Council Government to discredit the work started by Nkrumah. No money was allocated to the Association. Association matters were pushed to the background by the officials of the Ministry of Health.

It was not until Acheampong's military Government that the Association of Psychic and Traditional Healers was given a new life. In 1974 the Acheampong Government opened a Centre for Scientific Research into Plant Medicine at Mampong, in the Akwapim district of the Eastern Region (Newmann 1982). The main functions of the Centre were: (1) to conduct and promote scientific research into plant medicine; (2) to co-operate and liaise with the Ghana Psychic and Traditional Healers Association, research institutions and commercial organisations in any part of the country on matters of plant medicine; (3) to ensure the priority of drugs extracted from plants; (4) to undertake or collaborate in the collation, publication and dissemination of the results of research and other useful technical information; and (5) to establish, where necessary, botanical gardens for medicinal plants.

In July 1975 the centre was formally registered and opened by the Government as a statutory corporation with a council made up of the following members: a chairperson, appointed by the Government; a representative of the National Council of Higher Education: the Dean, University of Ghana Medical School; the Dean of Pharmacy, University of Science and Technology; one member to represent each of the three universities in Ghana; the Chairman of the Council for Scientific and Industrial Research or his/her representative; and the Principal Secretary, Ministry of Health or his/her representative.

The Centre for Scientific Research into Plant Medicine was an attempt by the Government to carry out systematic research into the potentiality of herbs used by indigenous healers. A physician with a considerable interest in cultural revival in Ghana was appointed by the Government as the head of the Centre, Dr Oku Ampofo, who is still the head of the Institute. His mandate was to find out appropriate ways and means to organise traditional healers to bring their herbs to the Centre for scientific analysis and testing; and to determine the treatment potentiality of each herb so analysed and tested.

When the authors visited his clinic during the course of this research Ampofo mentioned the steady progress the Centre had made in convincing indigenous healers to co-operate with him. He also mentioned that some healers did not want to expose their herbs to scientific testing because of various reasons known only to themselves. Some were afraid that they might lose their jobs or that their claims might not be authentic. Nevertheless, some healers co-operated and some were employed in the clinic to help to extract the preparations of herbs for public scrutiny. Some members of the University of Ghana's Departments of Chemistry and Botany were co-opted to help in the search for common medical herbal drugs which were genuine. Research work is still going on at the Centre. It must also be added that the Centre has a clinic for the treatment of various illnesses referred to it.

The healers who co-operated with the Centre were from the herbalists' group. It is worth noting that spiritualist/diviners and faith healers were reluctant to come forward to the Centre to subject their preparations to scientific analysis and scrutiny. Our findings supported the view that spiritualist-diviners and faith healers did not want to join national associations and co-operate with national institutions, because they do not wish to subject their preparations to public scrutiny, and to be controlled by an outside power.

Although the herbalist is often pictured as an individualist who refuses to co-operate with others for fear of having to share his/her 'secret trade', this image is not supported by the facts. Traditionally herbalists have co-operated with other healers in two important ways: (1) herbalists who were not able to treat particular illnesses often consulted with herbal specialists with experience in treating them; (2) herbalists in rural communities from pre-colonial days had formed occupational associations whose main business was to regulate healing practices, to establish moral codes of conduct and to outline proper occupational procedures for members to follow. The problem of individualism is rather found among faith healers and spiritualists. They claim that their sources of authority for treatment came from a supernatural source, and that they cure merely as intermediaries between the patient and the spiritual authority. It is therefore not within their power to be controlled by an outside association. However, there was a referral network among them through which they asked patients to see specialists and through which they made occasional consultations.

PART II: CASE STUDY FROM ZAMBIA

The population of Zambia is estimated at 6 million. Currently there are a total of 82 hospitals and 725 health centres which are operated by the government, missions and mining companies. There are 20,000 beds in the country and the doctor/patient ratio is 1:9,000. There are 700 doctors in the country, 500 of them expatriates.

This statistical information at first glance appears to present a favourable health care situation, but it should be noted that about 76% of the doctors are found in the cities and provincial capitals. Thus like other African countries, including Ghana, there is an unequal distribution of modern health resources. There is also a problem of unequal distribution of paramedical personnel. Of the 8,000 nurses in the country 80% are working in the large towns and cities. There is also an acute shortage of laboratories and midwifery personnel in rural Zambia (Kaplan 1979).

The policy of the Government is to encourage rural staffing as part of the priority to operationalise primary health care objectives. Yet there is an obvious difficulty in finding modern health personnel to go to the rural areas. Administrative and structural constraints have also hindered the governmental efforts. There is now an interest to seek co-operation from indigenous healers in the hope of improving and extending basic health care services.

A HISTORICAL ACCOUNT

The socio-cultural reawakening which occurred immediately after independence in African countries was felt in all sectors of national life in Zambia. As in most African countries there was an impetus in Zambia to re-examine local institutions and the wish was to encourage indigenous practices deemed to be effective in contributing to the health of the nation. There was also the wish to discourage practices which were harmful to national development (Mulungushi Hall Report 1977).

Traditional medicine was a term used in colonial times to refer to indigenous healing practices which people resorted to when left to their own devices. For the Zambian Government it was not an institution which could simply be ignored or discarded.

The Zambian Ministry of Health examined indigenous medicine in order to identify its detrimental practices. The Zambian Government has encouraged the positive aspects of indigenous medicine by providing support to legitimate healers to institutionalise their forms of healing. The Witchcraft Act passed in 1967 is an example of a legislative measure which was intended to eradicate practices perceived to be negative. Registration of healers was instituted. A conference was held in 1977 to open a dialogue between modern and indigenous practitioners. Indigenous healers were asked to form associations to standardise and control their practice. The formation of a national council was suggested by the conference participants.

The Witchcraft Act (Act 145) provides for penalties for the practice of witchcraft and for matters incidental to or connected with it. This Act refers to 'any death, injury, damage, disease or calamity, whether of an accidental or of a torturous character. Witchcraft includes the throwing of bones, the use of charms and any other means, process or device adopted in the practice of witchcraft or sorcery'.
The Act goes on to indicate

Whoever –

(*a*) names or indicates or accuses or threatens to accuse any person as being a wizard or witch or

(*b*) imputes to any person the use of non-natural means in causing any death, injury, damage or calamity or

(*c*) asserts that any person has, by committing adultery, caused in some non-natural way death, injury, damage or calamity – shall be liable upon conviction to a fine not exceeding one year, or to both such fine and imprisonment [Another aspect of the Act states] any chief or headman who directly or indirectly permits, promotes, encourages or facilitates the commission of any act punishable by this Act or who knowing of such act or intended act does not

> forthwith report the same to a police officer of or above the rank of Assistant Inspector or where there is no such police officer, to a District Secretary or an Assistant District Secretary, shall be liable upon conviction to a fine not exceeding one hundred kwacha or to imprisonment with or without hard labour for any term not exceeding three years (Republic of Zambia, Witchcraft Act, Chapter 145 of the Laws of Zambia, Government Printers, Lusaka).

The rationale behind the Witchcraft Act was to eliminate indigenous healing and medicinal practices deemed to be inimical to national consciousness and development. The Act in no way punishes a genuine healer who uses orthodox healing methods to support the growth and development of indigenous medicine.

During the 1977 Mulungushi Hall Conference, the Ministry of Health stated its interest in indigenous medicine. It wished to see indigenous healers continue to play their role in a well organised health structure. To this end the following issues were proposed:

(1) The possibility of retraining and replacement of genuine traditional healers in the development of Primary Health Care;
(2) to rid Zambia of quacks posing as indigenous healers;
(3) to develop an alternative institution of medicine which could play a complementary role in health care delivery;
(4) to establish a dialogue between practitioners of indigenous and cosmopolitan medicine in Zambia;
(5) to gain an understanding of the contribution being made to Primary Health Care in both systems of healing;
(6) to obtain insights into the modes of practice of indigenous medicine; and
(7) to promote the formation of a National Council of Traditional Healers.

The Conference demonstrated the interest of the Ministry of Health in supporting the growth and development of indigenous medicine. At the Ministry an established position for an officer in charge of traditional medicine has been created. The officer has instituted a system of registering traditional healers and traditional birth attendants. Nearly 600 traditional birth attendants have been provided additional training through UNICEF and WHO assistance. These refresher courses for traditional birth attendants are based on the recognition that about 80% of deliveries in Zambia are done by traditional birth attendants.

Joyce Leeson and Ronald Frankenberg studied the patients of indigenous healers in Lusaka (Leeson and Frankenberg 1977), and they came to the following conclusions:

that patients who were not satisfied with their treatment elsewhere visited these

healers;
that patients whose ills were of psychosomatic origin sought help from indigenous healers; and
that patients felt comfortable with these healers' holistic approach.

Faith healers in Zambia treat mainly psychosomatic diseases, insanity, epilepsy, sterility, impotency, chest asthma, infertility, bewitchment and spirit possession. They subject their patients to extensive interviewing, to discover how best the patients can be assisted to overcome their ailments. Apart from the interviews, faith healers diagnose through meditation, dreams, and prayers.

When a patient is brought to a faith healer, he or she goes with the patient into a quiet room, where a prayer is offered. In the quiet room the healer seeks for clues to find out why the patient is ill. The quiet room provides the faith healer with the opportunity to get in touch with the inner self of the patient, and the patient feels free to reveal confidential information to aid the therapy.

Faith healers seek spiritual help in diagnosis and treatment. At times the patient might be told to come back on certain specific days to continue with treatment. During the interim period, faith healers go through a series of prayers in order to discover what went wrong with the patient. To a faith healer if the patient was eventually cured, glory and appreciation should be given to God and the particular church supporting the practice.

One of the faith healers we interviewed was a leader of a popular church, the Mutumwa Nchimi Church. It has numerous followers and branches in Monze (Southern Province), Nambora (Western Province) and Chipata (Eastern Province). Patients, both church and non-church members, came from all places for healing purposes. The leader was known by them to have spiritual powers to heal epilepsy, sterility, impotence and asthmatic diseases. The healer had a clinic attached to the church building. Apart from treating out-patient cases he had many in-patients, among them those who were suffering from epilepsy. At the time of the research there were seven in-patients, young persons with ages ranging from fourteen to nineteen years. It was difficult to separate diagnostic and treatment procedures. In witnessing a case during one research period, a mother brought a boy of fifteen years to the healer. The mother was accompanied by her two sisters. On entering the premises, a church attendant came into the clinic to inform the healer (the leader of the church) that a mother had come to seek his attention with her sick child. He was asked to bring the child. They were given seats in the clinic.

The healer listened attentively to the mother who gave the medical and social history of the child from birth to the present situation. Without questioning, the faith healer took the mother and her child to an adjacent room. With the help of a lighted candle and a strong scented perfume which the healer sprayed in the room, he offered prayers to the mother and to the child. He gave the child a ritual mark (with a white powder) on his forehead and on the top part of his head. The mother and child were asked to report again in about a week's time.

In treatment the faith healer listened attentively to the whole story of a patient's life style, which had an important impact on the patient's illness. For example, if disordered social relations had existed the healer would ask the patient's relatives to go back to pacify the aggrieved person or persons. If an aggrieved relative had 'caused' the illness, he would also be summoned to appear before the healer. The healer would verify the situation before he would embark on a specific course of treatment. In treatment patients were given specific rules and regulations to follow, and in the final treatment phase patients were given herbal ointments and charms to protect them from evil forces.

Spiritualists or diviners interviewed in Zambia diagnosed through divination by seeking help from spirits. They diagnosed also through dreams and trances. When a spiritualist was satisfied that he/she had discovered what was wrong with a patient, the healer resorted to interviewing techniques to confirm the diagnosis and to obtain more details from the patient or the patient's relatives.

The healer sought to identify the social and psychological reasons for the illness. Enquiries were made regarding any social disturbances, disordered social relations, or inability on the part of the patient to communicate effectively with any household relatives. Later, the healer investigated any metabolic disturbances, lack of appetite, inability to sleep and whether there were other bodily symptoms and signs.

Spiritualists did not normally give patients any physical examination. They were usually satisfied that the diagnosis they gave was a correct one. They were healers who were full of self-confidence. After diagnosis the patient was given herbal medicine.

All types of patients visited spiritualists. Usually they were patients who had failed to receive appropriate treatment from a modern health facility. Others were those who felt that orthodox medical treatment would not be useful in treating their ills.

The common ailments diagnosed and treated by them were: impotence, epilepsy, overweight, high blood pressure, problems of unemployment, marital affairs, love medicine, rheumatism, mental diseases, delirium, forgetfulness, spirit possession, oedema, prevention of disasters, venereal diseases, and asthma.

When medicine was given to a patient to cure any of the above ailments, a ritual ceremony was usually performed at the healer's clinic to augment the potentiality of the medicinal preparation. The patient was also given advice on how to live with other members of the household, on how to take the medicine and on the type and nature of food to be eaten. Instructions of this nature were given to the patient, who was asked to report back to the healer within a specified time, usually five days.

Record-keeping, in the form of writing down of names, addresses, ailments, and cures, did not feature in the duties and responsibilities of spiritual healers. When asked how they were able to trace their patients or to know of what had transpired, they informed the author that they knew their patients very well and that it was also the responsibility of their patients to find them if they had encountered further problems. Of the few who kept records the information they kept was of a scanty nature. They recorded only names and house addresses of their patients. It was not common to find that they had recorded the types of diagnosis and the type of treatment they had given.

Most of the healers charged consultation fees of K2, at times K5 (about US $3) depending on the type of illness presented and depending on social-economic background of the patient. When the patient was cured he was asked to present an appreciation gift. Any amount might be given depending on the patient's ability.

Spiritualists have a deep-seated belief in the potency of spiritual powers. They kept in touch regularly with their spirits and they abided by the rules so established by the spirits in order to gain their favours and to obtain their support in healing, in diagnosis, and in treatment.

They relied more on a social causation theory of disease than on notions of the physical causes of disease. In most treatment sessions they used social analysis to get to the root causes of the patient's problems.

Usually in their clinic, children were seen playing around. But when a patient sought consultation, the children were asked to leave the immediate environment and the patient would be taken into a quiet room for consultation. In other words most spiritual healers often practised in their own home environment.

They were not usually available in the mornings for consultation but were almost always available in the evenings. Some of them had specific healing days for consultations and treatment sessions. The cases they could not deal with they referred to modern general hospitals.

The herbalists interviewed were members of traditional healers' associations, and were interested in protecting and advancing their occupation. They were more open-minded than the spiritualists. They were in favour of an umbrella national association and viewed it like a strong trade union organisation which could protect and advance their interests.

A herbalist interviewed saw his patient in his clinic in an open place in the inside corner of a market stall. In the clinic there were consultation chairs and medicinal tables. During the period of the fieldwork, it was noted that not many patients called to consult. The peak consultation period was in the late afternoon when not more than twenty patients saw the healer during a day's work.

This particular herbalist had a smaller patient load than a typical modern health practitioner in charge of an out-patient department. The herbalist therefore had more time to talk with his patients.

In a relaxed atmosphere the herbalist listened attentively to his patient's problems. After listening to the patient's complaints, he asked questions regarding the patient's ailment, mental state, relationship with relatives, and physical condition. When preliminary investigations had been completed, the herbalist examined the patient before he prescribed treatment. He touched the patient to find out if there were abnormalities on the body. He enquired from the patient if there was any pain. When he was satisfied that he would be able to cope with the patient's complaints, he reassured the patient psychologically not to worry. Then he accepted a consultation fee of about K5. After the payment of the consultation fee, he would prescribe treatment.

The herbalist acted in other roles. He performed the duties of a counsellor. He would advise the patient. At another period he became a pharmacist. He was also seen as a social worker, who talked effectively with the patient and his relatives on the effective way to rehabilitate the patient in his home environment.

The common complaints which were brought to the attention of the herbalist during the period of fieldwork were the following: love problems, marital discord, epilepsy, cough, rheumatism, persistent headaches, prolonged menstrual periods, abdominal pains, charms for good luck, infertility, back pains, diarrhoea, gonorrhoea, vomiting, asthma, lumps, impotence, child delinquency, worms, and spirit possession.

For traditional birth attendants (TBAs) interviewed, physical examinations took place within the context of the patient's environment. The TBAs were aware of the social and psychological background characteristics of their patients because they were resident members of the patient's community. They interviewed their patients in a relaxed atmosphere. At times the patients' relatives were present and they contributed effectively to give a fuller picture of what was presented. The TBAs raised questions which were rooted in the patients' social and psychological situation. They asked whether the patients were properly married, had children, had good households and were well looked after nutritionally by their relatives. They also noted whether the child was a wanted one or not.

Bodily examinations then took place to find out when delivery would take place, and if the baby was lying in the correct position. If all was well the mother would be advised to carry on with her normal daily activities. If a problem was detected she was given advice and appropriate herbal medicine. The pregnant woman would then be advised to report back in about three to five days time. If the problem was above the competence of the traditional birth attendant she would advise the patient to see a modern practitioner in a national health clinic. All three traditional birth attendants we interviewed in the course of the research took refresher courses in co-operation with nurses and doctors at a modern clinic in that neighbourhood. There was an ongoing organised training session for traditional birth attendants to upgrade their standards. Considerable goodwill existed between the traditional birth attendants and the modern hospital personnel.

Traditional healers in Zambia have their practice mainly located in the heart of where the people live and work. They are part of the social structure of the communities from where their clients come. They share in the value system and the entire cultural orientation of the people. We discovered that in Zambia indigenous healers took advantage of the fact that they were also part of the entire socio-cultural milieu of their patient. In terms of the social background characteristics of their patients they were not different. They did not set themselves apart from the people.

Most of the healers practised in the market-places where most people visited. All types of people had easy access to them. In the market-places, the healers, especially the herbalists, hired stalls and they displayed their medicine. In the market locations they held their consultations.

PART III: COMPARATIVE ANALYSIS

The Ghanaian and Zambian official policies towards indigenous healers in their determination to achieve national legitimacy are favourable ones. They are in line with the WHO decision which stated that national Governments must find ways and means to train and utilise traditional healers and to collaborate with them in providing primary health care. In line with WHO's decision the Governments of Ghana and Zambia have created avenues of collaboration.

In Ghana the Centre for Scientific Research into Plant Medicine is working hand-in-hand with indigenous healers in testing their medicinal herbs. This Centre is located at Mampong in the Akwapim district in Ghana.

In the years following independence the Ghana Government adopted a policy to extend health and other welfare services to rural areas in Ghana. Several committees were set up to study the existing health situation and to determine appropriate measures to deal with the situation.

The Brachott Committee Report (Brachott Committee 1961) recommended that long-term measures should be instituted to provide and extend sanitary facilities in rural areas. In 1966 the Easmon Committee drew Government attention to prevailing communicable diseases in rural Ghana.

It suggested the training of traditional birth attendants in hygienic practices and it suggested practical measures to upgrade their skills in order for them to contribute their quota in maternal and child health care in rural areas.

In 1971 the Health Planning Unit was instituted to update all the existing reports and to determine specific measures to tackle health problems. On the basis of the Health Planning Unit's report the Government decided to expand rural health services through the instrument of community participation and involvement. It was within this frame of thinking that the Danfa project (Danfa Report 1976) received full support from Government.

The Danfa project was a rural health experimental project. The Ghana Medical School, in conjunction with the School of Public Health, University of California, has assumed joint responsibility for the management of the project. The project provided a demonstration for an understanding of primary health care. It demonstrated the use of local people in community participation and it actually instituted a training programme for the training of traditional birth attendants, and other healers in the district.

The Danfa project is also seen as a practical contribution to the search for an alternative pathway in the provision of rural health and, as argued by Newmann, it was an attempt to seek local solutions to local health problems and a search in the utilisation of indigenous healers in national health programmes.

After the Danfa project the Government of Ghana and the World Health Organisation also collaborated in a community-based research project at Kintampo District in the Brong-Ahafo Region in Ghana. The aim of the project was to determine in a practical way the social processes that mould community health care. The project was financed by the Ghanaian Government and the World Health Organisation with Swedish International Development aid assistance. Traditional healers were encouraged through community discussions to train as community health workers.

Warren and others initiated the PRHETIH programme in the Brong-Ahafo Region in Ghana (primary health training for indigenous healers) in 1979 to upgrade the training of indigenous healers in Techiman District (Warren 1982, p. 1973). In order to extend basic health coverage to rural areas the PRHETIH programme was an important step in a collaborative approach between indigenous and modern health practitioners. In the project indigenous healers were given official recognition for training to upgrade their skills and knowledge in primary health care.

All these developments are indicators that in the evolutionary process, indigenous healers in Ghana have been influenced by modern health systems. Programmes and projects have emerged to upgrade the training of indigenous healers. In many areas in Ghana, traditional birth attendants have been given modern training and UNICEF has provided them with basic technology to improve their services. Ghanaian doctors and nurses in collaboration with expatriate staff have been involved in the training of traditional birth attendants and in upgrading the skills of herbalists.

In Zambia there is also governmental interest in upgrading the work done by indigenous healers. Apart from the passage of the Witchcraft Act, there is a Schedules Officer for Traditional Medicine at the Government of Zambia's Ministry of Health. Among his duties is to advise indigenous healers of all persuasions to improve upon their services by instituting refresher courses, seminars and conferences for them. The Officer is actively cooperating with THPAZ (Traditional Health Practitioners Association of Zambia) in visiting all healers. The main aim is to find avenues to standardise and upgrade their practices.

There is also an experimental training centre for traditional birth attendants. About 600 of them had already been given refresher courses to improve their existing expertise.

At the governmental level a National Council of Traditional Healers has been proposed and it is expected that an act will be passed for the formation of the National Council.

CONCLUSIONS

In this era of primary health care with the focus on health care as a social right, indigenous healers and traditional birth attendants of all persuasions are being regarded as national health care providers. The indigenous healers use cultural (social and psychological) holistic healing techniques, they are the first line of contact (after self-help) in most areas, they have been influenced by modern methods and ideas and modern health practitioners are more inclined to view them as collaborators in national health delivery efforts. Consequently, the indigenous healers are evolving with the help of the governments as an occupational group acceptable to modern Ghanaian and Zambian societies.

REFERENCES

Bannerman, R. H., *et al.*, (1981), 'Discussion of Oyebola's paper . . . Professional associations, ethics and discipline among Yoruba traditional healers in Nigeria', *Social Science and Medicine*, 15B.

Bennel, Paul, (1982), 'Professionalization: the case of pharmacy in Ghana', *Social Science and Medicine*, 16, 601–7.

Brachott Committee Report, (1961), Accra: Government of Ghana, Ministry of Health.

Brew-Graves, S. H., (1977), 'The evolution of traditional healing in Ghana', in *Report of The First National Workshop on Traditional Medicine in Zambia*. Mulungushi Hall, Lusaka (May).

Danfa Report, (1976), Accra: University of Ghana Medical School and University of

California, School of Public Health.
Easmon Report, (1966), Accra: Ministry of Health.
Ghana Population Census, 1970, (1980), Accra: Government Printer.
Health Sector Report, 1977, (1980), Accra: Ministry of Health, Health Planning Unit.
Johnson, T. J., (1972), *Professions and Power*. London: Macmillan.
Kaplan, L., (ed.) (1979), *A Country Study*. Washington, D.C.: The American University.
Leeson, Joyce, and Frankenberg, Ronald (1977), 'The patients of traditional doctors in Lusaka', *African Social Research*, June, 217–34.
Mensah Dapaah, K., (1968), 'Traditional healing', *Ghana Journal of Science*, 21, pp. 16–21.
Mulungushi Hall Report, Lusaka, Zambia: The First National Workshop on Traditional Medicine (May), (1977).
Newmann, Alfred K., (1982), 'Planning health care programmes in a pluralistic medical context', in Yoder, P. S., (ed.), *African Health and Healing Systems*. Los Angeles: Crossroads Press.
Oyebola, D. D. O., (1981), 'Professional associations, ethics and discipline among Yoruba traditional healers of Nigeria', *Social Science and Medicine*, 15B, pp. 87–92.
Twumasi, P. A., (1981), 'Colonialism and international health: a study in social change in Ghana', *Social Science and Medicine*, 15B.
Warren, D. M., *et al.* (1982), 'Ghanaiain national policy toward indigenous healers', *Social Science and Medicine*, 16.
World Health Organisation (1978), *The Promotion and Development of Traditional Medicine*. (Technical Reports Series 622): Geneva.

6 Carolyn Sargent

PROSPECTS FOR THE PROFESSIONALISATION OF INDIGENOUS MIDWIFERY IN BENIN

INTRODUCTION

The dynamic contradiction between historical consciousness and national unification which is prevalent throughout the developing world has reached acute proportions in the People's Republic of Benin since the 1972 socialist revolution which holds as a paramount aim the dissolution of ethnic boundaries. The creation of a socialist state, guided by the principles of 'scientific Marxism-Leninism', has precipitated efforts to render ethnic politics dysfunctional, to outlaw rituals and festivities which celebrate ethnic idenity and, in general, to eliminate vestiges of 'feudalism' and 'mystification' wherever these are in evidence.

The current relationship between the cosmopolitan and indigenous medical systems in Benin reflects these fundamental tensions. An examination of the status of Bariba midwives in northern Benin will indicate the dilemmas confronting indigenous healers in this region and the prospects for one indigenous medical speciality in the foreseeable future. The Bariba (*Baatombu*) represent one of the major ethnic groups of Benin and number approximately 400,000. Although primarily a sedentary agricultural society, the Bariba have established urban settlements since the seventeenth century in the Borgou Province of northern Benin. An increasing proportion of Bariba are Muslim – 25% of one district surveyed in 1977 professed adherence to Islam; however, Bariba religious practices persist and possession cults continue to flourish in spite of government restrictions intended to inhibit cult participation.

BARIBA MEDICINE

Elsewhere I have described Bariba medicine in some detail (Sargent 1982) and I will therefore present only a brief sketch of healers and specialisations in this paper. The Bariba consider the healer (*tingi*) to be a person manifesting the capacity to manipulate the forces of the universe and to wield substances with benevolent intent. It is this intent which distinguishes the healer from the sorcerer; both categories are known to have the potential for abusing power or applying it to socially desirable ends. Although there are few terms for specialists within the category of healers (one exception being bonesetters), most healers become renowned for expertise in one particular domain, for example, hernia treatment or respiratory disorders. Often, a healer will possess one primary medication with which to treat patients; if the medication is not useful, the patient concludes that failure to obtain a cure furthers diagnosis by elimination of one possibility and moves on to consult another specialist.

The category of midwife includes several varieties of birth assistant: the person who attends a delivery primarily in order to provide moral support for the parturient, or to offer such assistance as bolstering the mother from behind when she kneels to deliver. This supportive individual is usually a middle-aged or elderly female family member who rarely attends births outside the household, and is not designated by any term indicative of healing skill. A second category of attendant is the skilled technician, also a woman of advanced age, who may possess a medicine useful in accelerating labour or in stimulating delivery of the placenta. This person may also cut the cord subsequent to delivery of the child. This type of attendant may be referred to as *marusio* (one who does deliveries). Finally, there is the birth assistant who is referred to as *tingi*, the true healer. Those assistants falling into the category of healer as well as the *marusio* are usually elderly women, trained via apprenticeship to another healer, who have acquired substantial knowledge of medicinal substances. In addition, these healers possess a store of ritual incantations believed to be more powerful than the botanical preparations ubiquitous at midwife-assisted deliveries. The midwife-healer is also likely to be a member of a spirit possession cult such as *sambani*, which renders the healer clairvoyant and thus more competent to diagnose complications of labour and delivery. It is perhaps useful to note at this point that according to the Bariba ideal, a woman should deliver alone – unassisted – and should call an attendant only when the baby cries. A knowledgeable person should then arrive to cut the cord. A survey of 120 women of reproductive age in a Bariba village in 1977 indicated that approximately 43% did in fact deliver alone. The assistance of a midwife, then, is held to be most necessary for dangerous delivery complications, such as those provoked by sorcery or witchcraft.

BARIBA MIDWIFERY AS PROFESSION

The theme of this volume addresses the professionalisation of African medicine. It seems productive here, then, to consider whether and in what sense Bariba midwives can be said to constitute a 'profession' within Bariba society. In this discussion I will use as a framework Freidson's seminal work on the profession of medicine (1970). In delineating the characteristics of a profession, Freidson notes that it is difficult to agree on a definition of the term 'profession'. In moving towards such a definition, he cites that minimum conditions for the existence of a profession are that:

(1) 'the occupation has gained command of the exclusive competence to determine the proper content and effective method of performing some task' (1970, p. 10);
(2) 'the occupational group . . . must be the prime source of the criteria that qualify a man to work in an acceptable fashion' (1970, p. 10) and
(3) there be 'general public belief in the consulting occupation's competence, in the value of its professed knowledge and skill' (1970, p. 11). Control over training and licensing of membership and existence of a code of ethics are not considered indicative of professional status in this scheme (Freidson 1970, p. 69). Rather, 'the most strategic distinction lies in legitimate, organized autonomy' and it is this feature which distinguishes a profession from an occupation group, defined as a category of people who perform the same work and share common methods which are passed on to new recruits (Freidson 1970, p. 71).

Applying Freidson's model, it is difficult to consider Bariba midwifery as a profession. First, the problem of the differing levels of midwifery skill arise. Are all birth attendants to be considered members of the profession, or at the other extreme, should the profession comprise only those referred to as healers? Restricting membership to healers, one finds nonetheless that healing is a part-time occupation, and that competence is determined not by standards established as convention by the healing specialists but (a) by serving an apprenticeship with an experienced healer, concluded by death or replacement of the master, at which time the apprentice begins full practice and (b) by building a reputation among a potential clientele which observes and assesses the success of the specialist in treating afflictions, in this case, complications of labour and delivery.

Moreoever, a notable characteristic of Bariba medicine in general and one shared by the midwifery specialisation is an intense reluctance to share information or collaborate in order to treat a patient. Secrecy in diagnostic procedure, in preparation of medication, and in treatment is fundamental to the healing practice. The concept of 'legitimate, organized autonomy' is not applicable in this medical system, whose constituent units are primarily the master-apprentice dyad. Further, the criterion that the occupational group itself is the prime source determining content and method in task performance is not fully met in the Bariba case in that midwives draw on the general Bariba pattern of beliefs and practices regarding sickness causation and treatment. To this extent, broad understanding of diagnosis and treatment are shared by patients and healers, although healers do possess esoteric knowledge. Moreover, midwives share certain concepts and techniques particular to the demands of obstetrical practice, leading me to conclude that midwifery does in fact represent a therapeutic system (Sargent 1982, pp. 104–10). The idiosyncratic content of cures propounded by each midwife, however, again indicates the individual character of much healer practice and suggest that, in Freidson's terms, Bariba midwifery is closer to an occupation than a profession.

THE STATUS OF INDIGENOUS MEDICINE IN BENIN

Whether or not Freidson has determined that recruitment, licensing and ethics are peripheral to professional status, these criteria are of significant interest to national governments attempting to regulate and control indigenous medical systems. The position of the Government of Benin on this matter was initially set forth in a statement issued by the President of Benin on 30 November 1972, which declares the goal 'to associate modern and traditional medicine for the well-being of our popular masses and for the progress of medical practice in the People's Republic of Benin, while recognising the importance of our pharmacopoeia' (National Seminar on 'Méthodes et Moyens de Dépistage et de Traitement en Médicine Moderne et en Médecine Traditionelle,' INFOSEC, Cotonou, 10–15 May 1982). Two government offices have responsibility for policy in the domain of indigenous medicine – the Bureau for Health Education and the Division for Indigenous Medicine located within the Ministry of Health.

In conjunction with the creation of Government structures designated to promote indigenous medicine in Benin, a National Association of Traditional Healers (in French: L'Association des Guérisseurs Traditionelles du Bénin (AGTB)) was formed, with branches in each provincial seat. This association was composed of approximately 200 members, primarily southerners. Members were provided with a card demonstrating affiliation with the association. To date, few Bariba have joined the association, apparently due to certain features of the healing tradition in the northern region. First, Bariba do not sell medicine; medicines are offered to a patient, who may or may not present a gift in return to the healer. A gift, if preferred, is selected according to the 'will' of the patient. Northerners note with scorn the 'commercialisation' of medicine in the south. Second, Bariba healers have never had a comparable organisation, and tend, as previously explained, to engage in private practice. Young Bariba often complain that elderly healers are so secretive that too frequently, they choose to die without ever sharing their medical expertise with their relations. Thus participation in an association of healers holds little intrinsic appeal for most Bariba. Those 30 Bariba currently in the association were selected by the mayors and community delegates of northern districts, subsequent to directives issued at the provincial level.

In 1979, the Association was dissolved at the national level due to abuses by non-members. According to officials in the Division of Traditional Medicine, charlatans claimed membership in the association, fabricating diplomas and certificates to impress prospective clients, hence the government was obliged to disband the association to prevent exploitation of the population.

Currently, reorganisation of the association is in progress. Membership in the new association will be based on a census of 'legitimate' healers conducted at the neighbourhood level in each province. The definitive structure for the national association has not yet been determined but the core of the organisation will be local representatives who periodically attend meetings of the national collectivity.

Although the national association has been formally dissolved, units of the association continue to function at the provincial level. In May 1982 the Government of Benin sponsored a national seminar attended by forty six administrators and healers (of whom four were from the two northern provinces). The conference papers examined comparative methods of diagnosis and treatment in traditional and modern medicine and focused particularly on the study of divination and, more generally, mysticism, in traditional medicine. The importance of analysing the traditional pharmacopoeia was also emphasised. Those civil servants presenting papers urged close collaboration among doctors, nurses, midwives and healers, with one speaker advocating the creation of units for indigenous medical treatment to be housed within national hospital centres. Conversation with a Bariba healer who attended this seminar and several of his associates provided a revealing perspective on the concept of association and the perceived goals of the conference. This particular healer is son of the Land Chief of Parakou, and was one of a dozen healers included on a list of northern healing specialists compiled by the Land Chief at the request of the District Administrator of Parakou. According to the healer, the conference was held in order to find solutions to problems of adequate drug supply in the country. 'Things are no longer as before', he said, and indigenous healers must serve the country by supplying medicines to the people. In this sense, he expressed approval of the idea of 'associating'. When pressed to expand on the meaning of the association, he suggested that each healer would have his special medicine and would treat the disease in which he specialised. He did not foresee significant sharing of information among healers. He remarked that the Government had not clearly indicated what would be expected of the healers, but they had understood that healers would in the future work as consultants at hospitals throughout the country.

Although some seminar speakers (civil servants) assumed that collaboration between modern and traditional medicine already exists, there have in fact been only a few formal efforts to organise collaboration between healers and national health service personnel. Similarly, although the direction of traditional medicine foresees eventual licensing requirements, licensing and regulative measures have not yet been undertaken.

One ongoing effort at collaboration is that of the Centre Neuro-Psychiatrique de Jacquot, a psychiatric hospital which employs both indigenous healers and psychiatrists to treat the mentally ill. At Jacquot, patients often arrive with acute problems and are initially treated with cosmopolitan medications. Long-term care then involves both the cosmopolitan and indigenous systems; only one type of treatment is utilised at a time, with a one-week break between treatment modalities to eliminate possible negative effects of medication inter-actions.

A second collaborative centre is that of the Dispensaire de Cotonou 5 (Zogbo) where healers of different specialisations are grouped and receive referrals from dispensary staff; some healers, subsequent to Government training, participate in health education efforts together with dispensary personnel. In the north of Benin, no collaborations of this sort have been attempted. The major project forthcoming in northern Benin was to be held in September 1983, at which time the northern provinces of the Borgou and the Atakora planned to hold a seminar for selected physicians, public health officials and ten healers, to discuss indigenous treatment for diabetes, hypertension and sickle cell anaemia.

MIDWIFERY TODAY: THE CASE OF PEHUNKO

Interestingly, midwives are not systematically considered to be eligible for membership in the Association of Traditional Healers (few women of any specialisation currently hold associate membership). One explanation for this decision is that midwives are not classified as 'healers' but rather as mere 'birth attendants' (Director of Public Health, Borgou Province, personal communication June 1983). This bypassing of indigenous midwives in existing attempts at organising healers is indicative of a general lack of careful analysis of indigenous medical practice throughout the country. Data on healers from southern ethnic groups such as the Fon and the Yoruba is rather more widespread, due to the heavier distribution of southerners in the educational system and in the civil service.

The major thrust of government policy regarding maternal and child health has been and continues to be to encourage utilisation of Government maternity clinics for prenatal care and delivery assistance. Case studies from the Bariba village of Pehunko illustrate the current status of indigenous midwifery in a rural Bariba community, as well as delineating the dynamics of clinic use by a rural population. Pehunko, an historically celebrated Bariba chiefdom, has recently become a district seat, and continues to serve as a major grain and cattle market for the surrounding region. Periodic arrival of emigrants from Niger hoping to establish commercial ventures in Pehunko has led to a steady increase in population size (estimated at 2,000 in 1977). Local inhabitants are served by a dispensary, supervised by a male nurse with one assistant nurse, and a maternity clinic, staffed by a government midwife, a nurse, and an obstetrical auxiliary. The auxiliary received three months training in 1977 in a neighbouring district maternity clinic, as participant in a programme designed to train five young women to assist at deliveries in communities with no maternity clinic.

The training programme followed an earlier attempt to organise a training session for a dozen elderly Bariba midwives in the region. The initial session ended abruptly when the government midwife accused a participant of working with a dirty knife. The government midwife was disinclined to continue the training and the participants dispersed. When interviewed in later months, the indigenous midwives described their original interest in the programme and their eventual disillusionment with the attitudes of Government health personnel. This progression of events indicates the trend in Government policy to (a) recycle elderly traditional practitioners and (b) abandon the preliminary policy of retraining currently active midwives in favour of adopting a policy to train literate teenage girls to serve as obstetrical auxiliaries.

In the Pehunko example, the obstetrical auxiliary returned to the village and assisted at deliveries in the local dispensary, when women chose to deliver there. In 1982, construction of a maternity clinic begun in 1968 was completed and as of June 1983, a Government midwife had been in attendance in Pehunko for seven months. This midwife (as is often the case in the northern regions) is a southerner, who does not speak Bariba and who hopes to be transferred south in the near future. She has had no contacts with local midwives, although the male nurse has collaborated with several in the course of complicated deliveries at which he consulted.

The Pehunko population, according to several informants, initially responded with surprising enthusiasm to the opening of the maternity clinic – the Government midwife assisted at twenty five to thirty deliveries per month. However, in order to impress upon the local population the benefits of a clinic delivery, the community was informed via the town crier that any woman delivering at home would be assessed a fine of 1200 CFA (US$3.30). Community response to this decision reveals several suggestive reactions. During one week in June 1983, five women delivered at home – two alone, three assisted by birth attendants – and paid the fine after bringing the baby to the clinic 'to be washed'.

Women throughout the village expressed the sentiment that it is preferable to deliver at home and pay the fine than experience the indignities of a clinic delivery. Others noted that because a birth certificate is a prerequisite for a child to attend school, one cannot altogether ignore the clinic because the Government midwife is the official responsible for "giving papers". Thus far, paying the fine for a home delivery and receiving a birth certificate upon payment seems to meet prevailing goals among the majority of the population; clinic deliveries have dwindled to a fraction of the initial clientele. One specific example of maternity clinic use is that of Manou, daughter-in-law of a noted midwife. When Manou delivered, she brought the baby to the clinic shortly after delivery and claimed that she had gone to the fields to collect nuts and had delivered there. The Government midwife fined her, stating that in her opinion, Manou could not have delivered so precipitously. Rather, she had deliberately chosen not to deliver at the clinic. The midwife then kept mother and child at the maternity clinic until the husband paid the fine; the family expressed outrage at the incident and at the underlying policy.

In spite of the fact that women continue to deliver at home, indigenous midwives are pessimistic about the future of Bariba midwifery. One midwife, a possession cult adept, remarked that the Government sends girls to school, teaches them how to do a job, and then has to find work for them to do. Thus pregnant women are forced to deliver at the clinic in order to give the midwife something to occupy her time. Another woman complained that the clinic is engaging in commerce, rather than healing. Yet another popular midwife claimed to have retired, and when asked if she intended to train a replacement, she commented that apprentices would no longer be able to learn midwifery because pregnant women would be delivering at the maternity clinic, leaving the apprentices with no opportunity to follow an elder midwife, 'carrying her medicine gourds', to observe the techniques of midwifery practice. When asked if she would consider collaborating with Government health personnel, she replied that most of the practising midwives would be pleased to co-operate with the Government midwife and nurse, as in fact they have done informally over the years, referring cases beyond the competence of the midwife in attendance. However, given the 'heart' of the current health care staff, collaboration in the future is unlikely.

The case of Pehunko illustrates the extent to which local policy can be independent of national health policy. The fine procedure, for instance, has been adopted sporadically throughout the country in districts in the process of inaugurating new maternity clinics, but initiating a fine is not formally required according to established policy at the national level. Significantly, the local population is not aware of the Association of Traditional Healers and no regional healers are active members of the association. Clearly, no efforts are under way to develop channels of communication and collaboration between Government health personnel and local practitioners of any speciality. One Bariba midwife remarked, however, that patients forced to deliver at the clinic sometimes send out to a preferred midwife in the event of complications, requesting a Bariba medicine which is subsequently administered to the patient secretly, if possible. 'Collaboration', then, is found between patient and healers, against a backdrop of government health staff, viewed as adversaries.

THE IMPLICATIONS OF PROFESSIONALISATION FOR BARIBA MIDWIVES

Assuming a growing interest on the part of the Benin Government with regard to the integration of indigenous midwives into the national health system, what might be the probable effects of Government efforts at regulation on the speciality of midwifery among the Bariba? The concern of the state in this domain is ostensibly protection for the public against deleterious medical treatments. One approach to ensure such protection is to require licensing of indigenous practitioners. In addition, an association such as the Association of Traditional Healers of Benin may be formed with the intent of regulating standards, sharing information concerning techniques and practices and establishing methods of recruitment. Such efforts at systematic organisation have not yet received a major thrust in Benin. From the perspective of Bariba healers, including those midwives who might legitimately be categorised as healers, attempts at creating an association of healers would be diametrically opposed to Bariba concepts regarding the practice of healing.

The formation of an association essentially violates the individualism characteristic of Bariba medicine, while a movement to stimulate collaboration among healers – sharing of techniques or knowledge of substances, for instance – would sharply contradict prevalent views concerning secrecy in diagnosis and treatment as well as the tenets of the apprenticeship mode of recruitment. The one case of which I am aware involving collaboration among healers is that of one form of spirit cult, whose members, distributed regionally, meet periodically to hold a possession dance.

At such cult meetings, initiates are said to share esoteric knowledge with one another. However, non-initiates never have access to this information, nor is it routinely discussed even among cult adepts. Finally, unlike some southern healers, Bariba healers do not traditionally sell medications; thus an association to commercialise medicine or to regulate fees does not provoke immediate interest in this population. Creation of a structured association, then, does not seem to be especially relevant or advantageous to the 'professionalisation' of Bariba healers, in that the imposition of an association might dramatically alter essential features of Bariba healing practice.

I am not suggesting that collaboration between Bariba healers and Government health staff is impossible. Rather, I would argue that a more decentralised approach to integration is preferable. Elsewhere I have suggested, for example, that Bariba midwives be trained as participants in a regional screening and referral system designed to allow uncomplicated deliveries to occur at home, if preferred (cf. Sargent 1982, Chapter 10). Parental consultations held at district clinics are currently well attended. Thus clinic staff, in conjunction with indigenous midwives having received supplemental training in diagnosing high-risk pregnancies and problematic labour, could identify women likely to experience complications. Such cases might reasonably be encouraged to deliver at regional centres, together with those women selecting a clinic delivery based on personal preference. Inevitably, a means of obtaining a birth certificate in the absence of a clinic delivery would need to be assured for those who prefer home delivery. However, since until recently it has been possible to do so throughout Benin, the problem of registering births does not seem insurmountable.

Considering once again the state role in protecting the public interest, what is the rationale for accommodating current public sentiment towards obstetrical care in particular and with regard to indigenous healing in general? Trends in contemporary obstetrics in the United States provide an illuminating perspective on the situation in Benin. Growing pressures from advocates of home birth and others objecting to physician control of delivery and the general medicalisation of birth have resulted in increased alternatives for obstetrical care in the United States (Jordan 1978; Romalis 1981). Evidence from both the United States and Europe suggests that higher maternal and infant morbidity are associated with high degrees of medical intervention at birth (Jordan 1978). It would seem productive, then, for countries such as Benin, which are in the process of creating a national health system, *not* to adopt without modification an obstetrical care model which has proven to be unsuccessful in the long term in the United States and Europe. Aspects of obstetrical care characteristic of lay midwifery in Benin such as psychological support systems and attitudinal preparation of the mother might usefully be integrated into obstetrical care practice in the United States, rather than progressively eliminated from officially sanctioned obstetrics in Benin or elsewhere in the Third World.

I suggest, then, the widespread training of indigenous midwives to provide baseline services in a regional screening and referral system. The current policy of Benin to train middle-aged birth attendants rather than attempting to retrain the very elderly midwives or young girls may well prove to be the most practical approach to selecting midwives for collaboration. As I have argued in my previous work, extended periods of training at a central location (for instance at a district or provincial centre) have not proved to be feasible in Benin, where older women have responsibilities which do not allow long absences from home. An itinerant Government trainer, working at the village level, would therefore prove to be more efficient for the bulk of the training session.

The need for supplemental training is not limited to the indigenous midwife, however. Observations of Government midwives at work clearly indicate that clinic staff require additional preparation in serving the various ethnic populations of Benin. The policy of Benin is to station staff in regions of the country other than the region of origin of the staffperson. Although this policy may be beneficial to efforts at national integration, it does not enhance communication between health care professionals and the local population. A case in point is that of Bekegi, a mother of five in Pehunko, who sought counsel from the Government midwife at the Pehunko maternity clinic for a folk illness known as *tigpiru*. (*Tigpiru* refers to a condition which begins in the lower abdomen and when ripe, may protrude from the vagina or anus as a red, round form. The term seems to comprise haemorrhoids and various prolapsed organs.) The midwife responded that she knew nothing of *tigpiru* and could not treat Bekegi if she would not describe her symptoms 'correctly'. This type of occurrence is hardly limited to the Pehunko example, and results from the inadequate preparation of health care personnel to work with particular ethnic groups. Correspondingly, efforts at collaboration with indigenous healers cannot be expected to progress in such an atmosphere. One approach to the problem is to require language training for staff prior to being sent to a post. Improved language skills would go far in encouraging some grasp of indigenous concepts of sickness diagnosis and treatment among Government health care providers, and similarly, would render more promising any attempts at co-operation between clinic staff and local healers.

PROSPECTS FOR THE FUTURE

An analysis of the probable fate of indigenous medicine in Benin requires a brief commentary on the larger political context in the country. The policy of dismantling the indigenous political systems throughout Benin, and seeking to eliminate sources of ethnic identification seems to be in the process of modification. After several years during which the Bariba New Year was not publicly celebrated, for example, 1983 saw a gala fête on the streets of the Bariba capital of Nikki, presided over by the paramount chief, his attendant nobles and assorted praise-singers. Contrastingly, the chief of

Pehunko had not made a public appearance for almost five years prior to his death in 1982.

Significantly, by 1982 most Bariba nobles had sold their horses, claiming that Government restrictions on public processionals (usually conducted on horseback by nobles accompanied by praise-singers) made it too expensive to feed a horse. However, the recent celebration of the Bariba New Year signals an apparent relaxation of the policy of national unification. Correspondingly, the concession of the Land Chief of the urban agglomeration of Parakou (population 60,000) displays a large wall painting with the slogan 'Revalidation of Our Traditions' juxtaposed with 'Death to Traitors' and presented amidst a collection of figures representing heroes prominent in contemporary politics and in Bariba history. If these events represent a trend, one might see a resurgence of indigenous medicine – but evidence of a flourishing indigenous medical system would reflect only benign neglect on the part of the Government, allowing manifestation of public preference. Research throughout the developing world has demonstrated that consumers pragmatically utilise available medical care options, selecting from among indigenous and cosmopolitan health care alternatives, often using both systems to treat a single sickness episode. Thus from the perspective of the lay public, the indigenous medical system remains a viable alternative. As one elderly midwife in the town of Parakou remarked, Bariba medicine may become less popular in town, but in the rural areas, it will thrive for a long time to come. Government policy, on the other hand, does not portend any significant investment of resources in development or training programmes for the indigenous health care sector.

Finally, I would like to return briefly to a consideration of Freidson's work on the profession of medicine. Freidson suggests that the definition of an occupation as a profession is determined by analysis of the relations of occupations to one another in a social structure (1970, p. 186). Thus, '. . . we define the profession primarily as a special status in the division of labor by official and sometimes public belief that it is worthy of such status . . .' (1970, p. 187). Further, he notes that

> A profession attains and maintains its position by virtue of the protection and patronage of some elite segment of society which has been persuaded that there is some special value in its work. Its position is thus secured by the political and economic influence that drives competing occupations out of the same area of work, that discourages others by virtue of the competitive advantages conferred as the chosen occupation, and that requires still others to be subordinated to the profession (1970, p. 73).

Similarly, the investment of national resources in development of a medical system patterned after an imported model reflects the beliefs and values of the national elite in Benin. Indigenous medical practitioners such as Bariba midwives cannot hope to attain other than paraprofessional (subordinate) status in such a system.

REFERENCES

Freidson, Eliot, (1970), *Profession of Medicine: a study of the sociology of applied knowledge*. New York: Dodd, Mead and Company.
Jordan, Brigitte, (1978), *Birth in Four Cultures*. Montreal: Eden Press.
Romalis, Shelley (ed.), (1981), *Childbirth in the United States: alternatives to medical control*. Austin: University of Texas Press.
Sargent, Carolyn, (1982), *The Cultural Context of Therapeutic Choice*. Dordrecht: Reidel.

7 Carol MacCormack

THE ARTICULATION OF WESTERN AND TRADITIONAL SYSTEMS OF HEALTH CARE

LEGAL AND CONCEPTUAL BACKGROUND

LEGAL FRAMEWORK FOR CO-OPERATION

In some developing countries, parts of southern Africa for example, legislation has made the practice of traditional medicine illegal. Having enacted the legislation, however, those Governments were not able to provide approved health services that adequately covered the population, were reliably supplied with drugs and other essentials, or were adequately appealing to health needs as people perceived them. The people, faced with the choice of either no approved health care facilities, or inadequately located, staffed and supplied health posts, continued to consult traditional practitioners who had gone underground.

Furthermore, most rural people in the Third World conceive of health as it is defined by the World Health Organisation as a state of mental, social and physical well being. However, health workers are being trained primarily to treat diseases in an efficient technological way; a conception of health which denies the psychological and social context in which people suffer. Therefore, often when people do go to approved medical services for antibiotics they might also need to consult a diviner to determine the reasons for their misfortune, and perhaps a traditional priest and congregation to ameliorate disturbed social relations and regain a sense of psychological and social well-being.

The first step that must be taken by countries that have outlawed traditional practice is to repeal the legislation. Officials in the health service must make genuine gestures of collaboration to encourage the underground medical system to begin to practise in the daylight of full public scrutiny.

Much of the restrictive legislation comes from the colonial period and is at odds with countries' post-colonial nationalistic pride in indigenous culture. Christian medical missionaries often used medicine as a weapon for winning souls to a different cultural system, and trafficked in lurid tales of witch-doctors to colonial administrators in an attempt to deprive potential converts of alternative choices. Their evidence of the evils of witch-doctors was anecdotal and non-scientific for the following reasons:

1. They made no attempt to sample systematically traditional therapies and results.

2. If practitioners, traditional midwives for example, referred a difficult case they could not manage, they were blamed for seeing the patient at all. The midwife's successes – the vast majority – were never seen by hospital staff. If their practice was illegal, then they could not refer to hospital without risking imprisonment or fine, and lacking such life-saving techniques as the caesarean section, they could only resort to less effective methods in a desperate attempt to save the mother and/or child.

3. There was an exaggerated definition of the precision in scientific medical diagnosis and treatment, and a concomitant denigration of therapies which sought to heal and comfort people's psychological and social fears. Indigenous preventive measures and curative therapies were expressed in the local cultural idiom. Traditional management of illness was often either genuinely misunderstood by missionaries and administrators not well versed in the local language and culture, or deliberately distorted to enhance the colonial mandate.

4. Finally, there was the question of which medical system's assumptions, definitions and procedures would be used to evaluate the efficacy of therapies. Were the premises underlying the logic of the Western scientific tradition the only theoretical premises and logical system allowed?

Those battles fought between advocates of colonial and indigenous culture are to some extent past history; an orientation which lives on with only a few national elites and professionals. But that is not to say that peace will inevitably break out between qualified medical practitioners and their traditional counterparts.

PROFESSIONALISM

In a recent survey among the small elite group of Pakistani women university graduates, 40% of them gave birth with the assistance of a traditional midwife. Professional obstetricians, attempting to support themselves in private practice, are in direct competition with traditional midwives, even among wealthy, educated urban women. The medical profession is politically powerful, and although the Fifth Five Year Plan specified a change in the ratio of doctors to paramedicals from 1:2 to 1:5, the actual number of doctors between 1971 and 1978 increased more than four times over, while the number of nurses and lady health visitors increased less than two times over. Training of traditional midwives has occurred only in a few limited pilot programmes, and in-service training, supplies and other back-up services are negligible (MacCormack 1982b).

However, within all Third World countries the Western-oriented medical profession is not homogeneous and there may be sharp clashes between the professional aims of distinct factions within the country's medical association. The question for those concerned with equity in health care is whether physicians within the medical profession who are committed to primary health care and collaboration with traditional practitioners are politically powerful enough to override physicians whose main concern is professionalism in competition with other health systems. Some tactics used for excluding traditional practitioners from primary health care training and back-up are:

1. Requiring school qualifications for training programmes; a device which will exclude most traditional midwives in countries with low rural female literacy rates, and other practitioners as well.
2. Giving training at times of the year, in places, or with curricula that are so inappropriate as to discourage practitioners from coming forward.
3. Requiring a young age for trainees. This will exclude midwives who are universally middle-aged or elderly mothers, and all other locally respected practitioners who have built up their following through successful therapy over time. The better practitioners achieve respect and social status over time in a process that weeds out the less able. But if only young healers are eligible for training, more opportunists without skill or community acceptance will be chosen.
4. Requiring that practitioners form associations and present themselves with a well-organised hierarchy of officers where there is no cultural tradition for doing so.

The rationale for requiring traditional practitioners to form associations is so they might: be licensed or registered; assure patients that they have been well trained; be given legal protection when they perform doctor functions; maintain standards of practice through a type of 'General Medical Council'.

There are many problems here. With regard to the third point, legal protection has become a necessary part of professional practice for the very reason that the medical profession itself is not very good at peer review, closing ranks to protect incompetent colleagues with secrecy. Malpractice accusations are often resolved in public courts with opposed medical experts attempting to persuade a jury of lay people that one course of action was better than another. Traditional practitioners who have achieved a following do not need to provide further assurance to their patients. But most practitioners would like to further enhance their status by learning medical techniques and the use of drugs. These are the very skills physicians are least likely to relinquish if they perceive themselves as being in competition for patients and general social status. Finally, peasant practitioners, used to centuries of exploitation, will ask why they should be registered, as people are registered for taxes. Is it a device for the politically dominant group to control them more effectively?

Therefore, there is wariness that associations of traditional practitioners, should they be formed, will be politically weak 'junior' professionals of low status who might be legislated against at any time. There is a further worry that associations of practitioners, as in Nigeria for example, begin to confer rather notional professional qualifications upon each other and begin to charge fees that approximate doctors' fees. Indeed, when we think of professionalism, with its well known 'side-effects', we might query the merit of prescribing more professionalism – for the traditional sector – at all.

A final consideration is to question why any respected local practitioners would want to join a national health service in its lowest ranks. They will be at the bottom of the bureaucratic heap, poorly paid or asked to work for free, given least prestige, the last to be supplied with drugs and in-service training. If they remain independent, they can continue to work on a fee-for-service basis, and retain local respect by being readily available and able to use traditional herbal and other techniques when the supply of drugs to Government health workers dries up. They can also enjoy the job satisfaction of giving a range of services that is far more extensive than the job description of a medical auxiliary. Traditional midwives, for example, commonly give companionship, massage and ritual baths, and may even clean, wash clothes, cook and give child care. They often play an essential ritual role in beginning and concluding the birth period, which is a rite of passage for the mother and infant (MacCormack 1982a).

LEGITIMACY

Professional medical associations examine candidates, and if they reach an agreed standard, legitimise their right to practise medicine. This legitimising function has now largely been passed on to universities and state Governments in developed countries. However, in developing countries traditional practitioners are currently being asked to form associations for this legitimising function. We might therefore address directly the concepts of legitimacy.

In seeking legitimacy in healers, people reassure themselves that the system of healing has meaning and they can undertake the quest for health with conviction. Following Max Weber there are three types of legitimacy: rational-legal, traditional and charismatic. Rational-legal legitimacy in medicine is based upon formal examinations leading to legal entitlements. The purest, most efficient exercise of rational-legal authority is through bureaucratic administration, according to Weber. He maintained that bureaucracy converts spontaneous 'community action' into efficient methodically ordered 'societal action'. We of course know that the ideal of bureaucratic efficiency is seldom realised. What we often fail to realise, however, is that healers practise under other mandates of legitimacy in a manner that is not necessarily bureaucratically organised.

Traditional legitimacy develops through time as qualities of merit, valour and holiness become associated with a corporate group such as a congregation or a lineage. In the African context, traditional legitimacy is often associated with the wisdom of ancestral time; the residue of centuries of adaptation to an environment. 'Uncoerced obedience' arises from personal loyalty to those recognised as the heirs and bearers of legitimacy.

The third type of legitimacy, charismatic legitimacy, is analogous to the idea that God and His manifestations cannot be anything other than pure legitimacy. People of exceptional heroism and sanctity present a vision of hope and health. Believers follow in obedience to attain those goals. They have personal trust in the extraordinary qualities of the healer and his or her revelation.

Paradoxically, a medical system based upon traditional legitimacy may have more flexibility to respond to changing conditions than one based upon rational-legal bureaucracy. In the latter, people are loyal to the rules. But with traditional legitimacy the obligation of obedience is based on personal loyalty, free from cumbersome rules. In the case of traditional healers, as long as their action follows what Weber called principles of substantive ethical common sense, they are quite free to innovate. Their patients follow the regimen out of personal loyalty. Change does not come from legislation. Rather, knowledge is claimed to have always been in force but only recently to have become known through the wisdom of the healer.

Charismatic authority is potentially most flexible, even revolutionary. But it has the drawback of being unorganised and not amenable to replication or to systematic administration over wide geographical areas or through time. When charismatic authority becomes organised the system has been transformed into one of the other types of legitimacy (Weber 1947, p. 324–45; MacCormack 1981, pp. 425).

Healers who practise under a mandate of traditional legitimacy derive their legitimacy from membership in a congregation, sodality or lineage, not necessarily an association of the type envisaged by the World Health Organisation (1978). Their office in that group, and the entire corporate group's role in the local society, must be allowed for in health planning which seeks to achieve health for all through community participation. Plucking the practitioners, or the chemicals from their herbal remedies, out of the context of healing, and transfering them to the university, is a gesture of goodwill, but it is not a truly collaborative association of plural medical systems.

With this conceptual groundwork now laid, let us turn to types of collaboration already taking place, and techniques for engendering further constructive collaboration.

COLLABORATION BETWEEN MEDICAL SYSTEMS

REFERRALS AND 'DOCTOR SHOPPING'

If we take individual patients as the focus of analysis, we realise that there is already considerable informal integration of scientific and traditional medical systems. Younger doctors who have spent their childhood in rural areas are especially likely to refer patients with mental illness, fractures, skin diseases, infertility or addiction to traditional practitioners (see, for example, Heggenhougen 1980). Traditional practitioners with an acute emergency realise the superior techniques available in hospitals. Thus two-way referrals are integrating the separate systems without one unduly controlling the other (see, for example, Kimani 1981).

Most rural people have observed the efficacy of vaccinations, antibiotics and other medical materials. Both traditional practitioners and their patients want these to be part of the training programme for community health workers. However, this training of community-based traditional practitioners should not begin unless the secondary health care level of district clinics and hospitals is well staffed, well stocked, and functioning well as a base from which training, supervision and referrals can take place. Alas, in many countries, this secondary level is falling into decline at the very time the country is taking special grants for programmes in primary health care.

From the rural patients' point of view, inadequacies in either the scientific or the traditional system can be minimised by judicious shopping in either system for therapies. Quantitative studies suggest that in developed countries and developing countries alike, it is the wealthier, better-educated people who are seeking help in a plurality of systems (Vaskilampi and MacCormack 1982, Leslie 1980, Ademuwagun 1979).

Turning from purely individual choice to planned collaboration, some small-scale programmes may suggest further avenues for collaboration. For example, in a pilot programme in Sierra Leone tetanus immunisation was introduced as a ritual element in girls' puberty rites, with the full co-operation of high officials in the women's initiation society, who are also local midwives. Similarly, if local midwives were taught to give vaccines, they might administer them as part of the naming, or stepping-out ceremonies that often mark the beginning of an infant's social personhood.

TASK ANALYSIS FOR COLLABORATION

Primary health care planners must have a clear idea of what they would like traditional practitioners to do in the health service. The broad categories of 1) screening and referring only, or 2) diagnosing and treating linked together with preventive work, can be broken down into smaller tasks. The tasks suggest appropriate training and back-up to be provided. For example, weighing and recording the weight of a baby is one task. If the mother or midwife doing the task is illiterate then she should be trained, together with her daughter who goes to school or a literate village clerk. Or, the trainee might work with a simplified symbol system, or be designated as part of a target group for a functional literacy programme. These problems and options can only be identified and resolved if the desired tasks are explicit. A task analysis approach should also help to eliminate much of the abstract anatomy and physiology that seems to creep into the most simple of training courses.

Turning to the broad categories of tasks, traditional practitioners are often taught to do little more than screen and refer. They may not agree to play such an attenuated health care role. But if they do agree to collaborate with the health service on those terms, even these simple tasks are often not taught with realistic goals in mind. In many rural areas referring is easier said than done. Lewis describes a traditional midwife training course in Sierra Leone where women were taught little more than hand washing, screening and referring (1978). However, in one rather typical district in the country only 33% of the villages are on an all-season motorable road, and many villages on roads have only a lorry or two each week passing through at unpredictable times. The journeys are long and arduous. To refer a low-risk woman to hospital is unrealistic in villages without transport, where people cannot afford the cost of hospital treatment, where husbands (and often their mothers) may not agree to let a woman in labour leave the village, or where women themselves do not want to go because they fear the pain of unnecessary episiotomies and other hospital procedures. In Sierra Leone the major complications in pregnancy and birth arise from malaria and anaemia, but trained traditional midwives were not allowed to have chloroquine and iron tablets because they were illiterate and it was assumed they might confuse them. The assumption was quite incorrect, for these women commonly distinguish between hundreds of herbal specimens (MacCormack 1982a). They were explicitly taught not to use herbal remedies any more, and they were not given the most simple of scientific drugs.

If trained traditional practitioners are expected to diagnose and treat patients, and to link curative services with preventive initiatives, then they must: be given practical on-the-job training in their local area; be taught through actual consultation, diagnosis and treatment; be given frequent collaborative in-service training, perhaps by converting mobile clinics into village based on-the-job training (see MacCormack 1983); be regularly supplied with a few basic drugs.

PRIORITIES FOR COLLABORATION

Epidemiological techniques help to establish priorities for training types of traditional practitioners. If traditional midwives function as paediatricians, and if neonatal tetanus and general infant mortality rates are high, then midwives might be selected as the first category to train. Since traditional midwives often work in pairs or teams, it is best to train all in the village. At a minimum, the old woman with authority and her younger assistant might be trained. If only one is selected there is the risk of giving a certificate and 'rational-legal legitimacy' to one, setting her apart from, or against, the others, creating factionalism where none existed before.

Another approach to setting priorities for training is to begin with an informal survey of medical personnel who are enthusiastic to work with their traditional counterparts. Orthopaedic specialists, for example, may have come to respect the abilities of traditional bonesetters, and may teach them to promote the healing of wounds associated with fractures by keeping them clean. In turn, the doctor might be taught traditional splinting techniques. Or, gynaecologists who have few scientific techniques for treating infertility may want to work with spirit mediums who specialise in such problems, teaching them to use antibiotics for the treatment of sexually-transmitted diseases, encouraging the mediums to take on an educating and preventing role.

DATA-GATHERING TECHNIQUES

Manuals prepared by the World Health Organisation and other organisations often assume or recommend the use of formal, closed-question questionnaires (see, for example, WHO, 1978, p.49 *et seq.*). But such questionnaires are not the best way to find out who the traditional practitioners are, what practices they follow, or their willingness to collaborate with the national health service. The reasons are:

1. Formal, direct questions are usually perceived as rude by rural people who have not been conditioned to accept such questioning in school. Responses will be evasive or superficial.

2. Not only will questions be phrased indelicately, but the wrong questions may be asked if there has not been a pilot enquiry with interviews and open questions first. The whole domain of enquiry has been closed at the onset, before investigators could begin to learn practitioners' perceptions and constraints.

Recommended methods are:

1. *Key informant interviewing* in three stages. First, interview rural head men and senior women to learn the range of health care alternatives available. Take advice from them on how to approach practitioners. Next, interview

the practitioners using conversational techniques and a brief interview schedule so that four or five essential points are covered in all interviews. Use informal interviewing methods, allowing the interviewer to vary the order and the phrasing of questions, taking his or her cue from the flow of conversation. Finally, interview a representative sample of villagers to learn their views on their local practitioners, and what kinds of improved health services they wish. Use the methods outlined above.

Responses from open questions must be categorised and quantified. If a large sample is required, then the responses may be formalised into a questionnaire which is administered to additional people following this pilot exercise. Be sure that women and the politically powerless are adequately represented in the sample.

With this method of open-question interviews the ability of the interviewer is important. Interviewers should be as close in language, ethnicity, age, sex, and lifestyle to those being interviewed as possible.

2. *Direct observation*. If interviewers are tactful and respected, they may be allowed to follow up with direct observations. For example, it is much better to work with traditional midwives through some births than to give them a questionnaire about what they do. Or, in designing collaboration in an environmental hygiene programme (drinking water, latrines, etc.) direct observation of water sources, women's work patterns, etc., are superior to a formal questionnaire.

3. *Workshops*. Health service officials might usefully sit down at the early planning stages, in a representative sample of rural villages, and talk with local practitioners. Invite them to discuss the problems they experience and the things they would like help in doing. Data is immediately accessible, vivid, and working agreements can be arranged on the spot.

4. *Questionnaires*. Use only after more indirect and open methods are used as a pilot. Questionnaires are relatively easy to administer and interviewers do not need to be as adept as with open questions. Data is easy to process.

CONCLUSION: RESEARCH STRATEGIES AND PRIORITIES

Conclusions on research strategies and priorities are given under the following six headings:

1. Investigate the legal status of traditional practitioners.

Legislation that outlaws their practice should probably be repealed. But advocating legal entitlements for associations of traditional practitioners is a second step which might be regarded with caution. Consider carefully the advantages intended from their forming hierarchical associations. Are associations feasible for widely scattered rural part-time practitioners in countries with poor public transportation systems? Will associations encourage the wrong aspects of professionalism? Will the associations then be regulated and dominated by political elites, to the narrow advantage of the medical profession?

2. Modify curricula for doctors and nurses to include more community health orientations and methods
Perhaps having traditional practitioners within medical schools is one way to present a realistic picture of what traditional practitioners do and how they could be a valuable component in an articulated health care system. Beyond that, doctors and nurses need to be carefully taught methods for doing promotive and preventive work in a context of community participation that includes the community's folk practitioners. Thus they must be taught activity-based methods for training unschooled rural healers.

3. Use informal interview techniques to learn the full range of services traditional practitioners give
Respect for people's needs for services that go beyond scientific medicine would be implicit in such investigations. This research would seek to discover ways in which scientific medicine might enhance traditional competences. For example, diviners might be taught a range of scientific methods of diagnosis, to use in conjunction with their own methods for finding the cause of misfortune.

4. Use the above information to decide whether traditional medicine should be brought within the bureaucratic primary health care structure or informally linked with it through two-way referrals and consumer choices.
If the latter course seems most constructive, then specific planning and facilitating must be done.

5. Use the above information to examine the selection criteria for training programmes for community practitioners
Is literacy essential or might other training and record-keeping methods be used? Is youth essential? Rates of personnel turnover will indicate whether there is real economy in training young people with many potential years of service ahead of them. If only a half are still in post after a year, but all middle-aged mothers who were trained are in post after a year, youth may not be cost-effective.

6. Use the technique of task analysis and epidemiology.
These methods will help to set priorities in training. They will also help in developing the content of, and methods used in, training programmes.

SUMMARY OF RECOMMENDATIONS: THE ARTICULATION OF WESTERN AND TRADITIONAL SYSTEMS OF HEALTH CARE

National level

1. Repeal legislation which prohibits traditional practice.
2. Modify medical and paramedical curricula to include:
   (a) Understanding of folk therapies, and why people sometimes prefer them;
   (b) Techniques for community-based promotive and preventive initiatives;
   (c) Techniques for training traditional practitioners, who may be illiterate.
3. Do a quick national survey (perhaps through district medical officers) to determine:
   (a) Types of traditional practitioners, their numbers and distribution;
   (b) Their organisational structures, which may range from highly organised medical systems such as Ayurveda in India to widely-scattered bonesetters.
4. Consider whether there should be national associations of traditional practitioners.

Regional level

1. Do epidemiological surveys to establish priorities for collaboration with types of traditional practitioners.
2. Do task analysis to develop policy on:
   (a) Type of training and content of training;
   (b) Who should do initial training, and in-service training;
   (c) Where training should be done;
   (d) Back-up services that will be needed.
3. Evaluate pilot programmes for additional insight.
4. Encourage two-way referrals.
5. Day-to-day supervision and supply.

Village level

1. Interview to learn:
   (a) Who traditional practitioners are in local area;
   (b) Practitioners' views on additional training and types of collaboration;
   (c) Villagers' views of traditional practice and the government health services.
2. Collaborative training in villages if mobile teams are possible.
3. Improved curative and preventive work in a context of genuine community participation.

REFERENCES

Ademuwagun, Z. A., *et. al* (eds.) (1979), *African Therapeutic Systems*. African Studies Association. Waltham, Mass.: Crossroads Press.

Heggenhougen, H. K., (1980), 'Rural health care: Malaysian physicians' opinions about traditional Malay medicine and hospital assistants', *Medical Journal of Malaysia*, 34, pp. 238–47.

Kimani, V. N., (1981), 'Attempts to coordinate the work of traditional and modern doctors in Nairobi in 1980', *Social Science and Medicine*, 15B, pp. 421–22.

Leslie, Charles (ed.), (1980), 'Medical Pluralism', special issue of *Social Science and Medicine*, 14B.

Lewis, S. J. K., (1978), *The traditional birth attendant as a potential source of improved health care in Sierra Leone*. M.Sc thesis in medical demography, London School of Hygiene and Tropical Medicine.

MacCormack, C. P., (1981), 'Health care and the concept of legitimacy', *Social Science and Medicine*, 15B; pp. 423–428.

——(ed.), (1982a), *Ethnography of Fertility and Birth*. London: Academic Press.

——(1982b), 'Health education and community participation', for *Pakistan Water Supply and Sanitation Sector Study*, Alexandria: World Health Organisation, Eastern Mediterranean Region.

——(1983), 'Community participation in primary health care', *Tropical Doctor*, 13.

Vaskilampi, T., and C. P. MacCormack (eds.), (1982), *Folk Medicine and Health Culture*. Kuopio, Finland: University of Kuopio Press.

Weber, Max, (1947), *The Theory of Social and Economic Organization*. (Trans. and ed. by T. Parsons), New York: Free Press.

World Health Organisation, (1978), *The Promotion and Development of Traditional Medicine*. (Technical Report Series 622). Geneva: WHO

World Health Organisation, (1979), *Traditional Birth Attendants: A Field Guide to their Training, Evaluation and Articulation with Health Services*. Geneva: WHO.

PART II

PROFESSIONAL KNOWLEDGE AND ITS CONTROL

8 Pamela Reynolds

THE TRAINING OF TRADITIONAL HEALERS IN MASHONALAND

Pamela Reynolds

Just as the Secret movements of his understanding are manifested by his voice, so it would seem that the herbs speak to the curious physician through their signatures, discovering to him . . . their inner virtues hidden beneath nature's veil of silence.

Crollius, *Traité des signatures*, p. 4.
(Quoted by Foucault 1973, p. 27)

INTRODUCTION

This paper is concerned with the privileged possession of knowledge by traditional healers and the potential power that this possession offers. Who are these healers and how do they acquire their knowledge? What is the nature of their knowledge? And what are the consequences of professionalisation of traditional healers? In his introduction, Last points out that

. . . though 'professionalisation' is at one level all about power (and thus offers immediate scope for political solutions), at another level it is about the long-term structuring of a specific kind of knowledge and about how to transmit what is still relevant of it to the next generation.

According to Foucault (1973, p. xiv), attempts to understand the acquisition of knowledge should be subject to a theory of discursive practice. He explains his attempts to describe the order of things thus:

On what 'table', or according to what grid of identities, similitudes, analogies, have we become accustomed to sort out so many different and similar things? What is this coherence – which, as is immediately apparent, is neither determined by an *a priori* and necessary concatenation, nor imposed on us by immediately perceptible contents? For it is not a question of linking consequences, but of grouping and isolating, of analysing, of matching and pigeon-holing concrete contents; there is nothing more tentative, nothing more empirical (superficially, at least) than the process of establishing an order among things; nothing that demands a sharper eye or a surer better-articulated language; nothing that more insistently requires that one allow oneself to be carried along by the proliferation of qualities and forms. And yet an eye not consciously prepared might well group together certain similar figures and distinguish between others on the basis of such and such a difference: in fact, there is

> no similitude and no distinction, even for the wholly untrained perception, that is not the result of a precise operation and of the application of a preliminary criterion. A 'system of elements' – a definition of the segments by which the resemblances and differences can be shown, the types of variation by which those segments can be affected, and, lastly, the threshold above which there is a difference and below which there is a similitude – is indispensable for the establishment of even the simplest form of order. Order is, at one and the same time, that which is given in things as their inner law, the hidden network that determines the way they confront one another, and also that which has no existence except in a grid created by a glance, an examination, a language; and it is only in the blank spaces of this grid that order manifests itself in depth as though already there, waiting in silence for the moment of its expression.
>
> The fundamental codes of a culture – those governing its language, its schemas of perception, its exchanges, its techniques, its values, the hierarchy of its practices – establish for every man, from the very first, the empirical orders with which he will be dealing and within which he will be at home.
>
> (1973, pp. xix–xx)

In accord with a similar perspective on the acquisition of knowledge, I set out to discover how traditional healers in Mashonaland, Zimbabwe, learn. I tried to identify when they establish their empirical orders and in relation to what fundamental codes. Clearly, over time, traditional healers in Zimbabwe have ordered an impressive body of knowledge. I sought to discover from whom, at what age, with what leeway for innovation and in accord with what checks and balances they learned the use of plants, symbolic systems and social and psychological analysis. How did traditional healers learn of their culture's order?

THE HEALERS

Systems of knowledge are always in transformation, although the process may be greatly hastened or radically altered by formal intervention. Before intervening, we ought to know how traditional healers have ordered the distribution, acquisition, and recognition of knowledge. Among the Zezuru, it is difficult for researchers to discover how traditional healers acquire their knowledge because there is no formal apprenticeship or well-demarcated initiation ceremony at which competence and knowledge are either confirmed or tested, and there is no single body of knowledge that is passed on.

During 1982 and 1983, I worked with 60 traditional healers in three areas of Mashonaland where Zezuru-speakers predominate. The first area is in and around Musami, in the south of Murewa District, nearly eighty kilometres east of Harare. This area was chosen because every ten years since 1948 basic sociological surveys have been conducted in six villages there (see Bernardi 1950; Garbett 1960; Chavunduka 1970 and forthcoming). The surveys offer a sizable amount of background data on migrancy patterns, land holdings and kinship ties against which detailed studies in the life histories and practices of traditional healers could be set.[1] The second area is Mabvuku, a high-density suburb that was set aside in 1952 for blacks working in Harare (then Salisbury). It is situated twenty kilometres east of the city centre.[2] The third area is made up of the market places of Pedzanhamo and Mbare where traditional healers sell *materia medica* from stalls. The markets perch on the edge of Harare city centre, the industrial area, the main bus terminus and the high-density suburb of Mbare.[3]

I have gathered data on 47 traditional healers: 24 from around Musami, nine from Mabvuku and 14 from the two Harare market places; 28 of them are men and 19 are women (this does not accurately reflect the sex ratio among healers in Zimbabwe). The national sex ratio for healers is not known but a ZINATHA official estimates that 65% of traditional healers are women. Of the 884 entries in ZINATHA'S 1980 membership register that lists two full names, 447 were women. There are more men among those with whom I worked because all the stall holders at Pedzanhamo Market and all except two at Mbare are men. I did not uncover recurrent themes suggesting that men and women have distinctive styles in divining or healing. Both men and women were extremely generous and co-operative and I attended rituals at, and spent many nights in, the homes of healers of both sexes.

Of the 47 healers 38 are Shona-speakers, 25 of whom speak Zezuru, 7 Ndau, 4 Manyika and 2 Korekore. Of the other nine, three speak Nyanja, three Hilengwe, and one each Sena, Ndebele and Msenga. Forty-one of them were born in Zimbabwe: 27 in Mashonaland, 13 in Manicaland and one in Matabeleland. The other six came from neighbouring countries: three from Malawi, two from Mozambique, and one from Zambia.

Those living and working in Mabvuku and Harare grew up elsewhere. In Musami, 16 of the healers come from the district of Murewa. Five of the men are alien to the district and six live in or near their patrilineal homes. Eight of the women live in their husband's patrilineal home. Two of these women and another two live in or near their father's home, that is, the home of their childhood. Three women and their husbands are alien to the area: one came from Mozambique originally, one from Chihota, and one from Mount Darwin.

Forty-nine per cent are between the ages of 40 and 60, 19% are over 60 and 32% are under 40. The average age is 44. There are no clear differences in ages between men and women. The 47 healers claimed to draw their healing powers from three classes of spirits: early ancestral spirits (called hero spirits by Fry 1976, and referred to either as *mhondoro* or *gombwe*; they confer power over an area, a tribe or grant rain-making abilities); family spirits inherited from either the paternal or maternal line (*vadzimu*);

and alien spirits (*mashave*, including *njuzu* – the river spirits). Among them the healers have 72 spirits; of these, five are early ancestors, 27 are *vadzimu* and 40 are *mashave* (four of the last are *njuzu*). One healer in Mabvuku claims to be possessed by seven spirits; another by four; eight others in Musami and Mabvuku have three spirits each; the others have two or one each except for eight who have none (one is a foreigner with different ways, and the others sell *materia medica* in the market places). When pressed the latter say that their interest in healing and the efficacy of their treatment suggest that they must be guided by *mashave*.

Possession by one or more spirits is possible: for example a Mabvuku woman has one *mhondoro*, one *njuzu* and two *vadzimu* spirits. Thirty-two of the healers are actually possessed during trances. All but five of them use dreams for healing or divining and 12 use *hakata* (divining pieces) in their work. Of the spirits identified by name or sex, 33 are male and nine are female. No man had a female spirit. All of them use plants and animal parts in their medicines except one man from Musami who has a rain-making spirit and heals by using snuff and water. Methods of divination include actual possession, the throwing of *hakata*, and the use of dreams. Some use all three methods and some only one. A healer in Musami, who came from Malawi as a young man, divines with the help of the Koran, a looking-glass and a cabalash. A woman from the same area falls into trances but also uses a glass jar in divining. And a man, also in Musami, spits on his hands and divines by inspecting the patterns.

An ancestral spirit (*mudzimu*) usually brings with him or her a *shave* of the healing class to instruct the medium. (Of the ten or more classes of *mashave* only one bestows healing talents.) A healer may also be possessed by a *shave* of another class, for instance, a hunting *shave*. The *njuzu* spirits are said to inhabit water, have light-coloured skin and long hair. They take the one whom they wish to possess under the water for spells that vary (in this sample) from four days to four years. Four of the healers in my sample are possessed by river spirits. The river spirits are granted a higher status than either the *vadzimu* or *mashave*.

When a spirit is called out during the *bira* ritual, he or she should name himself and, if inherited, should identify his position in the family line. The family of the one being possessed will attempt to chase a spirit away if his claims are suspect. Each new spirit that possesses someone must be greeted with the proper ritual and gifts must be bought for him or the medium will be made to suffer. Spirits must be thanked at intervals and rewarded with gifts to ensure that the medium's healing talents are nurtured and his own health and well-being secured. In this way, ritual devoted to the exchange between a medium and his spirit(s) recurs.

Fifty-five per cent of the healers began to treat before the age of 40: indeed, 23% began to treat before they were twenty years old. Thirty-four per cent began to treat between the ages of 40 and 60, and 11% when over 60. In other words, 68% of them have been treating for over ten years. And the majority of them had signs in their childhood interpreted to them as indications of future possession.

All except two of them know of one or more healers in their lineages. One of the two who have none is possessed by a rain spirit and treats only with snuff and water: the other comes from Malawi but grew up in Zimbabwe and does not know her family's history. Eighty per cent of the persons identified in their families (dead and alive) as healers are patrilineal and only twenty-four per cent matrilineal. Seven named healers in both paternal and maternal lines, five of whom were men. In all, 94 persons of their parental (29), grandparental (47), and great-grand-parental (18) generations were named as healers. Five said that the art of healing went far back in their patrilineages: 16 members of their own generation were named as healers. It is commonly said that healing powers are inherited from the grand-parental generation and not from parents: among those with whom I worked, this held true for 50% but 31% had one or two parents who were or are healers. There is some overlap in these percentages as the parents and grandparents of some were healers.

The variation of patterns among healers is enormously wide. In the sample of 47, the following differences exist. There is a wide age range: one healer who is treating is in her late teens and another is in her early eighties. Some are men, some are women. They inherit their spirits from both or either the paternal or maternal lineage. Almost without exception, they have one or more healers in their families. Most are possessed by a spirit, some by two or three, one by seven, and some are not possessed. Most are informed about herbs in their dreams, some are not. A variety of divining techniques is used, including spirit possession, *hakata*, a glass, a mirror, spittle and dreams. One heals only and he uses herbs, another divines and heals but uses only snuff and water. Incomes differ: in the countryside some earn perhaps $20 a month and in town others earn up to $500 a month, one or two earn more. Some began to treat in their old age, others in their childhood. Some have acolytes, some do not. Some train family members to help them collect and prepare medicine, some do not. Some speak in strange tongues when possessed (one uses a locally invented 'language') and others do not. Some travel widely, often across the country, while others never go to a patient: one old man refuses to leave his village. Some strictly obey certain taboos while others have none or beg their spirits to waive the rule as occasion demands. Some see Christianity as compatible with their calling, others see it as antithetical. Some claim to have secret remedies; some foretell the future; some demand payment only once a cure is effected; some house and feed patients; some exchange information with other healers; some buy their herbs; some are members of traditional healers' organisations; some become possessed with ease; some specialise, others do not.

The variation is bewildering. Writers of books on traditional healers, however, seem to have found sound refrains applicable to vast territories. Has the nature of the anthropological enquiry glossed over these differences, or has recent socio-political revolution wrought such great changes in traditional spheres? Nevertheless, despite the variation there is a norm. The norm is found by talking to a broad spectrum of people and is reflected in the literature on traditional healers in Zimbabwe.

THE PROCESS OF ACQUIRING KNOWLEDGE

Leach (1982) sees the social anthropologist's role as that of a recorder of the way of life of a people (consisting of the acting out of an endlessly repeated social drama). He says that:

> The characters in the drama, the social roles, are more or less fixed, as are their mutual relationships which constitute the dramatic plot. But the way the roles are played varies from occasion to occasion according to which particular individual is playing which particular part at any particular time.
>
> The distinction between the roles in a drama and the actors who play the roles corresponds to the fact that the data of field research must always be looked at in two dimensions. The observer must distinguish between what people actually do and what people say that they do; that is between normal customs as individually interpreted on the one hand and normative rules on the other.

Leach focuses on the continuities and the variations in these underlying patterns, 'For it is the patterning rather than the superficial form of social behaviour which conveys "meaning" '. It is the patterning underlying traditional healers' 'apprenticeships' that I hope to trace. First I shall present the superficial form of social behaviour of the stated norm.

THE STATED NORM	ACTUAL PRACTICE
Childhood A: A healer *may* be selected by a spirit in childhood. Signs of calling in early childhood add authenticity to claims of healing ability.	*Childhood* 1: Prior to his death, a healer may designate his heir. The heir need not have been born yet; he or she is identified as, perhaps, the healer's son's first child of either sex. 2: Special ties are established between the child and the healer, often between grandparent and grandchild. As is customary the child may have been sent by his parents to live with the grandparent. Sometimes the child insists on living with a grandparent who is a healer, even against parental wishes. The child may spend much of his time in the healer's company, participating in trips to collect herbs and in treatment sessions. Most children are taught to classify plants into three categories: poisonous plants, edible plants, and

plants that must not be tampered with because they belong to the shades.

3: This instruction is enlarged upon from the age of nine. The healer instructs the child in the identification and naming of herbs. The child assists the healer in the preparation and administration of medicines. The child is expected to help during treatment sessions, including those in which the healer is possessed. First dreams are often recalled from this age and first hints of future possession are given in their interpretation.

Young adulthood B: In early adulthood illness initiates a process of consultation with healers and/or diviners. The illness may be presented as physical and/or mental, although a division between them is seldom categorically made. Typically, there is failure to recover that leads to a series of consultations, sometimes within the Western medical system. Consultations are organised by family members and continue until an acceptable diagnosis, followed by the remission of symptoms, is achieved.

C: The third stage is one of actual possession. It culminates in a ritual (*bira*) that is held for the emerging healer at which qualified persons bring out the spirit and question him or her. The spirit must name him- or herself and authenticate his or her position within the kinship system. The spirit makes demands for particular pieces of the paraphernalia of healing (cloth, dancing axes, skins) and identifies him- or herself as one who grants healing powers. He or she may promise to introduce another spirit (perhaps a healing *shave*) later on.

D: Soon thereafter, treatment of minor ailments or of a particular illness usually begins.

Young adulthood 4: At about the age of 13, the child begins to collect herbs and prepare medicines alone. He may begin to gather herbs on his own initiative. While the healer is away, the child often treats patients, according to the healer's instructions. Frequently, symptoms of illness are first connected to signs of a calling and incidents of odd behaviour are similarly interpreted. Sometimes the child rebels either against the order of things or specifically against the healing call. Refusal to attend school is quite frequent. Dreams are more openly interpreted as being messages from the shades. A ritual may be held on behalf of the child during which the shades are invoked and begged to leave the child alone until he grows a little older. Some begin to treat minor ailments on their own.

5: The process of 'matriculation' begins. It is characterised by illness and dreams, in which universal symbols like water, flying, and pythons appear, often as a test of courage. Western and traditional experts are consulted. The patient may stay with a healer for long periods, even for a number of years. Relatives are in charge of the procedure. There are suggestions that signs are linked to the life crisis through which the person is passing. For example, the life crisis might be related to adolescent rebellion, infertility in the first years of marriage or unemployment.

6: The spirit identifies itself, his demands are met and symptoms of illness fade away.

7: Soon thereafter the healer begins to treat in his own right. He gradually accumulates power and respect and a reputation for success in certain areas of divination and healing. The spirit introduces the healer to the treatment of progressively more difficult illnesses or problems. Patients are often referred to senior healers until the spirit reveals the means to treat a wider spectrum of problems.

Middle Age E: The healer reaches the peak of his or her career at middle age. The repertoire of illnesses cured is wide and a reputation for the cure of particular ailments is claimed. The healer is often a leading figure in ritual occasions, especially in bringing out the spirits of others.

Middle age 8: The healer is fully fledged. He begins to lead ritual occasions and bring out the spirits of others. In describing this stage of their life cycle, many healers admit training others but deny having been trained when they had their spirits brought out. The patients dream of herbs, the healer collects them and uses them in treatment. (If I am correct in claiming that many patients with emerging spirits have already worked with herbs as child assistants to kinsmen, then the process of exchange between healer and patients is a real one.)

Old Age F: Finally, the healer becomes old and the ambivalence in his status becomes exaggerated. He is widely respected, yet people suspect that his powers are declining. The spirit is seen to allow him rest periods. Some say the spirit begins to leave and he becomes mad. The stated norm emphasises that the healer is not expected to pass on his knowledge except as a shade, once dead.

Old age 9: A time of seniority follows. There is substantial evidence that grandchildren are trained to assume the healing role after the healer's death.

Death 10: Death is followed by the eventual possession of a kin member, often after a period of intense rivalry within the family.

The stated norm assigns an influential role to kin. Kin make decisions on when the patient (our emerging healer) should consult medical practitioners; who should be consulted (traditional or Western: local or alien); what treatment to follow (that is, which diagnosis to accept); and what family investment should be made in curing the patient. There is often conflict between affinal kin and cognate kin in handling the process of possession and in claiming rights to monies later earned by the healer. According to the norm, the healer plays a passive role: he is not credited with the expression of individual choice or the exercise of power. He is directed by either his kin or his spirit. Thus, he is a pawn in the kinship game for his spirit is usually an ancestor.

At various stages, sometimes in childhood, most often alongside illness, dreams play a part in the process of possession. For instance, in my work, all the healers who claimed to be possessed by *vadzimu* denied having been trained to identify herbs, classify plants, prepare medicines, diagnose patients, classify illnesses, or administer treatments. Each claimed that the spirit informed them either during states of trance or through dreams.

NOTES ON THE CYCLE

A healer does not necessarily go through all of the steps above. At each step, there is the possibility that training occurs. The process is long, complex and flexible. Within it there is the potential for the actor (patient) to make choices: his role is less passive than the stated norm leads one to believe. Let us consider the individual's role. In childhood, the process can be exploited as a means to express eccentricity, anti-socialism, bad behaviour or unhappiness at school. There are case studies illustrating each of these. In that the process of consultation and diagnosis is long, society attempts to ensure against charlatan claims. The process therefore allows for the expression of youthful rebellion and, at every stage, provides exits. For example, a patient may be diagnosed as having a *ngozi* (evil spirit), a family *mudzimu* (not a healing one), a *shave* of any of the numerous classes, or as being the victim of witchcraft. If the patient accepts the diagnosis, he can drop out of the qualifying process. The individual can direct family and community attention onto himself through illness (especially effective in a wage-earner or a woman responsible for both domestic and agricultural duties); or by behaving in a bizarre way; or by making direct accusations against a kin member saying that he or she is blocking the spirit or spoiling its emergence by means of witchcraft. The patient wields final control through the manifestation of symptoms. The above are some of the 'factors of recurrence' (to use Turner's phrase) that are revealed in an analysis of healers' micro-histories.

Why should we concern ourselves with the differences between the stated norm and actual practice in this particular instance? Because in childhood and adulthood the norm obscures the real nature of the learning process. Probably in all societies the real nature of learning is partially obscured because of the intrinsic complexity of the learning process and our ignorance of the actual mechanics of learning. Besides, a certain amount of opacity suits the *status quo* in upholding explanations as to how and why people must adhere to the established rules of training and qualification.

Undoubtedly, Zezuru traditional healers do acquire a significant body of knowledge about their culture's symbolic systems (its myths, patterns of dream interpretations, use of colours) and the classification of flora and fauna. For example, Mave (personal communication) estimates that of the 2,000 plant species found in Zimbabwe most healers use about 500. Gelfand (1964, pp. 26–7) makes an interesting comment on Zezuru patients' perception of healers' skills. He admits that he held the belief

> . . . that the *nganga* [the spelling of *nganga* has recently been officially changed to *n'anga*] was considered by his patients to have an inherent gift with which he could manipulate circumstances to bring about a desired effect and that the basis of his practice was magic.
>
> But when I asked the Mashona how they accounted for the cures attributed to the *nganga*, I found that they associated them with the potency of the medicines he prescribed and believed that it was the *nganga's* knowledge of the right medicine and not any special quality inherent in him that mattered.
>
> The *nganga* himself denies that knowing the right medicines or divining the causes of illness is a personal talent. He claims that his ability and skill are due to a special spiritual endowment.

Thus, the acquisition of special knowledge is intrinsic to the long, complex and flexible process of becoming a healer.

In summary, there is a wide variety of practice amongst healers. Yet there is a norm commonly proffered. The norm is used as a yardstick with which to measure individual claims to healing powers. While there is no monopoly, no guild that defines membership, the authenticity of those seeking to become healers is measured in terms of the norm. However, the norm does not fully represent the intricacy and complexity of the period of preparation that healers experience prior to the full exercise of their power as healers. Few attempt to set up as healers without going through the necessary preparation.

THE NORM AS THE CRITERION OF AUTHENTICITY

The following case illustrates what can happen if the attempt is made to avoid the preparatory stages. A man brought upon himself accusations of witchcraft when he overstepped the norm by claiming that three of his immediate family members were simultaneously possessed. None of the three had gone through the preparatory period before the claim was made. Because power that can be used in the interests of particular family groups is believed to accompany possession, often there is strong competition among family members to claim possession by the shades. Kin ties in this case are illustrated in Figure 1.

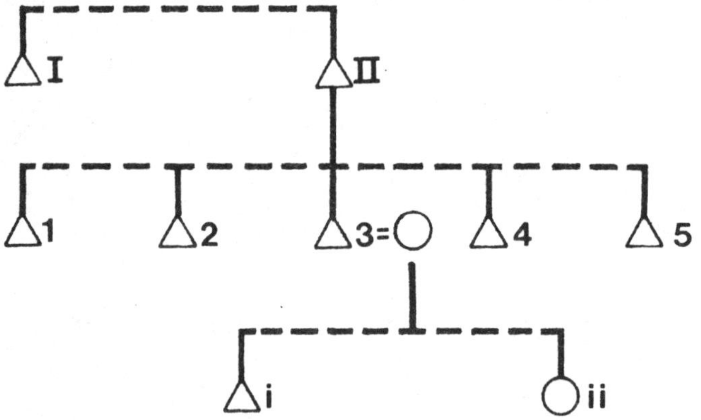

A man (II) now dead had five sons (1 to 5); the eldest two were ill (August 1983) and the third claimed on behalf of his wife and children that they were each possessed by a family spirit (*mudzimu*). The man's elder brother (I) has a family spirit that had recently been confirmed by the healer who related the case. Her information came from Son 1.

Son 3 prepared a ritual feast (*bira*) to welcome the spirits of his wife, his son and his daughter. At the *bira*, the father's elder brother's (Man I) spirit emerged. When Son 3 claimed that his wife and children were possessed by the spirits of, respectively, his father-in-law (wife's own father), his father and his mother, his father's brother's spirit challenged him. The latter asked how could he claim possession by the shades of three family members at once (an 'unnatural' occurrence), and why was he holding a *bira* for his wife's spirit at his home when it should be held at her natal home. The spirit possessing Man I demanded that the spirits speak for themselves. The man's wife's spirit said, 'I am the one who breaks legs'. The son's spirit said 'I am a fighter. Today no one will leave this house.' And the daughter's spirit said nothing. The uncle's spirit responded by saying that he knew that evil powers had been acquired and he warned that every member of the family would eventually be affected and the line might end. Son 3 was accused of obtaining the services of a *chikwambo* (faculty, conferred by *shave*, of recovering property and of punishing those who refuse to restore property (Hannan 1959). The healer used the word in a wider sense to imply any evil spirit), and of enlisting the aid of his wife and children in pursuing his evil intentions. Son 3's wife was accused of causing the paralysis of her husband's elder brothers.

After the *bira*, Sons 4 and 5 went to a diviner to request that he return the evil that had been placed on their two eldest brothers to the one who had sent it, that is, to Son 3. The wife of Son 5 asked the healer who related this story to take on the case. She refused, saying that a healer from outside the area must be consulted.

The Uncle (Man I) held a *bira* to which leading healers in the area were invited (including the story teller and two others with whom I worked). As he is the senior family member, all kin were obliged to attend; the confrontation occurred when the accusation against Son 3 was made public; he agreed to have the evil in his family chased, thus relinquishing his claims.

In another case a man did not want to admit that his younger sister was possessed by a *mudzimu*. At her *bira*, he ordered his daughter to act as if possessed and he placed her instead of his sister on the reed mat. The daughter did as she was told and named an ancestor as her possessing spirit. After the *bira*, she returned home and immediately became mentally confused. The rest of the case is complicated. The girl will probably remain mentally confused until a resolution accepted by the whole family is found.

THE ACQUISITION OF TECHNICAL KNOWLEDGE

The term 'technical knowledge' refers to healers' stocks of information about *materia medica*. Many healers know an impressive amount about flora and fauna. They have a wide range of information and show fine discrimination in their observation and classification of leaves, stems, roots, fruits, flowers and bark. They are able to distinguish plants on the basis of taste, touch, smell and their appearance across the seasons. Such a range of skill and knowledge is likely to have been acquired over time, under the tutelage of one familiar with the practice of healing. The ability to make fine discriminations is probably not acquired in adulthood; more likely, *some* children are provided the opportunity and encouragement to acquire specialised skills and information.

I cannot present all the evidence that supports this supposition here. The evidence includes data from the life-histories of healers, detailing their early learning experiences with healers within the family. There is also data on the children and grandchildren of healers currently practising who have been identified as having been 'called', or who act as acolytes, or who assist in the collection and preparation of plants for medicines. To determine whether children who have a healer in their families know more about plants than those who have no healer in their families, I tested 25 from each group, matched in terms of age, grade and sex. Although I have not yet fully analysed the results, it is clear that the former group knows more and that the knowledge acquired by children within families varies. To support my supposition that the discrimination and classification of plants begins in childhood, additional evidence comes from walks in the *veldt* with healers and their children and grandchildren.

In this paper, I shall refer to only one occasion during which I observed a healer teach her grand-daughter about herbs. My assistant and I accompanied an old healer, who had been treating for about 70 years, into the *veldt* to gather herbs. With her was her 16-year-old grand-daughter (her first son's child), her 6-year-old grand-daughter (her only daughter's child) and a patient's child, also aged six. The patient was a healer too. At the beginning of the walk, the healer knelt by a bush and invoked the shades by sprinkling snuff on the ground. She then addressed them, calling on Nehanda, Chaminuka, Gandera and many others. She begged the shades to guide her in finding herbs and to grant those herbs healing powers. The children stood before her. We searched for herbs for three hours in an arc from the healer's home. The 16-year old gathered herbs and returned with them to her grandmother. Once when she admitted to forgetting the name of a bush, her grandmother said, 'How can you keep forgetting? I am going to die soon.' The girl laughed shyly and repeated the name after her grandmother.

As we searched, we talked and the healer pointed out herbs. She gathered herbs to treat problems that included bewitchment (by a witch or an alien spirit), jealousy, madness, cleansing, the after-effects of adultery (if a person ccmmits adultery, he or she must take medicine to cancel the effects of a taboo which would bring harm to his children if he touched them), anxiety, violence in the mentally disturbed and physical ailments like diarrhoea. She interpreted signs in the environment, like the passing of a whirlwind, as messages from the shades. She took us to a sacred glade and explained what was allowed and what was taboo in the area and she told stories of the origin of violence between the races. We sat in the glade for an hour during which the 16-year old searched for rare plants and the 6-year old dug up roots for her grandmother. The woman told the child the name of each plant and its use. For example, when the child brought her a pink, plastic-like flower of an aloe, her grandmother told her that it should be burnt and mixed with snake oil (*shato*) and used to treat madness. She told the child to observe that 'a mad person moves just as the flowers hang and move on the plant'. The child worked with persistence and enjoyment and her grandmother accepted all her offerings.

The old woman told us a great deal and even discussed with us witchcraft among her fellow villagers. The children listened throughout and watched closely as she gathered herbs. Sometimes she would ask the older girl to find a particular herb or test her knowledge of a particular plant. Our presence rendered the occasion different but the children demonstrated their knowledge gained from many other walks.

On many occasions, one or two of the children or grand-children of healers would sit for long periods listening to our discussions. The topics often included witchcraft and its existence among neighbours. No one chased the children away. Yet when I asked healers if they informed children about aspects of their work, particularly the nature of the shades and of evil, they invariably said 'no, such matters are not for the ears of children.'

CODES OF CONDUCT AND FEES

Many Zezuru subscribe to the belief that healers are selected by spirits because of the purity of their hearts (*hana* – 'heartbeat' or 'conscience'). A particular spirit is said to search for a pocket, a medium, according to two sets of criteria. The spirit 'looks for the heart' and seeks a character that will match his own. *Hana* reveals itself in one who is strong-willed, well-behaved and stone-hearted. Bad dreams are frequently interpreted as trials set by the spirits to test one's will-power, calmness and strength in the face of adversity. When I asked healers why so many women were possessed by male spirits, they reasoned that men found that women had more reliable hearts and so sought them out as pockets. Thus, in affirming someone's genuine possession during a ritual (*bira*), the community is also recognising that person's moral purity. In turn, the one thus recognised is expected to live in accordance with a code of conduct that includes particulars laid down by the possessing spirit as well as more general restrictions.

According to healers, spirits trouble the children whom they later intend to possess, because they need to ensure that the children follow the precepts of the code. For instance, sometimes the spirit wishes to prevent the child from eating taboo foods (in the case of one man, his spirit prevented him from eating *sadza*, the staple food, from early childhood), or from being contaminated by Western ideas (as evidenced by fainting in class, dizziness when copying from the blackboard and other problems at school), or from contact with death (one girl who vomited when anywhere near a funeral was divined to be possessed by a spirit who hated death). Signs such as these are very likely recognised retrospectively; similar patterns can also be identified in the hero myths of other cultures. Nevertheless, I witnessed children receiving such interpretations; it therefore seems likely that some children whose behaviour, eccentricities, health or intelligence draw attention from adults are offered the opportunity to claim possession.

The following paragraphs outline the code. The process of becoming a healer involves much more than the acquisition of knowledge about flora and fauna. It involves an acceptance of given principles.

The symbols of office that a healer may wear (often copper bangles or black and white beaded necklaces) identify him as an initiated medium. They signify that he should not be angered or made to feel anger. His role is to advise. He should never beat or harm another, even in self-defence. He may not use his power to threaten others. To kill or cause an abortion is considered as an act of witchcraft. During the War of Liberation some healers refused to assist either side, saying that their spirits hated bloodshed and that they could not contribute to the war effort in any way. As a result some were beaten or imprisoned. One healer was accused by the comrades of having 'sold out' to the soldiers. He was taken by a *mujibha* (a young messenger) at night to the comrades' camp and beaten. As one comrade lifted his rifle to hit the healer it flew out of his hands. During the beating, the healer fell into a trance and the comrades begged his *mudzimu's* forgiveness because they knew the shades supported their struggle. They asked the healer for snuff as a symbol of forgiveness. Still angry, he refused but the comrades searched his clothing anyway and helped themselves from his *nhekwe* (snuff container).

In theory, the medium possessed by the area or tribal spirit (*mhondoro* or *gombwe*) has authority over healers in the area and can punish them (usually in the form of public reprimand or fine). Healers' organisations do discipline members through expulsion or recourse to the law courts. Healers say that the only effective discipline for committing sin is the loss of spiritual attention. The loss dilutes healing powers and the healer's number of patients dwindles. Thus, a person's moral standing and commitment is reflected in his or her success as a healer which, in turn, can only be judged by the number of patients who call.

While treating a seriously ill patient, the healer must keep pure. He must have no sexual intercourse. The herbs that belong to the shades and have healing powers must be touched only by someone pure. If herbs are tampered with by someone impure, the one who is possessed falls ill. In selecting a child to help him collect herbs, a healer looks for purity in the child's behaviour and manners. When someone begins to work with a healer, he or she is cleansed of impurities with water, incense and smoke. Misbehaviour in anyone annoys the shades even if it is 'natural' as in the sexual excesses of young men. If someone is impure, he cannot enter the *banya* (the healer's 'surgery') without bringing the shades' anger down upon his (the impure one's) family. If taboos are broken by a healer, even inadvertently, he will fall ill or lose his way home. Taboos broken by anyone may have the same result. I know of an incident in which young boys went hunting and, while passing through a sacred glade, one made a disparaging remark about the scarcity of the game. He disappeared at once and returned home some days later, after wandering aimlessly in the *veldt*. No one searched for him because they knew he was being punished by the shades.

The duty of a healer is never to forsake others. Some explained their support of the comrades during the war in these terms. Once a spirit has chosen someone there is no way for the individual to prevent possession. He who has been granted healing talents is obliged to use them for the good of others. If he does not, illness will follow or he will receive no more patients. One well-known healer recalls that she was given the power to heal when only 7 years old and would only tend patients reluctantly, wanting to play instead. As a result, she became ill at the age of 12 and was taken by the river spirits beneath the water for four days. Upon her return, she healed willingly: the shades had made their point.

A healer is perceived to experience advantages and disadvantages in his calling. Healing powers enable the medium to help others. In return, the spirit cares for the medium and prevents harm from befalling him. However, the healer often experiences illnesses that lead up to possession. And he must obey the code set by the spirit.

A healer is rewarded by the status that accrues to himself and his family from healing and from access to the world of the shades. Fees are considered as tributes of thanksgiving to the spirits and not as rewards for the healer. A fee must be charged, even to kin, or the medicine will not be effective. The poor are treated free but, if they are wise, they will pay something to ensure recovery. One healer treated his son's child for nothing. Lightning struck the healer's goats and a diviner revealed that the healer's spirit had been angered as he had received no thanks. The practical consequences of this belief are obvious. Some say that the spirit guarantees a cure so that the patient will be able to pay at the time of receiving medicine or later on. The spirit instructs the medium as to whether or not to accept a patient. The spirit does not allow the medium to charge a fee to one who is dying although he may treat him for nothing. Information given by the shades must not be divulged to others.

The code of conduct as outlined above is not articulated as such and aspects of it vary from healer to healer. In essence, however, the code is subscribed to by most healers.

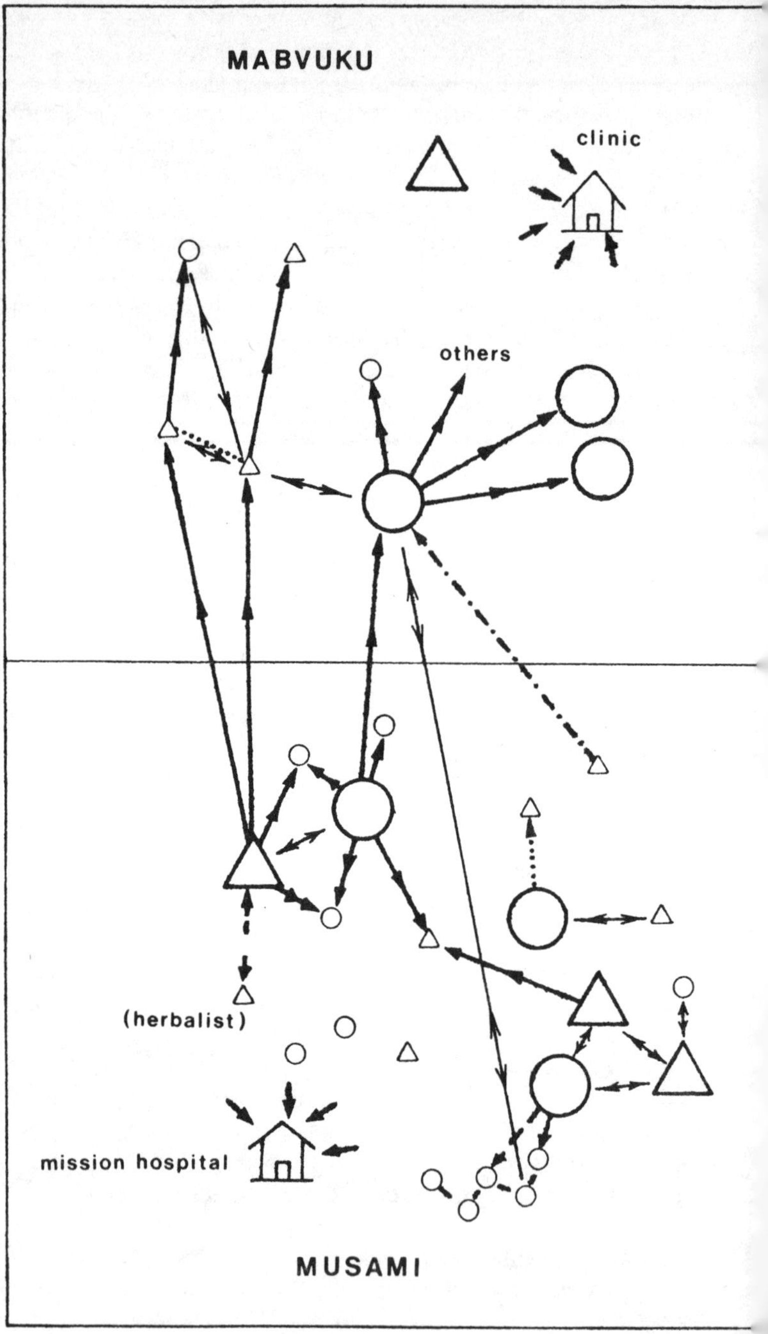
MABVUKU
clinic
others
(herbalist)
mission hospital
MUSAMI

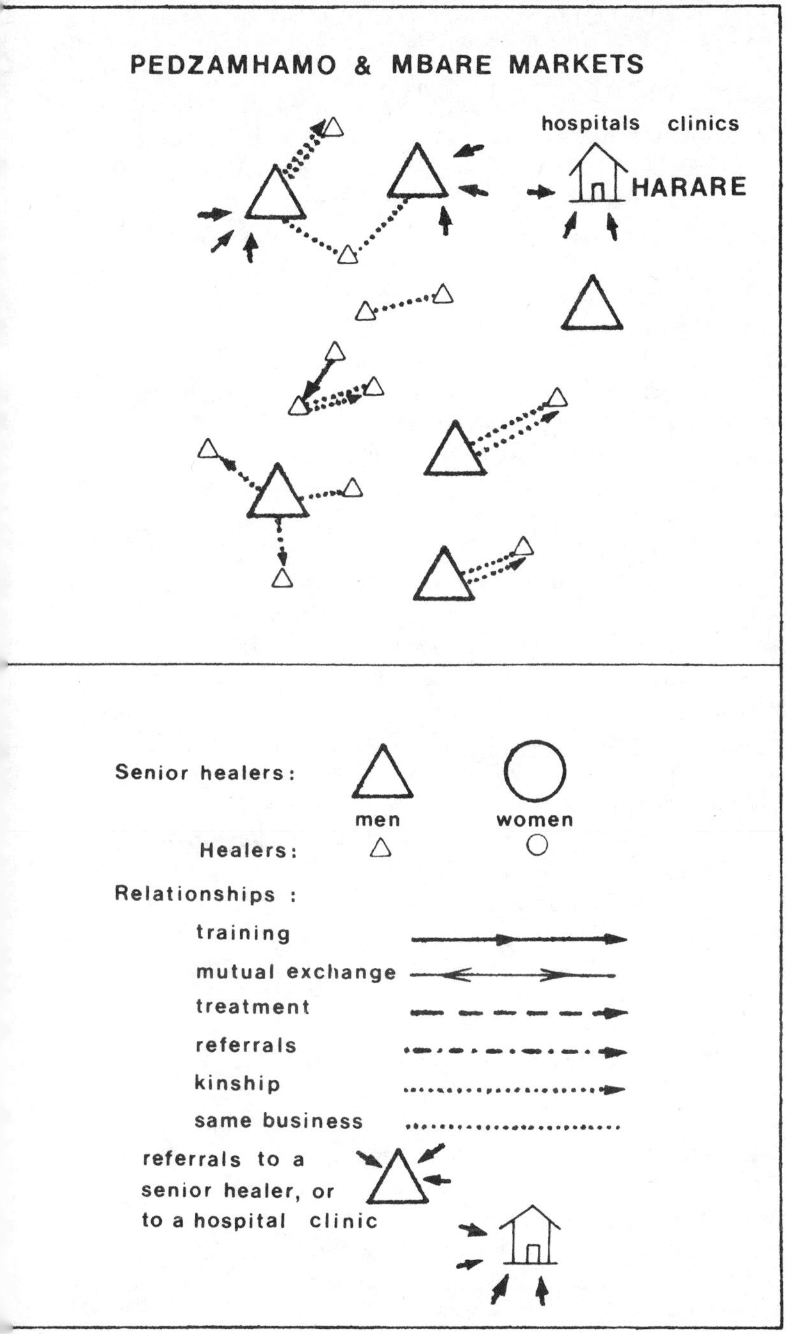
PEDZAMHAMO & MBARE MARKETS
hospitals clinics
HARARE
Senior healers:
men
women
Healers:
Relationships :
training
mutual exchange
treatment
referrals
kinship
same business
referrals to a
senior healer, or
to a hospital clinic

NETWORKS OF KNOWLEDGE, AND THE MARKET IN MEDICINES

In the literature, traditional healers in Zimbabwe are characterised as being secretive about their remedies. The uses to which they put their herbs are considered to vary too widely for a pharmacopoeia to be assembled. Healers deny that they learn from one another or exchange information about herbs. My evidence suggests otherwise. Figure 2 illustrates some of links between healers that I have traced. Each link represents an exchange or sharing of information. The circles represent the three areas of Musami, Mabvuku and the market places. The details of the exchanges are not pertinent to this paper, but it is worth noting how many links exist despite the healers' initial denials that any exist. Many healers refer patients to clinics and hospitals staffed by Western-trained personnel. I came upon no instance though in which the latter referred a patient to a traditional healer, perhaps because to do so would be an infringement of the code of the medical profession.

Among the Zezuru, there are different categories of healers and the boundaries between the categories are blurred. The categories include healers who claim possession by guardian spirits (*mhondoro* or *makombwe*), by ancestral spirits (*vadzimu*), and by alien spirits (*mashave*). A healer may be possessed by only one spirit or by one or more from all three groups. The subtle differences among mediums whose spirits have responsibilities for particular areas or functions (for example, a tribal or rain spirit) or among healing and family *vadzimu* or among the numerous classes of *mashave*, including the river (*njuzu*) spirits, cannot be examined here. They are all part of one system and they share an ideology that is common in essence, but varies in detail. For example, all those who claim to practise under spiritual guidance deny having been trained and all subscribe to the need to surround their practices with secrecy. However, once trust has been established, they are willing to reveal their networks and to share their knowledge. Organisations that represent traditional healers do not differentiate in their membership among the categories.

In part, an informant's place in his life cycle may influence whether he will acknowledge learning from another or teaching someone else. For instance, children talk easily about their learning and their roles as acolytes. Healers busy building their reputations deny that they were taught, but they may admit to teaching others. Old healers often talk openly about their efforts to teach members of a younger generation.

According to Turner (1967), among the Ndembu knowledge is far more literally 'power' than it is in the West. Knowledge confers some kind of mystical power on its possessor, giving him or her an affinity with the *materia medica* used, and enabling the herbalist to activate the latent virtues in the herbs he uses. The healers with whom I worked seemed to hold the same attitude towards knowledge. The curative strength of a medicine is believed to originate in a combination of the herbs' intrinsic qualities and the healers' spiritual power. Healers who do not claim to be possessed by spirits during states of trance more readily admit to having been taught their knowledge of *materia medica*. They do not need to establish that their knowledge is directly infused with power from the spirits. Nevertheless, they say that their very interest in herbs and their ability to collect, classify and use them testifies to their guidance by *mashave* (alien spirits). They describe in detail their early experiences in the company of kin-healers and the graduated nature of their learning, adding that without the guidance of *mashave*, the instruction would soon be forgotten.

The men in the market places who sell the *materia medica* and paraphernalia used by traditional healers are within the healing tradition, although their role is a new one. In the past, there must have been people who supplied healers with exotic objects like cowrie shells, even though procurement from a middleman runs counter to a widely held belief that a healer ought to find and prepare his own medicines. Some say the ingredients must be sought afresh for each new patient (both Evans-Pritchard (1937) and Turner (1967) give fine portraits of men who exchange *materia medica* across territories).

The men in the market places describe themselves as 'pharmacists' or 'wholesalers and retailers'. They subscribe to some aspects of healers' lore and reject others. For instance, all claim some form of spiritual guidance which bestows power through them on their remedies, yet they do not countenance the claim of many healers that the power of herbs is dissipated if they are collected by one not under direct spiritual guidance. Since they buy many of their ingredients, both plant and animal parts, from itinerants (including poachers) they cannot subscribe to that belief. Another belief that they refute is that if *materia medica* are exposed (placed on display), the power is ruined by evil airs that come from those that pass by. Again, they cannot afford to uphold that belief.

The attitude of other healers towards them is marked by ambivalence: on the one hand, healers in the city need a source for *materia medica* (particularly for items like lion's fat and baboon's fontanelle); on the other hand, the healers view with suspicion both the salesmen and their products because they infringe some of the tenets of their belief.

The 14 men with whom I worked in the market-places developed their interests and skills in healing in ways similar to those healers in Musami and Mabvuku. For instance, each of the men in the market-places identifies incidents in his childhood that were interpreted as hints of his future involvement with healing; each of them lived for part of his childhood with a healer; and each of them recalls dreams relating to his work. I have recorded the stock of four healers at the market-places of Pedzanhamo and Mbare and compared them with the remedial substances used by two men living in the countryside. A large portion of the stock of ingredients and their uses is the same for each man.

The men in the markets have established networks that reach across the country and into neighbouring states, via traders and practitioners. The market-places are also sources of information about variations in patterns of healing, different uses of *materia medica*, changes in fee structures, and reactions to Government measures concerning healing, especially actions toward witchfinders and charlatans. Stall-owners proudly claim knowledge of the far greater number of medicines than most healers have. Within and between the two markets stall-owners are linked by kin and friendships. There were no links between the healers in the countryside and the suburb (Musami and Mabvuku, respectively) and the market-places. Nevertheless, many traditional healers bought *materia medica* from the stalls, some on a regular basis and in bulk.

CONCLUSION

In Zimbabwe today the world of the healer is undergoing transformation. We have insufficient data to know exactly from what it is being transformed. The process is not without direction or social control, although the boundaries between types of healers are blurred, as perhaps they have always been. The difference in the networks outlined above suggests that transformation is occurring within the system in response to particular conditions that affect only certain practitioners, for example, the sellers of *materia medica* in the market-places are meeting new needs and in doing so are adapting traditional mores. The following queries will shed light on the process of change. Will the 'wholesalers' in the market-places find it in their interests to 'qualify' as diviner-healers? Will common membership in an organisation such as ZINATHA encourage diviner/healers to patronise the market stalls more openly and to cease being so disparaging of the stall owners' authenticity as healers? Will the distinctions among the roles and tasks of those possessed or guided by different categories of spirits become entrenched or will they be submerged? Can or should an organisation aiming to 'professionalise' traditional healers encourage existing variations? Or is a professional organisation more likely to formulate a particular philosophy and set of practices?

Most of the healers with whom I worked said that many new spirits began to possess hosts during the Liberation War, particularly between 1968 and 1972, in order to protect 'their children'. My data, drawn from the life histories of 47 healers, neither supports nor refutes the claim. Only in

Musami is there support for the healers' claims: one quarter of the healers began to treat during a five-year period between 1968 and 1972. The number who were called during the war years 1968 to 1979, the ages at which they were called, and the age composition of the sample reveal no particular bulge. Before we can endorse general statements on the increase in the numbers of healers, we need to document more carefully the numbers of healers, their life histories and the nature and size of their practices.

All but a few of the healers related incidents in their childhood that were interpreted to them as signs of future involvement in healing. All but a few had a close relationship as a child with a healer in the family. These two points suggest that even if the numbers of healers increased during the war, few who had not been prepared for the position joined their ranks. It is probable that at any one time in a given population there are many more potential healers than 'graduates'. I base this suggestion on my observation of the kin of healers during treatment sessions and on ritual occasions, when one or more demonstrated that he or she was well versed in the lore and rules of the art. Kin often act as midwives or specialise in curing a single ailment; given special circumstances, they too could be called. I suggest that the particular tension during Zimbabwe's struggle for liberation may have encouraged more people than usual to qualify as diviners and/or healers and that they were drawn from potential candidates well within the complex of the healing ethos.

While the learning process through which traditional healers in Mashonaland pass is neither formalised nor clearly demarcated, it is long, complex and flexible and cannot be replicated in the curricula of simple herbal courses. Nevertheless, traditional healers are not averse to courses, a pharmacopoeia or exchange among colleagues: they simply emphasise that knowledge thus acquired is but one step in the process, saying it is not 'deep' knowledge. Knowledge not infused with spiritual power is less effective. Ideally the necessary ingredients for accurate divination and successful healing include spiritual guidance, moral purity, a commitment to the client, and the possession of specialized knowledge. Traditional healers cannot envisage a system for themselves in which the acquisition of knowledge is accorded prominence over other aspects of their preparation and recognition as healers.

Among those who are interested in promoting traditional healers as medical practitioners, there is a tendency to ignore other aspects of the healers' work. Efforts are concentrated on documenting their knowledge of flora and fauna and on isolating the effect of their remedies, often suggesting that the healers' other concerns are the stuff of religion or superstition and their continuance need not be nurtured. I believe the various aspects of healers' roles are closely intertwined. If their work is not to be trivialised and their position undermined, a clear study of their techniques of social analysis and the tenets of their psychology must be made.

Abuses by healers must be stopped. Some abuses are criminal and need to be, and are being, policed: others arise out of ignorance or ill-advised beliefs. The healers with whom I have worked all expressed their willingness to learn Western medical ways and to co-operate with Western medics. Traditional healers could be taught to recognise symptoms that call for immediate referral to Western medical centres. Healers could be taught basic treatment schedules for handling child dehydration and similar problems. The many networks linking healers and the people could be utilised in the interests of the wider population. Information, new attitudes and techniques are already being passed along these networks. Government in Zimbabwe cannot carry the cost (financial or manpower) of incorporating traditional healers into the formal health system but the Government can enable the system to remain viable and to develop itself. It can facilitate organisations that research the systems of understanding that underpin traditional healing practices.

Professionalisation of traditional healers in Zimbabwe could facilitate the exchange of ideas, a pharmacopoeia, the monitoring of abuses, and referrals to Western medicine. There is, however, a danger that professionalisation could tamper with and dilute the existing learning process and trivialise the role that healers fulfil in their communities.

NOTES

1 In 1982 there were eight traditional healers in the six villages which had a total population of 1,428. Within the villages, there was one healer to 178 persons.

2 A ZINATHA (Zimbabwe National Healers' Assocation) official estimated that in 1983 there were 350 traditional healers in Mabvuku. In the same year the population was 34,000, which allows 97 persons to every healer. I cannot guarantee the accuracy of this estimate, as the municipality did not know how many healers were in the suburb.

3 In 1983 there were nine stalls selling *materia medica* at Pedzanhamo market and 22 at Mbare market. A number of stalls were run by two people. The 14 men with whom I worked either owned or assisted at stalls in Pedzanhamo, and some also owned stalls at the other market place.

REFERENCES

Bernardi, B., (1950), 'The Social Structure of the Kraal Among the Zezuru in Musami, Southern Rhodesia.' *Communications from the School of African Studies*, No. 23. Cape Town: University of Cape Town.

Chavunduka, G., (1970), 'Social Change in a Shona Ward.' *Occasional Paper*, No. 4. Salisbury: U.C.R.N.

Evans-Pritchard, E. E., (1937), *Witchcraft, Oracles, and Magic among the Azande*. Oxford: Clarendon Press.

Foucault, M., (1973), *The Order of Things: an archaeology of the human sciences*. New

York: Vintage Books.
Fry, P., (1976), *Spirits of Protest: spirit-mediums and the articulation of consensus among the Zezuru of Southern Rhodesia (Zimbabwe)*. Cambridge: Cambridge University Press.
Garbett, K., (1960), 'Growth and Change in a Shona Ward'. *Occasional Paper*, No. 1 Department of African Studies. Salisbury: U.C.R.N.
Gelfand, M., (1964), *Witch Doctor: traditional medicine man of Rhodesia*. London: Havill Press.
Hannan, M., (1959), *Standard Shona Dictionary*. Salisbury: Mardon Printers, (2nd ed.)
Leach, E., (1982), *Social Anthropology*. Glasgow: Fontana Paperbacks.
Turner, V., (1967), *The Forest of Symbols: aspects of Ndembu ritual*. Ithaca, New York: Cornell University Press.

9 Harriet Ngubane

THE PREDICAMENT OF THE SINISTER HEALER: SOME OBSERVATIONS ON 'RITUAL MURDER' AND THE PROFESSIONAL ROLE OF THE INYANGA

INTRODUCTION

This paper aims to highlight, by using a rather drastic sort of instance, the conceptual problems of relating indigenous and Western medicine, primarily in the southern African context. Lest this be taken to be mainly an abstract academic issue, it should perhaps be mentioned at the outset that a large part of the central argument is that the ethical boundaries of a system of medicine, and especially the line between what a practitioner may do for a patient or client and what he may not do, are derived from its conceptual systematics. As at the same time I seek to show that, in a definable part of southern African indigenous medical practice, the resultant ethics permit a practitioner to recommend in certain special cases a ritual killing, it will be realised that this is not a question of merely intellectual interest.

Ethical boundaries can hardly in practice be ignored in any attempt at incorporating indigenous medicine into national systems of health provision; but where this also means, as it is bound to mean, reconciling differing definitions of what is and what is not acceptable as professional conduct, the risks run by neglecting or overlooking such questions can presumably extend from recurrent misunderstandings to general breakdown. Although Western medicine certainly has its own problems of professional ethics, they plainly do not include the likelihood in particular that a practitioner will take part in any way in killing a fully functioning living person. If I am right in my contention that indigenous medicine, albeit in very special circumstances, does embrace this likelihood, we have here a stark example of the difficulties of combining or of reconciling the two systems.

Such difficulties, although most of course will not be of this order of severity, are not likely to be reliably overcome unless the reasons for these ethical differences are clearly understood. In the first instance they must be understoood *as* ethical differences, that is, as differences arising from the manner in which practitioners meet their professional obligations within different conceptual frameworks concerning the nature of health and disease. In other words, whatever we may understand by the 'professionalisation' of traditional or indigenous medicine, it should emphatically not be taken to imply that its practitioners have less than professional standing in their own eyes and in those of their clients, in this part of Africa at least. By that I mean just that they are seen as fully possessed of professional skills and professional responsibilities, in quite the same way as Western practitioners are. The difference lies in what is expected of them.

Second, it must be made plain that the question of how indigenous and Western medicine differ conceptually, and therefore in terms of ethical boundaries, cannot sensibly be answered in a blanket fashion. In southern Africa there are three principal types of indigenous practitioner, and each has a different kind of convergence with and/or divergence from Western practice, resulting from his or her conceptual and practical place in the traditional view of health and the sources of its impairment. In addition there is 'folk medicine' to be briefly considered, i.e. the home remedies generally known and applied without referring to a professional practitioner.

An account of these indigenous ways of handling disease – of endeavouring to cure or prevent it – can best be given in relation to conceptions of the nature of disease and how in general it comes about. What is expected of a healer must depend on beliefs about the nature of the condition which he is required to remedy or correct. As I shall try to show, the effect is that where indigenous and Western views of causation coincide or are similar there is not a lot of difficulty about reconciling or even combining methods of treatment. The difficulties arise when disease and its origins are viewed very differently, with unavoidably the consequence that approaches to treatment are equally different. This does not necessarily mean that the practical reconciliation of such different approaches is out of the question, but it does imply that an adequate understanding by each side of the other's approach, and especially of the conceptual base on which it rests, is virtually essential.

I have discussed at length elsewhere for the Zulu what might be called the logic of the traditional or indigenous conceptions (Ngubane 1977, esp. chs. 2, 6, 7). In going over much the same ground in outline here, I am assuming that the same broad principles apply not only to other Nguni but fairly generally in southern Africa. This kind of conceptual map should enable us to locate the ethical boundaries of each type of indigenous medicine and so to see rather more clearly where the fundamental problems of integrating it into national health systems are likely to lie. As I say, the special advantage of selecting ritual killing for attention is that it serves to illuminate these problems particularly starkly.

CAUSES, REMEDIES AND PRACTITIONERS

Bodily illness is traditionally not sharply distinguished from either misfortune or vulnerability to illness and misfortune; the word *isifo* in Zulu covers all three. Nevertheless a class of illnesses is recognized, to most of which the generic word *umkhuhla* is applied, which result from breakdown of the body or of specific organs, brought about, for example, by changes in the seasons, or due to a family susceptibility to certain complaints. The symptoms of such diseases are primarily somatic.

Medicines used in cases of this kind are believed to be potent and effective in themselves, without the need for any ritual in preparation or administration; and people are willing to try new medicines or to discard some for better ones. The home remedies mentioned earlier are entirely empirical in this sense, and so have been quite widely superseded by Western preparations, e.g. cough mixtures and aspirin.

In addition to widely known medicines for such illnesses, there are some which are only known to and available from specialists. Well-known examples are herbal preparations which make birth delivery easier (*isihlambezo*) or which make broken bones heal faster (*umhlabelo*). Such medicines are often used concurrently with Western forms of treatment, as when somebody with a fracture goes to a modern hospital to have the bone set but also obtains *umhlabelo* from an appropriate specialist. As with 'folk medicine' still in use, people go on resorting to the latter type of medication simply because from experience it is considered effective, again in a direct empirical sense. A specialist practitioner of this type is called an *inyanga* of the particular complaint, for instance *inyanga yomhlabelo*, the *inyanga* who deals with fractured bones. (The usage may be thought confusing, in view of the other medical meaning of *inyanga*, unless it is appreciated that the root meaning of the word is merely 'expert' – so that an *inyanga yensimbi*, for example, is a skilled metalworker.)

Natural conditions can also cause disease in a second and rather different way, the symptoms also extending to 'accident-proneness' or vulnerability to misfortune, as well as disorders of a social kind, such as *isidina*, persistent unpopularity. The conditions in question are environmental, or ecological, and are conceived in terms of a disruption of a normal or desirable harmony between an individual and his or her surroundings. Each country or region is regarded as having its own particular character, shown in its distinctive plants and animals which affect and are affected by the local atmosphere: they exude something of themselves into it and absorb something of it into themselves. The same applies to the human inhabitants, who thus have a distinctive relationship with living things around them and in general are adjusted to these particular surroundings. Hence if people go to a quite different region to which they are not so adjusted, they will become sick.

This normal adjustment or harmony with living surroundings is nevertheless constantly threatened by intrusive elements brought in from elsewhere by people or animals returning from distant parts, or by strangers. Another source of environmental danger is disease itself, of certain kinds (to be defined later) which in the traditional belief is removed from the sufferer as a definite material substance by successful treatment and may then remain in the atmosphere or stay otherwise localised until it attaches itself to somebody else. This possibility in itself poses ethical problems for practitioners and patients (or their families), to be discussed later. The immediate point however is that vulnerability to loss of harmonious equilibrium – that is, to disharmony or disorder – means that everyone must be frequently strengthened in order to develop and maintain resistance. In any case, whether it is used curatively or for prevention, the prime function of medicine is to keep or restore order; the word commonly employed in this context is *ukuzilungisa*, to restore order where there has been disorder.

In very general terms, of course, Western approaches to diseases and its causation likewise make basic use of such concepts as harmony and equilibrium, the loss of which is implied by the very words 'disease' and 'disorder'. However, Western *medicine* confines its attention largely to disordered functioning of bodily parts and organs, and views health mainly as a proper functional relationship or balance between such bodily constituents; even psychiatry does not commonly work with a conception of a comprehensive harmony between the individual and his natural and social environment. Such wider considerations, and above all the right ordering of one's relations with mystical forces and the supernatural realm, are not seen as being within the province of medicine at all but are treated as the business of quite other kinds of adept or specialist, such as priests for the mystical and supernatural as well as often for handling social relations.

Since in the African traditional view harmony with nature is continuous with harmony in society, so that disease or disorder can be just as much social as natural in origin, it must follow that diagnosis extends to disturbance in a patient's relations with other people. What expecially complicates this is, first, that the relations which must be rightly ordered include centrally those with deceased ancestors as well as with living kin; and second, that, as has already been indicated, the treatment of disease of social origin entails its removal in a manner which can harm other people if the disease then becomes attached to them. Ancestral spirits can withdraw the protection they normally provide against illness and misfortune if they are angered by non-fulfilment of social obligations; and some decision must be made about how to dispose of the evil from which a patient has been suffering once it has been removed by appropriate symbolic and ritual means.

Thus, although there are ailments which are considered to have a clearly identifiable bodily cause and therefore to be amenable to treatment by home remedies or by specialist practitioners, most disorders are such that diagnosis is far from easy and treatment commonly poses moral problems. On the one hand, disorder or disharmony can take so many forms and have such a variety of contributory causes that the task of accounting for a patient's physical or social suffering can be successfully tackled only by somebody with exceptional powers: the *isangoma*, aptly translated usually as 'diviner'. As a clairvoyant she can ascertain from her own ancestors what is at the root of her client's troubles; and having also a comprehensive knowledge of indigenous medicines she may go on also to prescribe a remedy. However, she does not do so simply as a matter of course, and if she does will charge an additional fee. Alternatively she may recommend the services of a male *inyanga*, or even of a Western-trained physician.

The *inyanga* on the other hand, lacking powers of clairvoyance, does not diagnose; he prescribes or provides treatment. Yet his medicine must act on social and supernatural as well as natural (including environmental) causes of a disorder, and of course he is expected to prescribe for misfortunes and social ailments as well as physical illness. This in practice means that it must have adequate ritual and mystical potency; but it also means that he has a measure of responsibility for what happens to the disease when it has been removed from the patient, especially for any effects it may have on other people. In other words, his profession imposes on him specific ethical responsibilities, as do all professions on their practitioners.

THE ETHICS OF DISPOSING OF DISEASE

Treatment which is ritual and symbolic in character has two purposes, for which two kinds of medicine are used, identified primarily by colour (Ngubane 1977, ch. 7). Black and red medicines are used in order to expel from the body what is bad and harmful, and also to strengthen it against future assaults by such evil; then white medicines are used in order to bring the patient back to good health.

Given the assumption that the evil thus removed is a material substance which does not just dissipate itself, it would be highly irresponsible merely to discard it without regard for what becomes of it. If it is merely left in the locality it may re-attach itself to the patient or else affect some other member of his family. What in practice is done depends on the seriousness of the affliction.

If it is mild in character and treatment for it is frequently provided (a good example is *isidina*), it may be discarded away from the family by leaving it at crossroads or otherwise on highways, where it can attach itself to a passing stranger and so be carried away elsewhere. While at first sight this may seem anti-social, a person's prime responsibility beyond his family is to his neighbours and the local community generally, and in any case it is reckoned as part of everyone's normal duty to see that he is adequately strengthened against just such environmental dangers, especially on a journey.

Evil of a graver kind, such as the polluting effect of a death, must be cast onto a scapegoat animal, which is not eaten but is left to die after its chyme, a ritually important substance, has been removed. Just as black medicines which remove disease must be followed by white medicines which restore health, so the use of a scapegoat must be followed by the sacrifice of another animal, usually white, in order to restore the protection of the ancestors. It is not feasible to be killing livestock every day for such ritual reasons, and therefore animals are used only where it would be quite unacceptable even for strangers to be at risk.

In addition to these quite familiar ways of handling the problem of disposing of disease or evil, it appears that there are exceptional circumstances where the evil to be removed and the good which is to be obtained are so great that the use of animals is not sufficient and nothing less than a human being will do. The indications are that the killing then serves a double purpose, in that the victim is both scapegoat and sacrifice.

Before citing evidence for this, I would observe that basically similar notions are to be found in Judaism and Christianity. In the Old Testament many instances can be found of both scapegoating and the sacrifice of animals, more particularly sheep, but when Jesus comes he dies, in Christian belief, both to take on all the sins of mankind and in order to bring salvation or the grace of God. Thus in his capacity as a sacrifice he has his body pierced and cries out, just as does a sacrificial animal. Subsequently the body and blood are consumed symbolically at a constantly repeated ritual feast which confirms at one and the same time the casting off of sin and the attainment of grace.

THE FUNCTIONS OF RITUAL HOMICIDE

Alarming as the suggestion may perhaps be that ritual homicide can be prescribed by a healer acting within the domain of his professional competence and obligations, I think that consideration of the facts obliges us to reach some such conclusion. It is regrettably the case that these days, at least in Swaziland, there is no shortage of such facts, although those to be found in the most readily available sources must be treated cautiously. Largely it has been the comparative frequency of such occurrences over the past decade or so that has led me to take a particular interest in them.

In less than five years in Swaziland, I have myself heard from friends of some thirty cases of what is usually, if misleadingly, called 'ritual murder', of which they had personal knowledge. Barely half of these have been reported in the local press. As could be expected, those which get the most news coverage are the cases of special interest – where a young child is the victim, say, or one of the participants holds a senior position; but it is evident that many other cases are mentioned very much more briefly or not at all. At the beginning of July 1983 eight people who had been convicted of taking part in such killings were hanged, and this of course was given publicity. However, not everyone accused of such crimes has been convicted, and there is reason to believe that not all ritual homicide has resulted even in prosecution. Persistent rumours even link the names of some highly-placed persons with events of this kind. Hence it is not suprising that wide concern has been felt about this.

Among those who have shown the most concern are evidently some of the *inyangas* themselves. In June this year *The Times of Swaziland* headlined on its front page the news that a new group of *tinyanga* meeting at Nhlangano in the south of the country but apparently including members from various parts of the country had called for the death sentence for 'those *tinyangas* who promote ritual murders'. They had submitted a resolution to this effect to the president of the local traditional court, to be passed on to higher authority, and a spokesman for the group was quoted as saying that they regarded themselves as 'professionally responsible' and that those they condemned degraded the image of other *tinyanga*: 'When people talk about *muti* murders today, the first thing they think of are the *tinyangas* who encourage them by promising to protect them, and improve them.' Such *tinyanga* were said by one group to have 'smeared their profession', and one of the group described them as 'a disgrace to our profession'.

Assuming that this report is reliable at least in its broad essentials, it is very evident from it that the *tinyanga* were not in any doubt about their professional standing and the consequent existence of professional ethical obligations. They appear to have been concerned about the good name of their profession much as we can imagine any group of members of an accepted profession being jealous of its reputation. Equally plainly, they were publicly dissociating themselves from those of their colleagues who might have been involved as *inyangas* in the kind of ritual homicide we are considering. While no doubt this is in itself commendable, it is not quite obvious that they themselves believed that it is unquestionably outside or beyond an *inyanga's* professional obligations to a client that he recommend ritual homicide. Contributing to their desire to express public indignation could have been a concern to avoid being targets for hostility, given that people who are perturbed, as many certainly are, about the prevalence of such killings are often inclined to place the prime culpability on the *inyangas* who recommend them. It is not impossible also that there was a touch of professional envy motivating the public pronouncements I have quoted, for one may be sure that cases of the degree of gravity to which ritual homicide would be appropriate carry very high professional fees.

I say this, not in order to adopt any fashionable posture of cynicism about the motives of professional people, but because I think there are good reasons for disagreeing with such public assertions. It is worth noting in passing, although of course it is not a conclusive point, that no justification was offered for these assertions; that is, apparently no attempt was made to say just *why* the encouragement of '*muti* murders' is disgracefully unprofessional – it was just publicly taken for granted that this is the case. As I say, if we examine such information as can be obtained about these cases, we can come to a different conclusion. We find that we are not confronted after all with an aberration or deviation from the true healer's course, a kind of left-hand path, to use the idiom of Western traditional magic. The *inyanga* who prescribes a *muti* homicide may well be seen as a sinister figure in the sense that his activities appear to be an alarming threat, but he does not follow a sinister path in the etymological sense. Rather, he arrives at his advice by considering the best interests of his client, as does any reputable healer of whatever background; the *inyanga* however does this within the framework of beliefs provided by the characteristic cosmology or world-view of African traditional medicine, as already outlined.

The most accessible information about the details of what in the press and elsewhere is usually called 'ritual murder' is of course that provided by the press itself, most often in the context of court prosecutions and hearings. Reliance on such sources must make my conclusions very tentative, until such time as adequate research has been done, using for example full court records as well as other forms of enquiry. Nonetheless, what emerges from a study of the newspaper stories is a striking similarity in almost all the reported cases. As will be seen, my view of the nature of ritual homicide is essentially a deduction from these recurrent details, when they are compared with what is known of the meaning that is attached to ritual killing of animals as I have myself described and analysed it.

In all cases, the killing of a ritual human victim is the work of a group of people, never of a single individual. The group is very seldom a family or other traditional set of kin; typically it is a set of people with some common interest in joint advancement, such as business partners, and in any case well-placed socially and evidently ambitious. The victim has personal qualities needed by the group for its advancement, and is always close to at least one member of the group, commonly a blood relative and obviously a loved one, even sometimes one's own child; it is very clear that it is never a stranger that is chosen, and least of all an enemy. The parts of the body needed for the *muti* are cut while the victim is still alive, so that he or she cries out in pain; but death appears to be by strangulation. The body is not buried afterwards but left somewhere in the open, often by a river.

Distressing and even shocking as the details of some of these cases can be in the Court evidence, it is very clear that what has been committed is far from just an act of wanton wickedness. In the strict sense it is not even an act of cruelty. It is especially for this reason that I query the use of the word 'murder' for these killings. While perhaps in a very strict legal sense any unlawful killing counts as murder, most of us would not readily use the word for, say, the act of putting to death a beloved person suffering from an incurable disease accompanied by constant agonising pain. What is missing in such an instance is malice toward the one killed. So it appears to be with ritual killing: the victim is a ritual victim, chosen maybe partly because the death means distress for at least one of the participants but also *as* a member of the group whose advancement is the goal of the performance. In other words, what is exhibited here is an extreme instance of the right invoked by all groups at one time or another to demand sacrifices from their members, in this case the sacrifice of a life.

Similarly, the victim is caused pain and so to cry out, not because anyone in the group wishes to inflict pain for its own sake, and even less because anyone delights in it, but because the pain and the cry are necessary for the sacrifice to be effective. As with sacrifice of animals, the cry arouses or summons the supernatural forces which will work for the good of the group. The cutting and removal of bodily parts has to do with their symbolic significance for the interests of the group. Both conceptually and behaviourally, the entire process is clearly structured, with nothing arbitrary about it.

This in itself provides an indication that '*muti* murder' is not quite outside the *inyanga's* professional domain. Well-ordered, clearly structured joint behaviour with a manifest ritual content is virtually certain to reflect a coherent conceptual system, and if what is done resembles what the same people do in other but comparable contexts, then it is more than likely that a common conceptual system underlies both sets of events. What we know of ritual homicide shows a definite conceptual continuity with ritual acts of less grim kinds which nevertheless have the attainment or preservation of collective well-being as their main purpose. It is not very difficult, at least in terms of conceptual principle, to see in particular why what is killed must be human and not animal.

In the first place, if the group seeking joint advancement are not kin, they have no common ancestor to whom a sacrifice can be made; and since it is to ancestors that animals are sacrificed, there would be no point in the group trying to promote its welfare by sacrificing an animal. Second, the ambitions of these people appear to be greater than can obviously be satisfied by the support of ancestors; if therefore they believe that they need supernatural assistance they must invoke a higher power which orders the affairs not merely of particular kin-groups but of all society. (That unusual ambition underlies ritual homicide is indicated also by what I find is a general belief among Swazis, expressed in many discussions, that it is again and again well-placed people seeking promotion, power, etc., who engage in these acts – not 'ordinary, poor people'.)

While for these reasons a group of such a kind must use a human victim in place of animals, the details I have cited indicate quite strongly that the general purpose of the ritual and the manner in which it is thought appropriate to pursue are essentially similar to those of rituals where animals are used. Whatever stands in the way of the group's realisation of its ambitions, and thus is evil from its point of view, must be put into a ritual victim; the ritual exercise however must also leave those who take part in it in a well-favoured state. Animal sacrifice achieves this where goals are more modest because the animal in crying out arouses the ancestors and because it is a food offering also. As already noted, the mystical force whose aid the ambitious group seeks is aroused by the human victim's cry, and presumably it is expected to work in the group's favour in the specific ways implied by the use of relevant parts of the body for potent *muti*; but the mystical force does not need feeding. Hence the human victim is partly a sacrifice, in so far as his or her cry of pain and bodily parts are to bring benefits to the participants in the ritual; but, since there is no need to consume the body, it can be used as a scapegoat. Thus the method of killing avoids opening the body or spilling blood – Swazis call it *ukosonta*, twisting the neck, as is done with the black bull used in the well-known *incwala* ceremony – and the body is not buried.

DEFINING PROFESSIONAL RESPONSIBILITY

An *inyanga* whose professional advice has been to employ such human *muti* takes no part himself in the killing or in obtaining the required bodily parts. All he does is to tell his clients (or possibly confirm their belief) that for their purposes they need a human victim; to advise them on the attributes the chosen one should have; and to prepare the *muti* subsequently when the required bodily parts have been obtained by the clients.

Given the beliefs which he and they share about the significance of misfortune and how it is to be countered and reversed, he has apparently little choice in the matter once he has agreed to be consulted. Like a Western physician, he is obliged to do his best for his patient or client, and this has in itself nothing to do with whether the manner in which the client's welfare is to be promoted is anti-social or morally objectionable.

Nevertheless, if *inyangas* were able to control one another by means of a professional body of some sort, it is imaginable that such a body could agree to redefine their professional responsibilities in such a way as explicitly to exclude the giving of such advice or preparation of such *muti*. However, if such professional self-regulation is not found within the traditional system, I think it is wiser to consider why this is the case before we decide that it is desirable. We should be wary of taking it for granted that, if healers are unorganised, it is because they are unable to get organised until people such as ourselves point out the advantages of organisation and urge it on them, perhaps with practical assistance to boot.

I say this more particularly because, at least in Zulu practice and among other Nguni, a form of indigenous organisation *has* been devised by the *izangoma* which certainly is not new and which owes nothing to Western example or practice. The account which I have given elsewhere of this (Ngubane 1981), and which I now summarise, refers in the first instance to the Zulu, as I have no reliable means of knowing just what obtains elsewhere, but I do have reason to believe that the kind of network I describe can readily extend beyond the Zulu area.

Once every year or two a diviner invites neighbouring fellow-diviners, along with the diviner who trained her and her own neophytes and ex-students, to a feast following slaughter and sacrifice. She herself will be invited likewise to similar occasions by her neighbouring diviners and ex-students, as well as by the diviner who trained her, so these meetings all told are quite frequent and can keep a diviner regularly in touch with several hundred others, visiting thereby many different localities.

Such an occasion is both a kind of professional conference and a means of disciplining and supervising professional activity. Participants dance and sing together, receive and welcome the newly qualified, exchange news about their localities and consider any problems posed by the occurrence of particular diseases. Mutual assistance is practised by divining for one another, and anyone who has fallen out of step in her explanations of clients' misfortunes with established beliefs about the realm of the ancestral spirits may be reprimanded and told that she must desist on pain of exclusion from the sorority. Such meetings thus control and serve to discipline diviners rather as churches control priests, or medical bodies doctors.

No such network of contact and regular meeting is found among *inyangas*, and it is not easy to see how it could exist, within the provisions at least of the traditional order. What occasions the diviners' meeting in the first instance is a religious or sacred event within the sorority, namely slaughter and sacrifice. The *inyanga* as a lay person cannot arrange any such event, and in any case he is not specially concerned as is the diviner with maintaining the moral and social order through communication with ancestors. *Inyangas* in fact compete with one another rather than practising mutual consultation and support, and one *inyanga* does not reveal the secrets of his trade to another unless he is training him. This is not mere perverseness, for if to cure and strengthen one patient is to endanger another with disease which has been cast out or which retreats from the one who has been strengthened, then those who are treating the two patients are necessarily in rivalry with each other.

Nevertheless, the decline or modification of traditional society in the face especially of industrialisation and urbanisation appears to be posing for *inyangas* problems of definition of their professional status which lead them to meet nowadays from time to time to try to clarify such questions. One recurrent problem is that of charlatanry in the townships and elsewhere. In rural society there is little difficulty about knowing who is and who is not an *inyanga*: public recognition exists in the form of supporting institutions and practices, as well as traditional authority, within which the position of the *inyanga* is clear and well-defined. Township life by contrast is anomic, with no such clarity of definition for any social role, and charlatans and confidence tricksters can flourish.

There is good reason to believe that the increase in ritual homicide is another outcome of social change – that is, a problem which arises within the modern rather than the traditional context, even though it reflects traditional kinds of understandings of the causes of misfortune. In other words, although the traditional conceptual framework permits or even in effect prescribes this kind of ritual killing, it is a means in terms of that framework of coping with troubles which in the traditional order were quite exceptional. I shall return to this point. Its relevance just now is that, as we have seen, some *inyangas* at least appear to view the comparative frequency nowadays of such killing, and public alarm in response, as a threat to the standing of their profession. Even so, the *inyangas* who met at Nhlangano in June 1983 were evidently not so much trying to organise themselves to stop all this happening as calling on public authority to do so – and in the first place on traditional authority.

The *inyangas*' predicament in this regard, then, is that whereas they are concerned about the sinister image which at least some of them have come to acquire in the eyes of the public, they have no obvious way of resisting what is presumably a growing demand for assistance with ritual homicide – since it is within the range of possibilities allowed by the cosmology – and cannot easily redefine by joint decision their professional responsibilities, as both in principle and in practice they customarily work in mutual rivalry, not in any normal sense in co-operation.

THE DEMAND FOR DEATH

This attempt, preliminary as it is, to explain how African traditional medicine can accommodate intentional homicide may give a seriously misleading impression if two further points are not explicitly made. The first is that most cultures in one way or another permit or condone the deliberate ending of the life of a human being, even aside from such obvious cases as warfare and self-defence; and that what is acceptable in one is frequently unthinkable in another. In many Western countries today abortion has become legally and in general socially acceptable, provided that the unborn child is young enough; if it is, then what counts is whether the pregnancy was wanted, whether it is possible to provide adequately for the child, etc. In other words, an unborn child has an inherent right of life if it is above a certain age but below that age its rights are only conditional and it may be permissible to terminate its life. Generally among southern Africans, by contrast, all unborn children of whatever age are entitled to life and it is not acceptable to deny that right. More strikingly still, in Western countries the increasing numbers of old people needing care has posed problems of how far they should be enabled to go on living in, say, a state of advanced senility; and it is not uncommon, although this is not quite publicly acknowledged as yet, for lives to be deliberately terminated in such cases, whether by passive neglect or more actively. Where on the other hand as in Africa generally people believe in respecting their elders and venerating their ancestors, it is unthinkable to convert an elder into an ancestor merely because it is too burdensome to keep him or her alive. Making the point more generally, in scarcely any society is there an absolute, inherent right of everyone to life under all circumstances; and life or death is acceptable or not for given individuals according to prevailing concepts of what decides that acceptability.

The second point, briefly put, is that it is not the *inyanga* but the client who decides whether a ritual victim is to be found. In other words, the *inyanga* supplies his distinctive services in these cases only when there is a demand for them. To limit our attention to the *inyanga* alone – if a perhaps unfortunate comparison may be permitted – is rather like trying to deal with prostitution by measures directed at the prostitute, without considering the demand for her services, that is, her customers.

The practical problem in this regard is not so much the mere possibility that ritual homicide can be committed by, so to speak, prescription, or even that from time to time this actually occurs; but rather, as already noted, that its frequency has increased to a point where it is no longer very rare. If in the end it is demand that counts, how can we account for the apparently greatly rising demand?

The demand comes, it seems, from successful people who wish to be even more successful – who desire promotion, wealth, power, business advancement etc. – but for whom the usual resources of traditional and modern society alike are not available. In traditional society the kind of success which is possible for you depends on who you are (that is, to which family you belong) and the degree of success you enjoy depends on your ability to do what is expected of you. If you encounter persistent misfortune, you seek divination in order to ascertain the cause and then use prescribed medicines to drive out the source of the trouble and/or sacrifice to your ancestors to restore good fortune and harmonious conditions generally. In modern society the kind of success you can enjoy depends mainly on the qualifications you have obtained, and your degree of success depends in principle on how competent you are in the kind of job for which you are qualified.

In modern Swaziland the traditional rules and understandings do not apply very directly in town business or employment, and it is often found that the rules which are supposed to apply to modern life do not in practice work. People discover that somebody less qualified and competent than you can be appointed above or ahead of you, and that you cannot rely on being able to continue in occupation of a favourable site for business if somebody more powerful or influential than you wants it. In a small country people even learn from the prior experience of relatives and friends that this is how matters stand and so do not even make any serious attempt at advancing themselves by improving their qualifications or working hard, perhaps. It becomes habitual to rely on *inyangas* for medicine to ensure that you get the position and rewards to which you feel entitled, and if your ambitions are high you seek proportionately more potent medicine, eventually with results of the kind we have been considering.

If it is for such reasons that ambitious people are led, once they can afford it, into seeking the most powerful *muti* of all, that obtained from a living, human body, it is not unlikely that they will find somebody willing to help them to obtain and utilise it effectively (according to traditional concepts), even if such assistance by *inyangas* has been emphatically proscribed and condemned. In other words, if social conditions engender the demand, action to prevent supply will be at best of rather limited effect (as we know from the traffic in drugs, for instance). To put it more bluntly: the popularity among the ambitious of ritual homicide is due primarily neither to the wickedness of *inyangas* nor to the overweening greed of those who employ such means to attain their goals, but rather to the sickness of the society which induces them to believe that there is no effective alternative.

CONCLUSION

If my argument and analysis are sound, there are two main conclusions which seem unavoidable. The first is that conceptually and therefore ethically traditional African medicine embraces the possibility, albeit in exceptional circumstances, of attempting to remedy ills by cutting flesh from a selected living person who is then killed. The second is that there are strict limitations on what is likely to be achievable in respect of integrating traditional medicine into national systems of health provision.

Neither of these findings is likely to be very welcome, and each can easily be misunderstood. The first provides no justification for any attempt at reviving the old missionary view of African beliefs as a manifestation of benighted savagery; but nor does it on the other hand condone ritual homicide. It is clear to me that in the past – as in principle today also – this was a provision for extreme and presumably very dire circumstances and that resort was made to such measures therefore extremely rarely. As I have tried to say, if we find that ritual homicide is no longer very rare we are certainly entitled to think that something is very wrong indeed; but what has gone wrong is not in any sense that old and evil practices are being revived, rather that measures formerly reserved for exceptional circumstances are now evidently being used constantly. It is rather as though a man who kept a gun in his house lest violent thieves broke in at night found that he was bringing it along to the door every time anyone called; it would imply that normal conditions of security in everyday life had broken down. Anyone who thought that what was wrong was either the availability of the weapon or the readiness of the man to use it would obviously have misunderstood the whole situation.

Equally, my second main conclusion should not be taken to signify that it is pointless going on trying to find an appropriate place for indigenous medicine within, or attached to, modern practice. As I have specifically said, part of indigenous practice, in so far as it aims to remedy bodily breakdown seen as due to specifically natural and empirical causes, is conceptually and otherwise in principle quite compatible with Western medicine – although of course we should expect various difficulties of detail, as well as problems arising from the secrecy of the indigenous practitioner about the specialised knowledge he possesses. The greater difficulties are those which arise where indigenous and Western medicine part company conceptually, as I have of course been saying at length. The widest gulf is between the diagnostic practice of the diviner and that of the Western physician; but it is plain also that both in the manner in which the essential nature of most disorders are conceived and in the means employed for setting them right the *inyanga* lives in a very different world from that of the Western-trained practitioner.

Although as far as I can see more is to be gained in general from leaving the two systems running in parallel, so to speak, with patients taking what they need from each as of course they do now, I would certainly not decry the continuation of attempts at finding a better mutual accommodation of the two medicines. There is no sign whatever that African patients anywhere in the subcontinent – and, I suspect, beyond it – are abandoning the traditional practitioners. Rather, they try to make the best of both worlds.

Who can reasonably blame them, if they find that neither world gives them entirely what they want? So by all means let us go on looking for better practical solutions. What I do insist, however, is that even modest forms of success will almost certainly elude us if we do not know properly what we are doing – that is, if we proceed without an adequate understanding of the rationale or conceptual logic of each system, and above all without recognising that each *is* a system, of concepts and consequent practice. So far, readiness of one system to accommodate the other has been shown most obviously by the so-called traditional (but evidently not very traditional*istic*!) practitioner, who is quite willing to advise his or her patient that the services of a Western type hospital or physican be sought, in what he or she deems to be appropriate cases. It is the Western side which has dragged its feet, resorting to disdain and scorn which in fact are based on ignorance. What should perhaps be first explored, therefore, is the possibility of systematically remedying that ignorance. The training of medical students, for instance, should as a matter of course include explanations of the kind of conceptual systematics I have myself endeavoured to elucidate and expound. For the sort of reasons I have given, detailed knowledge of actual remedies is much harder to come by; but at least if the next generation of Western-trained physicians understand better *why* their African patients are also going to traditional practitioners and what it is they think these can do for them, the prospects for finding the most effective forms of comprehensive treatment will have improved.

REFERENCES

Ngubane, Harriet (1977) *Body and Mind in Zulu Medicine*. Academic Press.

—— (1981) 'Aspects of clinical practice and traditional organization of indigenous healers in South Africa', *Social Science and Medicine*, 15B, 3 (July).

POPULAR CONTROL OVER THE INSTITUTIONS OF HEALTH: A HISTORICAL STUDY*

The professionalisation of medicine is a double process. It is first of all a struggle by one or more groups to establish control over medical resources. Groups sometimes compete, for example, to gain exclusive control over medical education or the use of specialised technology, to win the legal right to administer drugs or to receive payment for therapy. They also compete for the authority to certify medical conditions – whether the purpose is to establish a claim for insurance payments or to escape the stigma of witchcraft accusation. Secondly, professionalisation is the achievement of a degree of cultural authority, when a group of healers wins broad public acceptance of the efficacy of their practice and the validity of their knowledge. Public acceptance makes monopoly easier to defend; monopoly, by narrowing popular experience of unorthodox cures, makes public acceptance easier to sustain.[1]

A profession is created only after a long period of competition for control. In Britain astrologers, cunning men and wise women, all of whom treated illness in the seventeenth century (Thomas 1971), were later excluded from legitimate practice. At a later period, the American medical profession achieved full dominance only after resolving conflicts between homoeopaths and the regular profession (Starr 1982, ch. 3). In Africa today the competition unfolding between physicians and popular healers is leading to the development of professional organisations among popular healers. A new balance of control has not yet clearly emerged.

When groups compete we naturally focus attention on the outcome, on victory and defeat. But in the case of professionalisation the course of the contest has peripheral effects which shape the place of medicine in society. This essay will examine three of these effects, all of them by-products of the central competitive action.

First, some healers are left out of the new organisations, because not all of them achieve public recognition. Those who work closest to home, serving relatives and neighbours for little pay – who in other words make the greatest practical contribution – are the ones least likely to work towards recognition because they are secure within their local communities.

Second, professionalisation affects the relative balance of therapeutic control between healers and lay people. Ever since Janzen (1978) and Chavunduka (1978) described the role of lay therapy managers it has become increasingly clear that patients' relatives make many of the most important decisions on diagnosis and therapy (Janzen and Feierman 1979; Janzen and Prins 1981). This is a consequence of weak professionalisation. In a system without strong central control, a system in which many therapeutic options are available, and in which no one kind of therapy enjoys universal popular acceptance, the consumers of medicine must somehow find their way among the choices. In actual practice lay therapy managers from among the patient's relatives and neighbours exercise some authority over treatment. Increased professional control is likely to lead to a reduction of lay control.

Third, when the relationship between healers and the Government assumes a new shape, the scope of medicine is redefined. Medicine can, for example, be restricted to curing the sick; or it can integrate healing with control over public health conditions, as when healers supervise water supplies. In North America and Western Europe two relatively separate branches of the profession have emerged to deal with cures and with public health. Most of the literature on popular healing in Africa focuses narrowly on individual therapy. We need to understand African healing as a potential system of public health.

I propose to explore one case study, the history of healers in north-eastern Tanzania over the past century, with these three issues in mind. The account focuses especially on the Usambara Mountains of Lushoto District, where people speak the Shambaa language. My ethnographic research there in the 1960s included interviews with a number of healers, and a training period with one of them. Research in the late 1970s (together with Elizabeth Karlin, M.D.) concentrated on the therapeutic activities of all the households in a single village. Written historical sources are of course crucial to the interpretation.

CONTROL OVER HEALTH CONDITIONS

All across Africa in the years before colonial conquest healers, and the political leaders with whom they were allied, had a much wider range of control over the social conditions of health than they have had ever since. Maier, for example (1979), in a study of pre-conquest Asante, has shown the importance of street cleaning, careful maintenance of latrines, and variolation for smallpox, along with the organisation of healers under the stool of the Asantehene's doctor. Schoffeleers has studied Malawian cults as 'ritually directed eco-systems'. Cult mediums at times compelled people to plant particular crops, and restricted fishing and grazing so as to protect fragile resources (1978). Janzen has described the Lemba cult of Lower Zaire (1982) as a form of government, of trade organisation, and of therapy all at the same time. Ford (1971, pp. 333–35; 1979) demonstrated that the Nguni chief Mzila understood the relationships among tsetse, trypanosomiasis, and vegetation cover. He compelled his followers to 'draw near to the king' in concentrated settlements so as to establish a tsetse-free zone, and ordered the establishment of a game reserve outside which all wild animals (as trypanosomiasis hosts) were hunted.

These examples show that pre-colonial medicine in alliance with chiefs and elders (or at times in competition with them) had greater power over health conditions than it was to have under colonial rule. In the years of conquest, that power was systematically destroyed, as we can see from the history of the Shambaa kingdom in northeastern Tanzania (for the general history of the kingdom, see Feierman 1974).

Within the kingdom healers in co-operation with chiefs and local elders controlled a wide range of basic health conditions. Healers (*waghanga* in Kishambaa, *waganga* in Kiswahili) coordinated the cleaning of irrigation ditches and the distribution of water; thousands of hectares were under irrigation (oral traditions and Karasek 1911, p. 175). *Waghanga* advised on the choice of village sites; they normally selected defensible locations on high mountain ridges near clean water sources. In one form of divination the healer left a pot of milk out overnight to learn about potential insect problems at the village site. The mountain villages were built above the mosquito zone because people understood that mosquitoes brought malaria (LangHeinrich 1921, p. 259).

Healers, together with local elders and minor chiefs, insisted on isolating individuals who were seen as being in ritually polluted states, whether because they had been born under an ill omen, were lepers, or were infected with smallpox. In the mountains people with smallpox were required to move to the forest; at the Swahili-speaking coast the victims were isolated in separate houses. Shambaa speakers discussed smallpox as an *mvigha* – a 'rite of passage'. The parallels were clear: rites of passage took place in the forest; smallpox victims lived in the forest. Novices in rites of passage were in danger of death, as were smallpox victims. The person who passed through a rite of passage to become an experienced initiate (*kungwi*) learned the art of survival, and then taught it to novices. Anyone who had already suffered smallpox was called a *kungwi*, was known to be immune, and could carry food to the sick in the forest.[2]

Political leaders exercised some authority over the healing occupations. The king and chiefs controlled abuses among practitioners by deciding when accusations of sorcery were just. They either killed the guilty, required them to pay compensation to victims' relatives, or brought the sorcerers to live at court. Specialists in some healing skills, such as rainmaking, the making of war charms, the treatment of widespread epidemics, and the control of locusts, were required to work only at the chief's court, or with his explicit permission.[3] In all these cases political authorities became involved in regulating healers when sovereignty was affected in some way – either through a challenge to the royal monopoly over the power of life and death, or when the healer's speciality affected the welfare of the entire community.

German conquest (which in this respect was typical of all colonial conquest) destroyed the healers' control over the conditions of health, except for those few forms which could be hidden from view. The conquerors persecuted African healers because any African authority over collective action was taken as a threat to colonial sovereignty, because cult leadership had played a role in the great Maji Maji rebellion further south, because of cultural imperialism, and because some missionaries saw healers as the enemy. The district authorities arrested Magili, the most famous locust specialist[4], and they killed a local chief for making protective communal rites. In another case, missionaries committed a spirit possession healer to a newly established mental institution (Hosbach 1911). Karasek, a German planter who knew the Shambaa language, described an incident in which another planter seized an *mghanga* by his ritual hair lock, dragged him off and shaved his head. *Waghanga* began to give up their identifying hair locks, and placed their medicines in ordinary baskets so as not to be caught (Karasek 1911, pp. 155, 195). After the initial period of persecution, the Germans closely regulated medical treatment so as to exclude any practice capable of mobilising people at a collective level. In 1909 the District Officer began issuing certificates to *waghanga*, specifying the illnesses they could treat, the prices they could charge, and the localities in which they could practice.[5]

The breakdown of collective African control over the environment had disastrous effects.[6] When planters took land, and when *waghanga* were arrested, huge irrigated areas dried up (Karasek 1911, p. 175). The political upheavals led to intense famines in the 1890s. The forced removal of villages to the valleys, together with the movement of people searching for food, led to the spread of disease and a decline in population.[7] Compulsory porterage and plantation work forced men into the malarial areas which they had avoided. An oral narrative recorded in 1967 interpreted the sicknesses of the period as punishment meted out by the conquerors to ensure obedience. At the time of the actual events people said that the ancestor spirits were fleeing the land after planters had desecrated grave sites (Karasek 1911, p. 189).

Even though healers were under severe attack, and even though they lost much of their authority over communal affairs, local healing traditions survived through the entire colonial period. Healing practices, however, were now more narrowly curative, less concerned with general social conditions, than they had been before conquest.

In the 1920s the British, after taking over the colony, instituted a policy of indirect rule through hereditary chiefs. In the north-east this meant the restoration of a number of local dynasties, amongst which the rulers of the Shambaa kingdom were the most important. The British intention was to use chiefs in order to win the loyalty and 'free awe' of their subjects (Cameron 1939, p. 109). One of the bases of royal dominance in the Shambaa kingdom was control over rain. In the pre-colonial period rain charms would have been inseparable from the total body of medicines for public control over the conditions of health (Feierman 1972).

British administrators, however, encouraged rain magic while rejecting virtually all other public medicines. By the 1920s it was clear that irrigation, village placement, and control of water sources were under the control of colonial rulers. Healers were left with little to say over these.

At the same time chiefs lost some of their power to control people who ostensibly used healing powers for anti-social purposes. Control of witchcraft and sorcery became difficult public problems. In the nineteenth century chiefs and healers together would decide on measures for the control of witches. But chiefs under British rule had little say. After 1929 a chief could be prosecuted under the Witchcraft Ordinance if he publicly identified a witch (Tanner 1970, p. 27). The official compendium of Shambaa customary law did not mention witchcraft (Cory 1951).

Because of the vacuum in public authority, anti-witchcraft practitioners appeared all across Tanganyika during the years of British rule. These were experts in finding witches, or in protecting the innocent. The Government's response was ambivalent. The Witchcraft Ordinance gave power to the local British administrators, with the approval of the Governor, to deport without trial anyone 'causing fear, annoyance or injury by means of pretended witchcraft' (Larson 1976, p. 94).Governors used these powers primarily against witch-cleansers with large public followings (Larson 1976; 1973; Ranger 1966). The Government's fear was that witch-finding movements which spread rapidly across district boundaries could be the basis of large-scale rebellions (Ranger 1966, p. 6).

Nevertheless, at some moments local administrators welcomed and made use of the witch-finders. This happened within the Shambaa kingdom in 1946. Elsewhere, in two southern districts in the early 1940s the British district administrators were actually responsible for calling in Ngope, a famous witch-cleanser, because of the danger that sleeping sickness settlements would be destroyed by witchcraft fears and accusations (Larson 1973, p. 12). However, when a junior District Officer supported a witch-finder in 1958 he was reprimanded by his Provincial Commissioner.

The ambivalent, predominantly negative, response to witch-cleansers has continued under the Tanzanian Government. In 1973 a large group of women marched on the Lushoto TANU office to demand that a healer be allowed to administer protective medicines; the District Chairman replied that socialism and superstition were incompatible.[8]

Witch-cleansing, in an inconsistent and tense relationship with government authority, is the most important survival of public control African healers exercised over the conditions shaping health and disease. The other issues healers influenced – the siting of villages, the control of infectious disease, protection against invasion, irrigation – are all controlled by specialised agents of the Tanzanian government. The role of practitioners has been restricted over the past hundred years to intimate local healing.

HEALING IN VILLAGE LIFE

Current trends in the organisation of therapy within villages must be understood against a background of long-term continuity. Over the past hundred years the place of healers in the village division of labour has shown strong consistency. Healing and nurturing have been mostly the job of the old, and agricultural production the job of the young and able-bodied. This is often misunderstood by European observers who assume that men are productive and women nurturing. In northeastern Tanzania, as in much of Africa, both men and women do farm work, with a heavier share falling on women. The division between production and care-giving is therefore based on age. Men and women in their twenties, thirties, and forties devote themselves largely to productive jobs. People beyond their productive years heal the sick, provide nursing, and oversee childbirth. Care of infants is divided between young mothers (despite their enormous range of other responsibilities), children, and the old.

A further persistent division separates two kinds of healers from one another – one provides care for relatives and neighbours, and the second treats strangers for pay. The contrast is best illustrated with descriptions of two actual healers, both from the same village in Lushoto District. The first, who is in his seventies, I will call Hamisi (not his actual name). He spent many of his younger years working for wages in a distant town. When he reached about 60 he gave up his job, moved back to the village, and spent more time farming. This was also a time when he began to take over his father's medicine gourds. Hamisi had worked alongside his father over the years, but now moved towards becoming a full-time healer. The division between production and care-giving is clear in Hamisi's career. For him, the transformation from wage-earner to healer was part of ageing.

Hamisi charged his fellow villagers a shilling or two, rarely more, for treatment. He claimed to be a particular type of healer – one who inherits most of his medicines and uses them to treat neighbours irrespective of their ability to pay. Healers of a second type, he argued, purchase medicines and then treat illnesses for pay. It is not always true that healers with large fees have purchased their medicine. In any event, Hamisi fits his characterisation of the first type, although occasional visitors from far away came for Hamisi's help and paid large fees.

Hamisi stood at the juncture between two worlds: the world of concerned lay people – the patient's relatives and neighbours – and the world of specialised practitioners. Relatives and neighbours lacked specialised knowledge; practitioners lacked intimate understanding of the patient's household. Hamisi combined the two. He therefore served as a gatekeeper. He often sent patients and their relatives to the hospital or to specialised healers.

The second healer, one who treats strangers for pay, I will call Juma (again not the actual name). It would be impossible to know the differences between Hamisi's practice and Juma's by asking villagers about their respective reputations. However, a survey of hundreds of illnesses in the village over the course of a year showed that whereas Hamisi was often the first healer consulted, Juma gave no consultations except to his immediate relatives. Some neighbours explained Juma's indifference to practising locally by saying that most consultations within the village are not adequately lucrative.

Juma also worked for wages earlier in life, but quit his job in his late forties. His medicines, which are partly inherited and partly purchased, are said to be effective in countering the effects of sorcery. Juma spent part of the year in the village, some months attending to his medical practice in Dar es Salaam, and some time travelling around Tanzania treating difficult cases. He supplied a list of 102 places in northern and central Tanzania where he had practised medicine.

Hamisi and Juma represent polar types of healers. Hamisi treats people in his own village; is consulted early in an illness; directs patients to other healers; charges little or nothing; and combines the roles of therapy manager and healer. Juma treats patients far from home; deals with cases which have gone for a long period without improvement; treats most patients himself; and charges substantial fees.

Midwives are even further along the continuum towards altruistic care-giving than Hamisi. These older women charge no fees but are given gifts. No women in the study village were *waghanga*, and in general a small proportion of the region's healers are women. One female *mghanga* explained that she had begun practising only after overcoming the determined opposition of her male colleagues. She ultimately succeeded because her speciality was spirit possession. It was impossible for the men to prove that her relationship to her spirit, which was the source of her healing power, was inadequate.

Altruistic healing is the job of the old. Of the six full-time healers in Juma's and Hamisi's village, none are under the age of 50. All except one have adult children who help with farming. That one practises in the village, but specialises in a form of healing with high fees, in which onerous food prohibitions are not set aside until after payment. From this very small sample, and from impressions of a wide range of data, it seems that healers who make the transition to full time practice at early ages are more likely to charge stiff fees. For them, healing takes the place of farming or wage employment. For older men (and for midwives) it is the occupation of the care-giving years.

The division of healers between Juma- and Hamisi-types is not something new. Some pre-colonial and early colonial healers travelled widely, collecting large fees; others received trifling payments for treating neighbours. Much of the best information on healing in that period comes from Karasek, a German planter who lived with a local woman named Makihio. Her father suffered a long illness, leading the family to call ever more distant healers. The more distant the *mghanga's* home, the more esoteric his treatment, the higher were his fees. Karasek also described Shambaa healers who made fortunes travelling through Bondei and Zigula, far from home. Villages without known healers simply relied on their old men. And in any case the sick person's relatives tried every home cure possible before resorting to a famous professional (Karasek 1911, pp. 195–97; 1923–1924, pp. 13, 36). In addition, 'the midwife and the other women who help', Karasek wrote, 'are not paid in money, but take part in a splendid meal served in connection with childbirth' (1918–22, p. 89). Missionaries of that period were also in a position to observe healing among their converts and neighbours. Rösler described how people began treatment at home with herbs, and then moved out in a widening circle at ever-increasing cost if the illness persisted.[9] 'The healer working at home', a proverb of those years went, 'is paid only a cup of beer' (Johanssen and Döring 1914–15). Magili, a famous travelling healer, took three cows in payment for his locust medicine (Gleiss 1898). Hosbach met a travelling healer who had once taken a young woman as his fee (1911).

In the years after colonial conquest prominent travelling healers were persecuted, as we have seen; at the same time the burden on women and on healers who helped relatives at home grew substantially. In north-eastern Tanganyika, the heart of the German settler zone, new demands on men's labour must have increased women's responsibility for food production. Beginning in the late 1890s each settler was allocated a certain number of villages from which to draw male workers (Iliffe 1979, p. 152). This system was abolished and then replaced with a requirement that every local man keep a labour card showing that he had worked 30 days for a European in each four-month period. Missionaries complained that proselytisation was impossible because most men were off doing compulsory labour.[10] They did not mention the effect of this system on women's work. Depriving households of men's work time must necessarily have placed more of the subsistence burden on women, shifting care-giving, in turn, to the old. The effect seems clear, even though we have no precise data on household work time in the German period.

After World War I the new British rulers did not retain the system of labour cards and compulsory employment, but did try to keep subsistence as women's work while using men's labour for export production. The new rulers used taxation to encourage men to work on plantations or grow cash crops, but insisted up until about 1949 that each household be self-sufficient in food. In 1948, for example, at a time when food was short and cash relatively plentiful, the District Commissioner prohibited the importation of food into Lushoto District because it would undermine self-sufficiency. The reliance on women's subsistence labour was continuous in British Tanganyika, but most extreme during World War II when all non-salaried men in Tanga Province were classified as either fit for military service, fit to be sisal cutters, or for estate work, with only the weakest to remain for food production.[11] The great changes since that time have led to important inequalities among village women, with an impact on their work time. But on the whole the gender-based division of labour and authority established in the colonial period continues.

The high-colonial economic system placed the burdens of food production on women without providing substantial help with medical care. During the 1930s Usambara District (later Lushoto District) had nine or ten so-called 'Tribal Dressers', each with minimal education, each expected to spend no more than two hours a day on medical care.[12] The Medical Officer at the District Hospital was responsible for all public health needs and served as a private physician to European settlers. He was expected to provide medical care for a hundred thousand Africans in the time left over. Tanganyika's Government encouraged missionaries to fill the gaps left by Government medicine. But most of the missionaries in Lushoto District were Germans whose efforts were interrupted by two World Wars.

Except for limited areas near Government or mission hospitals, healers-at-home provided the only effective health care system for the population of north-eastern Tanganyika until the 1950s. Most people of the region would probably have preferred the widest range of options – to retain home and travelling healers, but to gain access to biomedical care. In 1947 local peasant leaders complained, as part of their case for removing the Paramount Chief, that 'Usambara has no midwifery. Shambaa women give birth in circumstances of great difficulty. Many Shambaa women die in childbirth. Why is there no special place for instruction in midwifery?'[13]

Health services in north-eastern Tanganyika expanded during the last decade of colonial rule, and have continued to expand even more rapidly since then. By 1978 Tanga Region had 12 hospitals with 1629 beds, 220 dispensaries, and 12 health centres (Tanzania, Ministry of Health 1979). In addition, in the years since the Arusha Declaration of 1967, the creation of villages as legal instruments of socialism and development has made it possible for local people to have a significant impact on their own conditions of health for the first time since the German conquest. Villages can take measures to improve sanitation, to establish co-operative child care or child feeding arrangements, or to improve water supplies. The great value of voluntary villages as creative institutions has been obscured by the disruptions attendant on forced villagisation in some regions, and by the economic crisis of the late 1970s and early 1980s.

At the same time Government health authorities have tried, in ways described by Dr. Semali in this volume, to establish links with popular healers. The National Union of Traditional Healers had a brief troubled life. The Faculty of Medicine at the University of Dar es Salaam established a Traditional Medicine Research Unit in 1974, with its strongest emphasis on clinical trials and chemical analysis of local medicines. In addition, the Ministry of Youth and National Culture has organised seminars for popular healers, with the intention of learning about local remedies and opening discussion between hospital and popular practitioners.

Government policy directed specifically towards popular healing – whether initiated by the University, the Ministry of Health, or the Ministry of Youth and National Culture – has not had any fundamental impact on the shape of medical practice. Profound Government-sponsored changes have emerged instead from villagisation, and from general health policy, especially in building a network of hospitals, health centres, dispensaries, and village health posts all across the country.

Government health institutions place a high value on youth and education. They have the practical effect in the northeast, and undoubtedly in the country as a whole, of excluding the older men and women who give much of the actual health advice and provide much of the health care. The older men and women are not being harmed by their exclusion. Their system of health care is preserved outside the formal governmental structure. But Government health education and public health practices are being weakened, because the old people who are most influential in forming village health opinion are not consulted.

The institutions of local health care and local government have been changing quite rapidly. I will therefore describe institutions as they existed in 1979–80. More recent Government actions have shown awareness of the problems, and some improvements are being made within the constraints imposed by the difficult economic situation.

Maternal and child health clinics are among the most important instruments of Government health education at the village level. These clinics tend to be located at centres of curative care so that mothers who bring their children for treatment are also encouraged to chart the nutritional status of their children, and to improve child care and child nutrition. In 1978 13% of dispensaries in mainland Tanzania had MCH aides, as did 59% of health centres, and 52.7% of hospitals (Tanzania, Ministry of Health 1979, p. 126). Since many maternal and child health clinics travel in a regular circuit, from village to village, the actual contact with the rural population is probably somewhat higher than these figures indicate. In the village we studied, the MCH had a substantial impact. Well over 70% of village children had received many of their immunisations. Most mothers saved MCH growth charts for their younger children.

MCH organisation, however, appears to assume a division between productive and reproductive activities more characteristic of the upper middle class in nineteenth century Europe than of peasants in twentieth century Tanzania. The MCH aides are young women, and MCH patrons are assumed to be young mothers who devote their attention to infants and children. In the actual case, however, the young mothers care profoundly for their children but must spend most hours of their day farming and carrying firewood, with some time spent in cooking. Their children are often cared for by other mothers, by young children, and by older women. The rainy months, the time of the year when food supplies are low, when labour demands on young women are the highest, and when illnesses among the children are especially frequent (see Chambers, Longhurst and Pacey 1981), are the months when women can least afford the time to attend MCH, but are most in need. I asked the great majority of women in the village about their experience at MCH clinics. More attended for brief periods and then gave up. A small minority continued. In a number of cases the young mother could not attend and sent the child's grandmother or aunt in her place. The older women, acknowledged village experts, found it intolerable to be given brusque instruction on child care by school leavers. In most cases the old women left, did not return, and instructed young mothers not to return. Young women in the village continue to get most advice on child rearing from older women, and advice for the treatment of sick children from older male *waghanga*. The older people maintain a separate health care system largely unseen by the Ministry of Health.[14]

Conflict between health policy and the facts of Tanzanian production and reproduction can also be seen in the experience of village health workers and in health planning by villages. It has been impossible for the Tanzanian Government to provide every village with a dispensary. The village health post was therefore planned as a stopgap. Each village was encouraged to send two school leavers, one young man and one young woman, for training at the district hospital. The Government would then provide a supply of simple medicines, and the village would pay the health workers. We saw from our own experience in training health workers (confirmed by reports from other places) that village pay was irregular, that young men after school and before marriage are at a time of life when they need to work hard to earn money for marriage and for establishing a family, and that mature adults look for health advice to those who are older. The village health workers appear to be trying to establish an alternative to the medicine of the elders, not a supplement to it. This is the conclusion I draw from the responses to a survey of village health workers by the Ministry of Health: 'All said they do not cooperate with the traditional healer' (Tanzania, Ministry of Health 1980, p. 129).

Finally there is the question of public recognition of healers. The healers who have come to the attention of friendly Government authorities have been those with distinctive specialities who travel widely, not the stay-at-home village healers who provide diagnosis and therapy at low cost. For officials who want to preserve national culture, or to find medicines of practical value, specialised healers often seem to hold the most promise, as in the case of Kabwere and Partners Herbalists of Moshi, who announced to the press that they possessed a herbal cure for cancer.[15] The National Union of Traditional Healers and its offshoot organisations have mostly been led and staffed by healers who travel, who practise in towns, and who do not specialise in caring for relatives and immediate neighbours. The Planning Office of the Ministry of Youth and National Culture argued, in a very thoughtful seminar document for traditional healers, that old men who provide therapy in the villages where they had always lived have no need of Government recognition, for they are known and their work is trusted.[16]

Those people who provide the most important rural services on a day-to-day basis are neither hospital workers nor famous and specialised popular healers; they are old people with medical expertise who live and practise in their own villages. They have not been pushing towards professional recognition because they do not use medicine as a path to wealth, and are protected by their patients' trust. The danger is that increasing Government control by hospital-based healers along with greater recognition of the most prominent popular healers will leave this special set of locally-based practitioners more vulnerable than they have ever been. If popular healers were licensed, some of these local practitioners might be left out, not recognised, or unable to pay licensing fees. This would be a loss for the health of the entire nation.

Midwives, stay-at-home *waghanga*, and older women who care for the sick could play an important role in the hospital-based health system in three ways, while continuing the services they already provide within their villages. They could, first of all, discuss with orthodox medical authorities ways to improve their work at referring patients to hospital. It would be useful, for example, for them to distinguish between malaria, which is usually treated within the village, and meningitis – a disease for which hospital care is effective and delay dangerous. Second, popular healers could use their influence to introduce new techniques into everyday prevention and cure. They would be happy, I am sure, to learn that oral rehydration saves the lives of young children with diarrhoea. Third, the old people could help to improve government health services. The *waghanga* and midwives understand the failings of clinics, dispensaries, and hospitals. They know, for example, when bad manners are driving women away from maternal and child health clinics, or when careless diagnosis is making a dispensary unpopular. They lack only the authority to set matters right. Each dispensary or clinic needs to have local old people, who themselves provide health care, serving as the community's advocates with enough authority to demand changes.

Giving the old people authority *over* health professionals is crucial. They are the ones who actually decide on the course of therapy in most illnesses. If health workers see them as powerless and ignorant recipients of expert advice they will continue to use the clinics and hospitals in the way they know best, but will be unable to shape these institutions to meet community needs. Village work for community health, if it is to advance, will have to acknowledge the responsibility, authority, and knowledge of older women, midwives, and stay-at-home *waghanga*. Learning from the *wazee* (the old people) is, after all, one of the central ethical requirements of village life.

*This material is based upon work supported by the National Science Foundation under Grant No. BNS–7825336. Any opinions, findings, and conclusions or recommendations expressed in this publication are those of the author and do not necessarily reflect the views of the National Science Foundation.

NOTES

1 On professionalisation as a struggle for control over medical resources see Unschuld 1979, p. 4. On cultural authority see Starr 1982, pp. 13–17.

2 For the description of someone who has had smallpox as an immune *kungwi*, see LangHeinrich 1921. On rites for other epidemics see Karasek 1911, p. 203. The treatment of smallpox and ill-omened births at the coast is described in Erhardt's

journal, Church Missionary Society archives, CA5/09, 5 April and 24 July 1854.

3 On the killing of sorcerers see Krapf 1964, vol 2, p. 110, and Church Missionary Society archives, Erhardt's journal, CA5/09, 21 September 1853. Karasek 1923–24, p. 27 discusses rites for the control of epidemics. Locust control is described by Gleiss 1898. All of these issues, along with rain and warfare, are the subject of Feierman 1972.

4 Bethell Mission archives, Tagebuch Neu Bethel, 22 January 1894.

5 *Usambara Post*, 11 December 1909.

6 For a general description of this process see Ford 1971; Kjekshus 1977 relies heavily on Ford, whose argument he extends beyond trypanosomiasis.

7 For a similar process in Kenya see Dawson 1979.

8 *Daily News*, 15 September 1973; for another case see 'Eight Held for Causing Chaos', *Daily News*, 14 May 1980.

9 *Nachrichten aus der ostafrikanischen Mission*, vol. 7, 1906, p. 111. For further evidence of the same pattern see Dale 1896, p. 229; Markus 1902; Riese n.d.; Tagebuch Neu Bethel 10 March 1894; Wohlrab n.d., p. 47.

10 *Usambara-Post*, 29 August 1908, 'Missionen und Arbeiterfrage'. H. Dupré n.d., p. 63. Iliffe 1979, p. 153. *Nachrichten aus der ostafrikanischen Mission*, September 1905, p. 140; October 1907, pp. 174–75; January 1912, pp. 20–23. Tanzania National Archives (TNA), German Files, XI A3, Wilhelmstal, Bezirksamtmann Meyer to Trappists at Gare, 18 June 1903.

11 TNA (Tanzania National Archives) 72/62/6, Lushoto District Annual Reports 1948, 211G. 72/3/1a Lushoto, Increased Production by Natives, Vol. I. For a fuller account see Feierman 1982.

12 TNA 4/706/1 Volume I, PC's Office Tanga. Medical: Tribal Dispensaries, 1929–1938.

13 'Maulizo Mbele ya Bwana'. TNA 72/44/16 Lushoto Native Affairs. General Usambara Associations.

14 Tobisson (1980) described a similar situation in Mara Region. Aged midwives there provide care without payment, would like further training, but do not get it.

15 One example of a list of specialised healers is the one compiled at the Lushoto District Office of the Ministry of Youth and National Culture. Description of the herbal cancer cure is in *Daily News*, 5 June 1980. 'Kabwere' is a name used by witch-finders; healers who travel widely collecting large sums.

16 The planning document was provided for a seminar at Korogwe, document dated 1 December 1979.

REFERENCES

Cameron, Donald C., (1939), *My Tanganyika Service, and some Nigeria*. London.

Chambers, R., Longhurst, R., and Pacey, A., (eds.), (1981), *Seasonal Dimensions to Rural Poverty*. London.

Chavunduka, G. L., (1978), *Traditional Healers and the Shona Patient*. Gwelo.

Cory, Hans, (1951), 'Sambaa Law and Custom.' Typescript. Revised and edited by E. B. Dobson. Cory Collection, University of Dar es Salaam.

Dale, Rev. Godfrey, (1896), 'An Account of the Principal Customs and habits of the Natives inhabiting the Bondei Country, compiled mainly for the use of European missionaries in the country,' *Journal of the Anthropological Institute*, 25, p. 181–239.

Dawson, Marc, (1979), 'Smallpox in Kenya, 1880–1920', *Social Science and Medicine*, 13B, 4, pp. 245–50.
Dupre, H., (n.d.), 'Land and Volk un Usambara: Selbstgeschautes und Selbsterlebtes.' Manuscript. Bethel Mission Archives, Bethel bei Bielefeld.
Feierman, Elizabeth Karlin, (1981), 'Alternative Medical Services in Rural Tanzania: A Physician's View', *Social Science & Medicine*, 15B, 3, pp. 399–404.
Feierman, Steven, (1972), 'Concepts of Sovereignty among the Shambaa and their Relation to Political Action'. D.Phil. thesis, Oxford.
——(1974), *The Shambaa Kingdom: A History*. Madison; Wisconsin.
——(1981), 'Therapy as a System in Action in Northeastern Tanzania', *Social Science Medicine*, 15B, 3, pp. 353–60.
——(1982), 'Production and Reproduction in Lushoto District.' History Seminar Paper, University of Dar es Salaam.
Ford, John, (1971), *The Role of Trypanosomiases in African Ecology*. Oxford.
——(1979), 'Ideas which have influenced attempts to solve the problems of African trypanosomiases', *Social Science and Medicine*, 13B, 4, pp. 269–75.
Gleiss, F., (1898), 'Magili, der Herr der Heuschrecken', *NaoM*, 12, 8, pp. 128–30.
Hosbach, W., (1911), 'Eine Geistergeschichte', *NaoM*, 25, 11, pp. 209–13.
Hughes, Charles C., and Hunter, John M., (1970), 'Disease and "Development" in Africa', *Social Science and Medicine*, 3, pp. 443–93.
Iliffe, John, (1979), *A Modern History of Tanganyika*. Cambridge, England.
Janzen, John M., (1978), *The Quest for Therapy in Lower Zaire*. Berkeley.
——(1982), *Lemba, 1650–1930: A Drum of Affliction in Africa and the New World*. New York.
Janzen, John M., and Feierman, Steven, (eds.), (1979), 'The Social History of Disease and Medicine in Africa'. Special issue of *Social Science and Medicine*, 13B, 4.
Janzen, John M., and Prins, Gwyn, (1981), 'Causality and Classification in African Medicine and Health', Special issue of *Social Science and Medicine*, 15B, 3.
Johanssen, E., and Döring, P., (1914–15), 'Das Leben der Schambala, beleuchtet durch ihre Sprichwörter', *Zeitschrift für Kolonialsprachen*, pp. 137–50, 190–226, 306–18.
Karasek, A., 'Beiträge zur Kenntnis der Waschambaa', (1911), *Baessler Archiv*, pp. 155–222; (1922), *Baessler Archiv*, pp. 69–131; (1918–22), *Baessler Archiv*, pp. 56–98; (1923–24), *Baessler Archiv*, pp. 1–53.
Kjekshus, Helge, (1977), *Ecology Control and Economic Development in East African History*. Berkeley.
Krapf, Johann Ludwig, (1964), *Reisen in Ostafrika*. Stuttgart.
LangHeinrich, F., (1921), *Schambala-Wörterbuch*. Hamburg.
Larson, L. E., (1973), 'Witchcraft Eradication Sequences among the Peoples of the Ulanga District, Tanzania.' History Seminar Paper, University of Dar es Salaam.
——(1976), 'Problems in the Study of Witchcraft Eradication Movements in Southern Tanzania.' *Ufahamu*, 6, 3, pp. 88–100.
Maier, D., (1979), 'Nineteenth Century Asante Medical Practices', *Comparative Studies in Society and History*, 21, pp. 63–81.
Markus, (1902), 'Markus und sein Tagebuch.' *NaoM*, 16, 7, pp. 98–100.
Ranger, T. O., (1966), 'Witch-Craft Eradication Movements in Central and Southern Tanzania and their Connection with the Maji Maji Rising.' History Seminar Paper, University of Dar es Salaam.
Riese, F., (n.d.), 'Die Opfer der Schambala'. Manuscript, Bethel Mission Archives, Bethel bei Bielefeld.
Schoffeleers, J. M., (ed.), (1978), *Guardians of the Land: essays on Central African*

territorial cults. Gwelo.

Starr, Paul, (1982), *The Social Transformation of American Medicine*. New York.

Tanner, R. E. S., (1970), *The Witch Murders in Sukumaland: a sociological commentary*. Scandinavian Institute of African Studies, *Crime in East Africa* No. 4. Uppsala.

Tanzania, Ministry of Health, (1979), *Inventory of Health Facilities 1978*. Dar es Salaam.

Tanzania, Ministry of Health, (1980), *Evaluation of the Health Sector 1979*. Dar es Salaam.

Tanzania, Ofisi ya Waziri Mkuu na Makamu wa Pili wa Rais. (1975), *Sheria ya Kuandikisha Vijiji na Vijiji vya Ujamaa*. Dar es Salaam.

Thomas, Keith, (1971), *Religion and the Decline of Magic: studies in popular beliefs in sixteenth- and seventeenth-century England*. Harmondsworth, Middlesex.

Tobisson, Eva, (1980), *Women, Work, Food and Nutrition in Nyamwigura Village, Mara Region, Tanzania*. Report No. 548, Tanzania Food and Nutrition Centre, Dar es Salaam.

Unschuld, Paul U., (1979), *Medical Ethics in Imperial China*. Berkeley.

Wohlrab, K., (n.d.), 'Die Religion der Schambala und die christliche Missionspredigt'. Manuscript, Bethel Mission Archives, Bethel bei Bielefeld.

Wohlrab, P., (1913), 'Ein neuer Dämonen Kultus in Usambara', *NaoM*, 27, pp. 186–89.

Abbreviation:

NaoM Nachrichten aus der ostafrikanischen Mission. Berlin, 1887–1914.

11 D. D. O. Oyebola

NATIONAL MEDICAL POLICIES IN NIGERIA

It has been recognised for quite some time now in most developing countries that if they are to meet the WHO minimum acceptable standard of health personnel to population ratio, alternative forms of health care delivery system, apart from Western medicine, must be sought. Historical, cultural and sociological factors have consistently identified traditional medicine as this alternative source of health care delivery. Indeed, it is known that traditional medicine provides health care for about 90% of the rural population of many developing countries (WHO 1975). The rural population constitutes up to 80% of the population of Nigeria (Olatunbosun 1975). Apart from the factors of availability, accessibility and cultural acceptability, the other advantages of traditional medicine (TM) have been well documented. The problems and prospects of utilisation of traditional medicine in Nigeria have also been examined (Ademuwagun, 1975, 1976). The purpose of this paper is to focus attention on the recent attempts by the Federal and State governments, practitioners of Western medicines and herbalists' associations in Nigeria to involve traditional healers in the health care delivery system. This chapter hopes to draw attention to how the question of whether to grant official recognition to the traditional healers or not has been politicised.

SOURCES OF HEALTH CARE DELIVERY IN NIGERIA

Nigeria is a medically pluralistic society. Thus, when they fall ill, there are many sources from which Nigerians can seek help. These sources are the hospitals, health centres, dispensaries, pharmacies, patent medicine stores, traditional healers, spiritual churches (as typified by the Cherubim and Seraphim Church, Christ Apostolic Church, Celestial Church of Christ and many Evangelistic groups), Mallams (Muslim priests/healers), herbal stores (usually located in the local markets) and street hawkers. Very often, the health consumers 'shop around' the different sources of health care delivery until they find solutions to their problems. The pattern of utilisation of the different health care services and the factors that determine which service patients choose in various illness conditions have been documented (Ademuwagun, 1976, 1977). Although this chapter will focus mainly on Western-trained doctors who practise in hospitals and in health centres and on the traditional healers, a brief comment on the healing practice of the Aladura Churches is made. This is considered necessary because some scholars regard the healing activities of the Aladura Churches as part of traditional medicine, a view with which this writer disagrees.

FAITH HEALERS

Although, there are some similarities between the healing practice of the Aladura churches and traditional healers as Turner (1967) and Omoyajowo (1982) have pointed out, there are however marked differences in the two systems of healing. Many of these differences were highlighted by Turner (1967) and Omoyajowo (1982). Specifically, in Omoyajowo's reference to the third clause of the by-laws and regulations of the Aladura Praying Band Section's Memorandum and Articles of Association, the following healing methods are prohibited by the Aladura:

> Members shall neither keep nor use Shigidi (clay idols used in sending bad medicine to kill people); sokuro (medicine hung up with intention to prevent death); Tira, Igbadi and Onde (charm and Talisman sewn in leather or parchment put around waist or neck for self protection); Arimole (burying of medicine in the ground for self-protection); Epe or Ase (Imprecation); Apeta (Power used to cause poisonous boils or carbuncles); Oruka ere (ring soaked in bad medicine for slapping the face or shaking the hands of foes); Akaraba (charms used to hypnotize and to cause mischief); Agadagodo (juju padlocks . . .); Gbere sinsin (skin marks by incision with juju powder for prevention against witchcraft or snake bite); . . . Madarikan (medicine or charms trusted upon as a means of protection against enemies); Agbelepota (medicines or charms to kill enemies unawares); . . . Doctor's treatment is not disallowed.

Omoyajowo (1982) also noted that clause 5 of the same by-laws prohibits consultation of *babalawo*, *Ifa* priests, soothsayers and Mohammedan priests, especially for purposes of knowing the future. However, none of the sections of the memorandum of association is averse to the 'judicious use of native herbs, the engagement of medical practitioners or doctors or the use of patent medicines or other drugs'. Thus, the above prohibited methods of healing for the Aladura Church and the WHO definition of traditional healers below (WHO 1976a) show that in spite of similarities in some aspects, traditional medicine is not the same as spiritual healing as practised by the Aladura churches. My field experience with the two healing systems concurs with this conclusion. This conclusion is consistent with the view of Omoyajowo (1982) who stated: 'The Cherubim and Seraphim, having repudiated the traditional religion, has rejected most of the traditional means of healing.'

WESTERN MEDICINE AND HEALTH CARE IN NIGERIA

The beginning of scientific medicine in Nigeria dates back roughly to 1419, that is, with the advent of the Portuguese traders (Schram 1971). Medical practice at the time was largely empirical and was little different from traditional African care. There was no organised medical service for Nigeria in the first half of the nineteenth century. Apart from military hospitals, which catered primarily for the interest of sailors of the naval squadrons, the first hospital in Nigeria, the forerunner of the Lagos General Hospital, was built in 1873. The second hospital to be built in Nigeria was by the Roman Catholic Mission. This was the Sacred Heart Hospital at Abeokuta, completed in 1895. Apart from a tiny makeshift temporary civil hospital built in Asaba in 1888, government itself did not erect its own full hospital, St. Margaret's Hospital in Calabar, until 1898 (Schram 1971). Thus, before the missionaries brought 'modern medicine' into Nigeria towards the end of the nineteenth century, delivery of health care in Nigeria was the sole responsibility of the traditional healers. Even today, as we move through the ninth decade of the twentieth century, most of the 80% rural population in Nigeria have no available alternative to the traditional healers for health care. The few medical doctors (when related to the population they are meant to serve) that are available prefer working in the cities and shun rural postings. Osuntokun (1975) noted that 70% of the doctors in Nigeria live in seven cities (Kano, Zaria, Enugu, Benin, Ibadan, Lagos and Ife) with a population of roughly 5–6% of the country's population. The majority of the remaining 30% stay in the other large towns leaving the rural majority with very few doctors. The uneven distribution of doctors is aggravated by the absence of basic amenities like piped water, electricity and good access roads to many of the rural areas. The introduction of a compulsory one-year national service in 1973 in Nigeria by the then Federal Military Government solved a little of the problem of acceptance of rural posting by doctors. The National Youth Service Corps Scheme (NYSC) provides for a compulsory one-year service to the nation by all graduates of institutions of higher learning, including doctors and pharmacists. Through this scheme, it has been possible to send some doctors to the rural areas after the one-year internship. The number of doctors available for this scheme is however too few to cope with the demands of the rural majority; moreover, these doctors invariably return to the cities after the year's national service. All these point to the need to explore alternative sources of health care, especially for the rural majority.

TRADITIONAL MEDICINE AND HEALTH CARE

It is common knowledge to medical practitioners in Africa that many diseases that afflict the population can be avoided or treated by simple methods applied by people, who, while not specially qualified, are accessible and available, particularly in rural areas. The traditional healers can fulfil this role adequately in the villages and hamlets. Moreover, they live and work among the people and have profound knowledge of the dynamics of the people's culture and their environment.

THE WORLD HEALTH ORGANISATION AND TRADITIONAL MEDICINE

In spite of the sanction of long usage, the exact definition of who a 'traditional healer' is has not been easy to establish. While individuals who refer to traditional healers know exactly whom they refer to, there is no universally accepted definition of who a traditional healer is. However, the World Health Organization (WHO 1976a) defined a traditional healer as

> Someone who is recognised by the community in which he lives as competent to provide health care by using vegetable, animal and mineral substances and certain other methods based on the social, cultural and religious background as well as the prevailing knowledge, attitudes and beliefs regarding physical, mental and social well-being and the causation of disease and disability in the community.

This committee gave the following synonyms for a traditional healer: 'Traditional therapist, healer, practitioner of traditional medicine, fetish healer . . .'

The fact that this list of synonyms was not closed emphasises the awareness that there could be great variation in the titles by which the traditional healer may be identified by various persons. As long as his roles fall within the scope of the above definition, which seems sufficiently comprehensive, regardless of slight differences in titles, the identity of the traditional healer within this framework is easy.

The WHO, through its various expert committees, has repeatedly focused attention on the importance of traditional healers in health care delivery in the African sub-region. Thus, the WHO executive board, at its 57th session in November 1975, produced a paper on 'Health Manpower development: training and utilization of traditional healers and their collaboration with health care delivery systems' (WHO 1975). Also, the WHO regional committee for Africa at its 26th session in Kampala in September 1976, deliberated and produced a paper on: 'Traditional Medicine and its role in development of Health Services in Africa' (WHO 1976b). Also in 1976, at the Regional Office for Africa in Brazzaville, a group of experts produced Afro Technical Reports Series Number 1, entitled 'African Traditional Medicine' (WHO 1976c). Another group of WHO experts also met in Geneva in December 1977 and produced Technical Report Series No. 622, entitled 'The Promotion and Development of Traditional Medicine' (WHO 1978). The latter committee of experts maintained that all medicine is modern in so far as it is satisfactorily directed towards the common goal of providing health care, despite the setting in time, place, and culture. They also observed that the essential differences among the various systems of medicine arose not from the difference in the goal or effects, but rather from the cultures of the peoples who practise the different systems. They further noted that traditional medicine is nothing new, since it has always been an integral part of all human cultures. The main reason traditional medicine in some developing countries has not made substantial progress as compared to Western medicine, they maintained, is because traditional medicine has not exploited the rapid discoveries of science and technology for its own development unlike medicine as practised in the industrialised countries which keeps abreast of scientific and technological innovations to the extent that it is often exclusively referred to as modern medicine.

The common themes identifiable in all the WHO deliberations on TM referred to above are that, apart from attempting definitions of TM and traditional healers and making some attempts at classifying the various categories of healers, they were unanimous that TM provides health care for 70–80% of the population of developing countries. They tried to identify the 'positive' and 'negative' aspects of TM. They emphasised the need for better understanding and mutual respect between practitioners of Western medicine and traditional healers. The need to improve the quality of health care provided by traditional healers through further training was stressed. It was also the consensus of opinion of these experts that TM had a good potential in drug research and the need to utilise traditional healers in national health care systems with a relationship in the form of co-operation or integration between practitioners of Western medicine and traditional healers was highlighted. Each of the reports of these expert bodies contained 'recommendations' or 'proposed approach' to the achievement of the latter objective, i.e. utilisation and integration of TM in national health care systems.

For the purpose of this paper, the most comprehensive recommendation with respect to integration was that contained in the Technical Report Series Number 622 (WHO 1978). This recommendation provided for four levels at which action can be taken to effect integration of traditional healers. These are at the international, national, professional and consumer levels. The recommendations most pertinent to the present paper are those that relate to the national level. It was recommended that national policies should be formulated; overt recognition should be given to the existing systems of traditional medicine; legal recognition and social equality, employment opportunities and mobility should be provided by TM; all systems of medicine should be institutionalised, and budgetary support should be secured for them.

The rest of this paper will be devoted to the efforts the various governments in Nigeria, practitioners of Western medicine and traditional healers' associations have made to promote utilisation of TM in the National health care team. Special attention will be focused on recent political developments and their effects on TM.

NIGERIA FROM INDEPENDENCE TO AUGUST 1983

The early history of Nigeria is sufficiently documented in the work of Ikime (1980) and need not be repeated here. A brief account of her political history from Independence to date is, however, pertinent as background to the theme of this essay.

Nigeria became independent on 1 October 1960. She was ruled by a civilian government from independence till January 1966, when the civilian rule was terminated in a military *coup d'état*. Nigeria was under military rule for thirteen years (January 1966 to September 1979) including a thirty-month period of civil war between 1967 and 1970. Although both the civilian and military governments were aware that most Nigerians seek the help of traditional healers when they are ill (Johnson 1973), not much was done to promote the utilisation of TM in health care delivery. It is an open secret however that many of the top politicians and military rulers engaged the services of renowned traditional healers to procure charms and all sorts of traditional medicines which they believed would guarantee them success in their political ambition in the case of politicians or protection at the battle front or elsewhere in the case of soldiers. The traditional healers tried to get government support by organising symposia, and leading delegations to top government functionaries, especially during the military regime. Their efforts were however attended by little success. Neither the government nor the scientific doctors gave serious thought to the possibility of bringing traditional healers into the health care delivery team.

When the ban on political activities was lifted in 1978, five political parties fulfilled the conditions for registration and were thus registered to contest the 1979 elections. Provision of health care was one of the important campaign issues for the election. Indeed, one of the political parties had, as one of its main programmes, provision of free health service for all the citizens. During this period, prominent traditional healers became political activists in the different parties. Apart from their traditional role of supplying protective 'charms' to top politicians, they helped to canvas for votes for their parties. Available information indicates that a few of these healers who are literate got important political appointments at the local government or state level after the elections. This marked the turning point for the fortunes of traditional medicine in Nigeria.

Although the political party that promised free health service for all citizens did not win the Presidency, it won governorships and the majority of the seats in the houses of assembly of some states. This party nonetheless decided to go ahead with the execution of its electoral promise of free health service to all citizens in the states it controlled. Apart from limited funds, a major constraint on the fulfilment of the promise of 'free health' scheme was manpower. This political party was therefore to the forefront of efforts to explore utilisation of alternative sources of health manpower, including traditional healers.

Hence, shortly after power was handed over to an elected civilian government in 1979, the move to use traditional healers gathered momentum. Motions to support this move were tabled in some state houses of assembly. In arguing in favour of such motions on the floor of parliament, it was not unusual to find television news coverage of assembly proceedings showing a member with a profound Traditional Medicine background rehearsing long incantations in support of his case, to the approval and ovation from many of his colleagues. Lagos State was the first to pass the traditional medicine bill and set up a traditional medicine board. Membership of the board is made up largely of traditional healers with Chief J. Lambo, a traditional healer, as chairman. Oyo State had recently passed a similar bill called the Advisory Board on Traditional Medical Practice Law, 1983. The bill also provided for majority representation of traditional healers on the Board. The composition of these boards is consistent with the views of Oyebola (1981) and Bibeau (1981).

In 1981, the question of the adoption of a national policy on utilisation of traditional medicine was discussed by the National Council on Health (NCH). The latter body is a council whose membership includes the Federal Minister for Health, the Commissioner for Health from each of the 19 states in Nigeria and the Chief Health Officers of the Federal and state governments. Available information indicates that the NCH unanimously agreed that traditional healers should be utilised in health care delivery. The council further agreed that a national traditional healers' board with representatives of the Federal and state governments (mostly traditional healers) should be established. Each state was urged to pass a traditional healers bill and set up a traditional healers' board. The state boards were to work closely with the national traditional medicine board. The NCH set up a committee to work out the details of implementing these decisions. The first and perhaps the most crucial is that since most traditional healers are illiterates and speak solely their local language, there was the problem of what language to adopt in the deliberations of traditional healers who come from different ethnic groups in the country. What will be the language to use at meetings? How will healers who speak their local dialects understand each other at meetings? In what language will minutes of meetings be kept and how will it be possible to circulate this to members for checking for correctness or making amendments before proposing ratification? There are no easy answers to these questions. The role of the traditional healers' associations in these developments will be discussed later. The NCH considered it appropriate to find out the reaction of the Western-trained doctors to the plan to use traditional healers. Thus, the two bodies that control the practice of Western medicine in Nigeria – The Nigeria Medical Association (NMA) and the Nigerian Medical Council (NMC) – were asked for comments on this proposal. It was the view of the NCH that the issue of traditional medicine should be studied carefully before final decisions are taken.

The NCH is similar to the General Medical Council (GMC) of Great Britain while the NMA is similar to the British Medical Association (and presumably to equivalent professional bodies in other countries of the world). The composition and functions of the NMC and the NMA are similar to those of GMC and BMA respectively. There is abundant literature on the GMC and BMA which makes detailed description of the NMC and NMA superfluous.

Another important indicator of the commitment of the Federal Government in Nigeria to the promotion of traditional medicine was a decision in the Senate to set up a Senate Committee on health and social services. The committee was given the responsibility of finding a lasting solution to the problem of the health care delivery system in Nigeria and the formulation of a national drug policy. In pursuance of its assigned duties, this committee, through paid advertisements in the national dailies, called on members of the public to submit memoranda on traditional medicine that would assist it to arrive at the best recommendations on the role traditional medicine should play in national health care delivery. The committee undertook a nationwide tour and individuals or groups were encouraged to give oral evidence before its members.

From the foregoing, it is obvious that the Federal and state Governments in Nigeria have been very active in recent times in their attempts to legalise and utilise practitioners of traditional medicine in the health care delivery team. This posture is consistent with the WHO (1978) recommendation of 'formulation of national policies' on traditional medicine. Promising as these recent developments may appear, the Federal and state Governments are still a long way off from taking the ultimate decision to legalise and utilise traditional healers in the country's health care delivery team.

WESTERN-TRAINED DOCTORS AND NATIONAL POLITICS

Some of the earliest Nigerians to be educated studied medicine. The first set of Nigerian doctors who have been appropriately described as 'Nigerian pioneers of modern medicine' (Adeloye 1977) were James Africanus Beale Horton (1858), William Broughton Davies (1858), Nathaniel King (1879), Obadiah Johnson (1884), John Randle (1888), Orisadipe Obasa (1891), Sodeinde Leigh-Sodipe (1892) and Oguntola Sapara (1895). All these men qualified in medicine in the nineteenth century in the years shown in parenthesis. Many of these men, apart from having successful medical practices on their return from the United Kingdom where they studied medicine, also became famous as political luminaries. Africanus Horton wrote extensively on West African politics; John Randle, after a short stay in the colonial medical service in Lagos from 1888 to 1893, took up politics. He, together with Dr. Orisadipe Obasa, founded the People's Union in 1908. This was the first political organisation in Lagos and indeed, in Nigeria (Adeloye, 1974, 1977). Obadiah Johnson and John Randle served in the Legislative Council of Lagos on the invitation of the colonial governors of their time. Thus the early Western-trained doctors in Nigeria, apart from being pioneers in medicine, were also pioneers in political consciousness and in the formation of political parties. Since these early times, Western-trained doctors have maintained their leadership position in their society and have remained very influential politically. Up to the time Nigeria attained independence, such was the political pre-eminence of the Western-trained doctors that whenever the colonial governor was away from the country, the Chief Medical Adviser to the government acted as governor.

Since independence, Western-trained doctors have continued to show keen interest in National politics. Some of them have held important political appointments. Indeed, a Western-trained doctor is one of the state governors in the present civilian administration, while others hold ministerial, adviser or commissioner appointments. The views of the Nigerian Medical Association (NMA) continue to be important in influencing government decisions on matters relating to health care delivery. It is necessary to emphasise the latter so that the contribution of the NMA to the current debate on traditional medicine can be placed in proper perspective.

THE ROLE OF WESTERN-TRAINED DOCTORS IN PROMOTION OF TRADITIONAL MEDICINE (TM)

For several years, the practitioners of scientific medicine in Nigeria have looked down on traditional medicine (Ademuwagun 1975). While a few scientific doctors have acknowledged that traditional healers have a role to play in health care delivery, several have not only felt that they have no role to play, but that their practice is positively harmful. The WHO experts have recognised and stated consistently however that the two medical systems can be complementary in health care delivery.

It would appear however that the scientific doctors have sensed the changing political climate with respect to traditional medicine since the inception of the civilian government in October 1979. In this regard, it is of interest that a major theme of the NMA conference at Ilorin in April 1980 was a symposium on 'the place of traditional medicine in basic health care delivery' in Nigeria. While many members who contributed to that symposium felt that the traditional healers could be useful in health care delivery, there was little doubt in their minds that available information on several aspects of traditional medicine was too scanty to allow for a meaningful decision at the governmental level. It was the opinion of the majority of members that recognising traditional healers at that time was like licensing killers.

Consequent to the seeking of the opinion of the NMA and the NMC by the NCH on plans to utilise traditional healers, both bodies indicated that they were not opposed to the idea. They were however of the view that it was important to know the number of healers available, and how to assess the quality of their knowledge; they also stressed the need for registration of healers, the need to know their speciality areas and that the secrecy surrounding their practice must be removed.

At the recent Senate committee hearing, contrary to speculations, the traditional healers, in seeking recognition, received the support of the NMA. In presenting the NMA's memorandum, the NMA's president said his association appreciated the services of traditional healers but warned that their herbs and drugs must be subjected to rigorous scientific analysis to identify their specific medicinal potential and potency. The NMA, in recommending government recognition of traditional medicine, said that such recognition must entail the certification of its practitioners by their local governments through the State Ministries of Health to enable them to practise only in their local government areas. The NMA advised further that traditional birth attendants, bone setters, mental health therapists and circumcision 'surgeons' should be registered following recommendation by their village heads. They suggested that herbalists, like conventional doctors, be subjected to annual inspection and renewal of registration certificates by appropriate authorities.

In addition, the NMA further recommended that all the traditional healers must attend regular refresher courses and workshops conducted in the vernacular by State Ministries of Health during which new apprentices would be identified. The NMA further suggested that new entrants must have a pass in WAEC (equivalent of Ordinary level GCE) in at least three subjects, including one science subject. The NMA further proposed that state and Federal governments should establish an Institute of Traditional Medicine with corresponding management boards to ensure a minimum of five years' training for trado-medical students. Also, they suggested establishment of research institutes in traditional medicines and encouragement of research projects on traditional medicine in Universities. Dr Adeniyi-Jones, the health management consultant to the Senate committee, was reported to have suggested that before a traditional healer is certificated, he must practise for five years, be able to read and write and keep records. He further suggested that traditional healers should not be allowed to issue death and sickness certificates yet. The NMA objected to the recognition of witches, sorcerers, extortioners, soothsayers and practitioners of homoeopathic and acupuncture medicine.

The position of the NMA is open to question. It is not the intention of this paper to discuss the merits and the demerits of the NMA recommendations to the Senate committee. The present position of the NMA however underscores the changing attitude of practitioners of scientific medicine to traditional medicine in recent times even if some of the terms on which they are recommending recognition may be considered unrealistic.

THE ROLE OF TRADITIONAL HEALERS' ASSOCIATIONS IN THE STRUGGLE FOR LEGALISATION AND INTEGRATION

Traditional healers exist in all parts of Nigeria. There is however, a dearth of information on the activities of traditional healers in most parts of Nigeria, except among the Yoruba where many studies have been carried out (Lambo 1954; Leighton *et al.* 1963; Maclean 1971; Oyebola 1977). The heterogeneous nature of Yoruba traditional healers is well recognised and attempts have been made to classify them (Margetts 1965; Maclean 1965; Odebiyi 1976; Oyebola 1980a). Oyebola (1980a) identified seven categories of traditional healers:

> Babalawo, Onisegun, Alasotele (Soothsayer); Olorisa, Awon leku-leja (traditional 'pharmacists'). Specialists such as traditional bonesetters, traditional 'psychiatrists', traditional birth attendants or midwives, the Olola and a miscellaneous group which included Afaa (mallam) and Aladura (spiritual healers).

The criteria for the classification and the functions of each category thus identified were clearly enunciated. My discussions with some traditional healers from non-Yoruba-speaking parts of Nigeria and academic colleagues from different parts of Nigeria at the University of Ibadan revealed that traditional medicine as practised in different parts of Nigeria has a lot of similarities to that of the Yoruba.

Traditional medical associations exist in all parts of Nigeria. The organisation of these associations in the major ethnic groups in Nigeria is similar to that of the Yoruba which had been previously described (Oyebola 1981). Apart from laying down some guidelines for the practice of their members, these associations are responsible for the discipline of erring members. The associations are not given financial support by the federal or state governments. Members contribute money to support their associations.

The traditional medical associations have tried to respond to the demands of improved educational, economic and political awareness in Nigeria by attempting to 'modernise' their practice. Apart from the need to keep abreast of social trends, such modernisation attempts are geared towards correcting some of the criticisms some of the elites have persistently used in opposing government recognition of their profession. Thus in order to counteract the criticism of lack of uniform standards among their members, some traditional healers' associations now issue certificates to their members (Illus. 3). This is meant to serve as accreditation of professional competence. Although the recipients of such certificates must have undergone a period of apprenticeship, the healers have no uniform way of testing professional competence. Moreover, the issuance of a certificate is not common to all healers' associations. The traditional healers have also started putting some of their medicines in bottles that are well labelled (Illus. 7). At the 'research centre' of the Amalgamation of Nigerian Medical Herbalists at Oyo Road, Ibadan, attempts have been made to manufacture tablets from traditional medicine (Illus. 7). Many of the healers' associations have tried to meet the legal provisions of the companies act by engaging lawyers who help them in drafting constitutions for their different associations (Illus. 3).

A few healers have set up traditional medicine hospitals where girls with little education are given uniforms and function as 'nurses'. Instances of traditional healers owning and using stethoscopes have been reported in a national daily. I consider the latter to be extremes of modernisation which may have serious implications for traditional medicine. The privacy in consultation which traditional medicine offers and the rich cultural heritage which enhances the therapeutic effectiveness of TM may be lost in these attempts to copy Western medicine.

My recent investigations however revealed that in most of the states in Nigeria there are several associations, with a lot of rivalry for leadership. Even factions of the same association exist in many instances. Attempts to get these healers to form a single body even at state levels have not been too successful. At the national level, in addition to local rivalry as witnessed in the states, the factors of ethnic loyalty, what language to use at meetings where mostly illiterates speaking different native languages meet, and how national officers will be elected are some of the problems that have so far not been easy to solve. It would appear that this writer, in his reply to the comments of Dr Bibeau (1981) on an article published in 1981 (Oyebola 1981) underestimated the difficulties that may be involved in forming a National Association of Traditional Healers. This is not to say that a national association is not important or desirable. Indeed, the Federal Government of Nigeria finds it difficult at the moment to discuss the various issues that need to be resolved before taking the important step of granting recognition to traditional healers because of this non-existence of a national professional herbalist association.

This non-existence of an all-embracing national professional association notwithstanding, it is necessary to emphasise that the several state traditional healers' associations and individual traditional healers have been in the forefront of canvassing for the recent changes in attitude to traditional healers. They have made their greatest impact through persistent lobbying of the politicians. Traditional healers had frequented the offices of Ministers/Commissioners for Health, Chief Medical Officers, Chief Public Health Officers at the Federal and state levels either individually or in groups soliciting support for their practice. For instance, my investigation revealed that in Ondo State, their early success at the beginning of the civilian administration in 1979 led the governor of the state to approve the opening of seven traditional medicine clinics. Squabbles among members of the association in that state and the need to monitor the performance of those clinics opened caused the government to cease such action forthwith (Akinyosoye, personal communication). In Imo State, a trado-medical research centre was opened in May 1982. The Honourable Federal Minister for Health was expected (and I learnt had agreed) to preside on the occasion. Unfortunately, he could not attend. In a speech titled 'The World will come here to learn' presented on that occasion, Chief Anyioha, a traditional healer (who is apparently well-read), said, *inter alia*, 'Imo State Ministry of Health, around September 1978, issued a circular letter calling on local government secretaries to submit names of good native doctors in their areas for integration in the state's Rural Health Care Institutions'. It has not been possible for this writer to contact all the state Ministries of Health for development on traditional medicine at the state level, but deliberations at the federal level referred to earlier seems to support a nation-wide favourable disposition to traditional medicine by state Governments.

There is perhaps no more vivid example of the traditional healers associations' role in recent developments on TM than the representation the traditional healers made to the Senate Committee on Health and Social Services. The report of that committee is yet to be submitted and many of the memoranda submitted to it are still confidential. However, on 16 June 1983, one of the national dailies carried the story 'Native doctors take their case to Senate'. The paper reported that the National Assembly, instead of its usual guests of Ministers, special Advisers, labour leaders and state agitators, played host to scores of traditional healers from all over the country who had come to seek legislative stamp for their trade which, although they have been practising it for decades, is yet to receive government recognition. The Senate Committee had a week-long hearing session with the trado-medical men before they left Lagos on a countrywide tour to take more evidence and inspect the clinics and laboratories of many of these traditional healers.

Present at the Senate hearing in Lagos, among the scores of other traditional healers all of whom addressed themselves as doctors, were Chief (Dr) J. O. Lambo, National President of Nigeria Association of Medical Herbalists (NAMH) and Chairman of Traditional Medicine Board, Lagos State, Dr H. O. T. Ajala, Secretary of the Nigeria Health Physicians, Dr J. O. Mume, based in Warri, and President of the Bendel State Trado-Medical Association, representatives of a group that identified itself as the African Medical Herbalists and the Nigerian Union of Medical Herbal Practitioners. In making his case for recognition of traditional medicine, Chief Lambo inundated the committee with the history of many trado-medical conferences he had attended in Cairo, Ghana, India, China etc. on the order of the WHO or the Federal Government. In his submission, Dr Mume, who was reported to have spoken in fluent English, suggested that the Federal government should form a National Council on traditional medicine. The council should be headed by a seasoned traditional doctor. In a tortuous memorandum, Dr Ajala prayed the Federal government to allow traditional healers to practise alongside orthodox medical doctors, establish trado-medical departments in all Colleges of Medicine and form a national research centre to investigate the nation's medicinal herbs and plants. The African Medical Herbalists, armed with their nineteen-page constitution, spoke in the same vein. The Nigerian Union of Medical Herbal Practitioners, realising the use of legal practitioners or knowing the limit of its members to convey their views vividly, hired the services of a lawyer. Even at that meeting, it was easy to notice the cold power rivalry among the various groups.

The campaign for the 1983 national elections is at its height at the time of writing this (end of June 1983). The Senate committee has not had time to write its report and submit it. The various governments are pre-occupied with their election fortunes. The traditional healers are waiting anxiously for the Senate Committee report. The practitioners of Western medicine are at least not in stiff opposition to traditional medicine being recognized as long as certain conditions, some of which were mentioned above, are met. The *Daily Times* (a national daily) of 23 June 1983 carried an article written by Professor Falaiye of the University of Lagos College of Medicine. It was entitled: 'There is nothing to quarrel over; Traditional Medicine could be an advantage'. This writer had consistently maintained the latter view (Oyebola 1980b). There is very little doubt however that the last three and a half years have witnessed a change in the attitude of government and practitioners of Western medicine to traditional medicine. It has also witnessed an intensification by traditional healers of their clamour for government recognition. The final decision on whether government will recognise and legalise traditional medicine and its practice in Nigeria is a matter for time to decide.[1]

NOTE

1 Subsequently there have been the military coups of 31 December 1983 and 26 August 1985. No nation-wide decisions have been made.

REFERENCES

Adeloye, A., (1974), 'Some early Nigerian doctors and their contribution to modern medicine in West Africa.' *Journal of Medical History*, 18, 275–93.

Adeloye, A., (ed.), (1977), *Nigerian Pioneers of Modern Medicine*. Ibadan: Ibadan University Press. See pp. 1–22.

Ademuwagun, Z. A., (1975), 'Problems and prospects of legitimatising and integrating aspects of traditional health care systems and methods with modern medicine therapy: the Igbo-Ora experience'. *Nigeria Medical Journal*, 5, pp. 185–90.

——(1976), 'The challenge of the co-existence of orthodox and traditional medicine in Nigeria'. *East African Medical Journal*, 53, pp. 21–32.

——(1977), 'Determinants of pattern and degree of utilization of health services in two divisions of western state, Nigeria'. *Israeli Journal of Medical Science*, 13, pp. 508–13.

Bibeau, G., (1981), 'Discussion on "Professional Associations, Ethics and Discipline among Yoruba traditional healers of Nigeria" ' by D. D. O. Oyebola. *Social Science and Medicine*, 15B., 94–5.

Ikime, O., (ed.), (1980), *Groundwork of Nigeria History*. Ibadan: Heinemann Educational Books for the Historical Society of Nigeria.

Johnson, His Excellency, M., (1973), Opening Speech delivered by His Excellency Brigadier Mobolaji Johnson, Military Governor of Lagos State. In: *Proceedings of the International Conference on Traditional Medical Therapy – a Critical Appraisal*, held at the University of Lagos, Akoka, Yaba, Lagos, Nigeria. 10 Dec. 1973.

Lambo, T. A., (1954), 'Observations on the role of cultural factors in paranoid psychosis among the Yoruba tribe (a study in comparative psychiatry)'. M.D. Thesis. University of Birmingham.

Leighton, A. H.; Lambo, T. A.; Hughes, C. C.; Leighton, D. C.; Murphy, J. M. and Maclin, D. B. (1963), *Psychiatric Disorder among the Yoruba*. Ithaca, New York: Cornell University Press.

Maclean, U., (1965), 'Traditional medicine and its practitioners in Ibadan, Nigeria'. *Journal of Tropical Medicine and Hygiene*, 68, pp. 237–44.

——(1971), *Magical Medicine: A Nigerian case-study*. Allen Lane, The Penguin Press.

Margetts. E. L., (1965), 'Traditional Yoruba healers in Nigeria', *Man*, 102, pp. 115–18.

Odebiyi, O. O., (1976), 'Yoruba folk medicine, its practice, research development and relation to modern therapy', *J. Pharm.*, 7, pp. 151–5.

Olatunbosun, Dupe, (1975), *Nigeria's Neglected Rural Majority*. Ibadan: Oxford University Press.

Omoyajowo, J. A., (1982), *Cherubim and Seraphim: the history of an African independent church*. New York, London, Lagos & Enugu: NOK Publishers International.

Osuntokun, B. O., (1975), 'The traditional basis of neuropsychiatric practice among the Yorubas of Nigeria', *Trop. Geog. Med.*, 27, 422–30.

Oyebola, D. D. O., (1977), 'Studies on the traditional medical care among the Yoruba of Nigeria'. M.D. Thesis, University of Ibadan.

——(1980a), 'Traditional medicine and its practitioners among the Yoruba of Nigeria: a classification', *Soc. Sci. & Med.*, 14, pp. 23–29.

——(1980b), 'Intra-natal care as practised by traditional healers/midwives of Nigeria', *Int. J. Gynaecol. Obstet.*, 18, pp. 295–99.

——(1981), 'Professional associations, ethics and discipline among Yoruba traditional healers of Nigeria', *Social Science and Medicine*, 15B, pp. 87–105.

Peel, J. D. Y., (1968), *Aladura: a religious movement among the Yoruba*. London.

Schram, R., (1971), *A History of the Nigerian Health Services*. Ibadan: University Press.

Turner, H. W., (1967), *History of an African Independent Church*. Oxford: Clarendon Press.

WHO (1975), 'Health manpower development: training and utilization of traditional healers and their collaboration with health care delivery systems'. WHO 57th Session. Paper EB57/21 Add. 2.

WHO (1976a), 'WHO Press release.' AFRO 76/0005, Regional Office for Africa, Brazzaville, March 1976.

WHO (1976b), 'Traditional medicine and its role in the development of health services in Africa.' WHO Regional Committee for Africa. 26th Session, Kampala 8–15 September 1976. Paper AFR/RC 26/TD/1.

WHO (1976c), 'African Traditional Medicine.' WHO Regional Office for Africa, Brazzaville, *Technical Report Series* No. 1.

WHO (1978), 'The promotion and development of Traditional Medicine.' WHO, Geneva, *Technical Report Series*, No. 622.

PROFESSIONAL INTERESTS AND THE CREATION OF MEDICAL KNOWLEDGE IN NIGERIA

INTRODUCTION

My interest in the role of indigenous African medicine on the continent centres on the need to analyse the relationship between occupational/ professional interests and the development of medical knowledge. The present emphasis on the professionalisation of indigenous health workers touches these two separate issues. I believe that each group of practitioners has professional interests to protect (Pearce 1982; Oyarebu 1983), and that the means used to accomplish these goals must be understood as a separate problem from that of the type or amount of knowledge at their disposal for healing. In focusing on these two issues, this paper will look at the production and dissemination of medical knowledge within the two competing systems in Nigeria. Regardless of the claims of the occupational groups, what type of knowledge is being developed and what suggestions can be made for the welfare of the consumers in the future? To accomplish this, the paper is divided into three sections. In the first, I will focus on what I consider to be important aspects of the professional competition between Western-trained practitioners and their indigenous counterparts. In this competition reference is often made to the lack of scientific knowledge within the indigenous sector. The second section will therefore compare the production and dissemination of medical knowledge within the two types of medical systems. This will be followed in the last section by a discussion on the type of medical knowledge which needs to be uncovered within the indigenous system.

PROFESSIONAL INTERESTS WITHIN MEDICINE

It is well recognised in the West that along with the clergy, the military officer and the lawyer, the physician ranks as a member of an established profession. Today the profession possesses a high degree of specialised and abstract knowledge which when applied to the problem of healing is believed to give the best service to the client. Hughes has argued that 'professionals *profess*. They profess to know better than others the nature of certain matters, and to know better than their clients what ails them or their affairs. This is the essence of the professional idea and the professional claim' (1965). While it is true that by the twentieth century the university-trained physician had emerged as the undisputed professional within the medical sector, the literature shows that the rise to the top and the legitimacy given the position came as a result of struggles with other competing groups and not just as a result of the type of knowledge the doctor possessed. The process of professionalisation involved negotiations with the State, with other groups (e.g. surgeons), as well as the ability to take advantage of certain social and economic developments occurring within Europe (technology developed during the industrial revolution, urbanisation, the rise of hospitals, etc.). There was also the incorporation of the new scientific approach into medicine. For, as we know, science did not develop within medicine, but was incorporated into it. While this was important for securing 'control over the practice of healing', the learned physician had been a recognised professional (similar to the clergy) before this occurred. Both his status in society and his dominance over the other healing occupations were legitimised as early as the sixteenth century (Freidson 1972).

The struggles which physicians had with the barber surgeons, midwives and apothecaries reveal that the enhancement of a group of health workers within the medical sector is not intrinsically tied up with the body of knowledge the group possesses. At the time, many of these other groups had more specialised and more practical knowledge than the physician. They performed much-needed services to the general community, the university physician's theories notwithstanding. If one were to make use of Lee's (1981b) recent theoretical distinction, one would say that the physician's *structural superiority* was not initially matched by his *functional importance*. Today, he claims both structural superiority and functional importance because of his knowledge of science. This point is important because I believe that although physicians continue to draw attention to the problem of science, they are quite aware that the indigenous practitioner presents a challenge on two distinct fronts. There is the question of professional status, autonomy and control of the client and market. Professional status gives the authority to determine for others, in the medical sector, what are medical activities, when they are to be carried out and by what methods (Pearce 1982). There is also the separate problem of what Freidson refers to as the technology of medical work. This deals with what is to be accepted as medical knowledge – i.e. the place and role of 'science' in medicine. While for example physicians are being challenged by nurses on the matter of professional status, there is no argument between the two groups as to the proper approach in the acquisition of medical knowledge. The problem of indigenous healers goes beyond that of nurses. An observation of other occupational groups will reveal that there are 'professions' which maintain their autonomy but do not depend on a body of scientific knowledge (e.g. the clergy). There are also distinct occupational groups which do depend on scientific knowledge but as yet have been unable to attain the status of professions (e.g. pharmacists, draughtsmen).

With respect to the status of indigenous practitioners we can see that there are several options available. Within a national medical system, indigenous healers could be included as *colleagues* to the university-trained physician. This is the option dreaded most by the physicians, as it assumes full professional status and a sharing of responsibilities. There is also the additional problem of which of the groups within the indigenous systems should be given this status. Those who presently have the highest status locally (i.e. the diviners) are the most likely to be rejected. Indigenous workers could also be included as *junior health workers* or semi-marginal professionals. In this case, the physician remains the undisputed professional. However, the case of nursing is a reminder that those who enter the medical occupation ladder at an inferior level (as did nurses during the Nightingale era) may soon begin to agitate for a higher status. Lastly, outside the official medical system, indigenous workers could be officially recognised as health practitioners (the separate development thesis). One of the conclusions from my data (Pearce 1982) on the Western-trained physicians in Nigeria was that they do not want healers as health *personnel* included in the official system of medical care. When the physicians were given the option of accepting healers as colleagues or as junior workers, the majority were not interested in either form of co-operation with the healers. There were no psychiatrists in my group of respondents. However, it is interesting to note that data collected on psychiatrists in Bendel State supported my findings. Oyarebu (1983) interviewed all six qualified psychiatrists and the four clinical psychologists in the state. None of the 10 were in favour of integration, although the psychologists favoured some sort of consultancy between Western-trained and indigenous practitioners. Since the treatment of mental illness is often cited as one area where the two groups of workers can readily work together, it is significant that at least this group of psychiatrists appear to be totally against integration. The idea of *ad hoc* collaboration and consultation would leave the indigenous worker outside the mainstream to be consulted at the discretion of the physician.

If we now return to the issue of scientific versus non-scientific medical knowledge, the situation of the Western-trained physician becomes clearer. As noted above, doctors have insisted that the recognition of indigenous healers should depend on whether or not their (the healers') work can be submitted to scientific analysis. Aspects which defy experimentation should be 'castigated' (Iginla 1983). No doubt many individual physicians are genuinely apprehensive about the incorporation of 'non-scientific' systems of acquisition of medical knowledge. Nevertheless, the issue of professional interests suggests that 'science' is also a convenient rallying-point for preserving the present status/legal differences.

One major problem facing physicians here is that the profession looks beyond national boundaries to the 'international community'. The standards set by the Euro-American medical groups are the models. In those countries, the Yoga teachers, faith healers or *curanderos*, etc., still exist outside the official system. Even in Communist China, the work of magico-religious healers was made illegal. Not all the various types of practitioners of old China were integrated into the new system. Those incorporated were basically from the ancient, literate and secular medical tradition (Leslie 1980; Lee 1981a). Thus as professionals, physicians in Africa may fear they will be devalued, as medical personnel, on the international scene. In addition, the acceptance of magico-religious theories and beliefs at their face value, without any serious attempts to uncover the medical message embedded in them, poses some philosophical problems which challenge science itself (Hospers 1956). For example, the belief in supernatural beings or forces suggests that there are creatures with enough power to suspend or interfere with the very laws of nature and physical events on which science depends and which it seeks to uncover. Modern medicine has gained so much of its present prestige because of its adherence to the scientific perspective; thus it will be difficult for its professionals to be seen by other scientists (e.g. those in the physical sciences) as wholeheartedly embracing non-scientific perspectives.

At this point, it is pertinent to ask what the attitudes and views of indigenous healers are to collaboration with the Western-trained workers. I believe that there is a mixed reception. On the one hand many individuals and representatives of indigenous associations have approached the Federal Government concerning the need for official recognition, the building of schools and colleges and the establishment of joint clinics. Up till now the relationship between the two modes of healing differs from state to state in Nigeria. In some states (e.g. Bendel) indigenous healers are allowed to practise under restrictive Governmental laws. In other states, such as Lagos, Borno and Gongola, indigenous clinics are not recognised by the Government (Igun 1982). At the Federal level however there has not been official recognition. In comparison to all of the above, many healers are known to be apprehensive about integration. Some have expressed the legitimate fear of being wiped out 'as practitioners' while their knowledge is absorbed by various members of the Western team (Pearce 1982). In Oyarebu's study cited above, 95 indigenous healers in Bendel state were also interviewed alongside the physicians. Only 35 favoured integration. Twenty-seven favoured consultancy only. The remainder did not favour integration or consultancy (33 healers). Akintunde (1980) interviewed 10 healers in Oyo State (from Ogbomosho, Ile-Ife and Ibadan). These healers were generally uninterested in any programme of integration. They preferred to remain as consultants outside the orthodox system. There was a fear of interference and control by Western-trained practitioners. Given the issue of professional interests, there is no doubt that the latter are poised to do just this.

One important dimension affecting professional competition is the socio-historical setting within which the negotiations occur. When the learned physicians were struggling for structural dominance in the Middle Ages, the struggle existed within a particular context. None of their competitors had an undisputed knowledge base from which their practice flowed. In the medical arena, there was as yet no single group of workers who had already risen to a position of eminence. This is not the situation today. However this does not mean that the outcome of the present competition is a foregone conclusion. As Hindess (1982) has argued, the result of any struggle between rivals cannot be predicted solely in terms of the estimated imbalance of power (wrongly conceived of as merely the capacity to secure objectives) between the two parties. The actual outcome depends upon a group's ability to state its objectives, assess the particular context and situate itself in such a way as to be able to mobilize the means at its disposal. In any given context, obstacles could include the opposition of others. There is also the important relationship between the group's intrinsic capacities (e.g. status, skills, knowledge) and any outside or extrinsic resources which could be mobilised (e.g. third parties whose behaviour can be decisive). The implication of Hindess's paper is that the outcome of a struggle is the result of a social process in which potential assets may or may not be employed by each party. The ability to use assets depends on a variety of factors including divisions within one's ranks and conditions existing outside the immediate arena which may or may not be to one's advantage.

Following this position, one can analyse some of the things which are already occurring between the Western-trained physicians and indigenous healers in Nigeria. For example, some indigenous healers are attempting to take advantage of government interest in planned development. The belief in most African nations, for the past two decades, has been that rapid development can best be accomplished through conscious planning. In Nigeria, one of the present points of focus is the development of its own pharmaceutical industries. In 1983, the Senate Committee on Health and Social Services began its deliberations concerning a national drug policy in which Nigeria is to try and produce 75% of its own drugs in the future.

Taking advantage of this new development, various representatives of indigenous associations have sought for an audience. It is argued that herbal practitioners have a lot to offer in this area and many physicians agree. However, the favoured position of the physician *vis-à-vis* others has already ensured that his opinion will be sought in this matter. Physicians as members of the educated elite are closer to the centres of power than their indigenous counterparts. They have sought and won the right to evaluate critically the work and prospects of indigenous healers. The indigenous system is also faced with the conflicting interests of the elite, which leads to a certain amount of ambivalence. While there are nationalistic interests encouraging the development of African medical traditions, there are also professional, financial, and deep personal interests in the way medicine is presently organised. Thus the programme which develops in the future may not depend solely on the intrinsic capacities of either of the two groups.

THE DEVELOPMENT AND DISSEMINATION OF MEDICAL KNOWLEDGE

In evaluating the work of indigenous healers, Western-trained physicians believe that the standards of science should be the yardstick. I shall therefore review briefly the process by which scientific knowledge is produced and disseminated before a comparison is made with the process of knowledge development within the indigenous system.

THE PRODUCTION OF KNOWLEDGE

The orthodox view of the nature of scientific knowledge rests on the assumption that there is a real and objective physical world out there which can be understood through the discovery of natural laws. The following quotation from Mulkay is a good example of the view most people hold:

> Science is that intellectual enterprise concerned with an accurate account of the objects, processes and relationships occurring in the world of natural phenomena. To the extent that scientific knowledge is valid, it reveals and encapsulates in its systematic statements the true character of the world (Mulkay 1979, p. 20).

Scientific information is developed through empirically tested hypotheses derived from well-reasoned and logically consistent theories. Even though scientists often refer to non-observable entities in their work, these are expected to make sense within the vast system of observable material already accepted as part of reality. Thus the unobservable objects of the religious healer (i.e. supernatural beings) belong to a realm about which the scientist has no accumulated empirical knowledge. Scientific information is believed to be reliable and rational; scholars can arrive at the same results in an experiment, regardless of their beliefs or personal qualities. The facts so accumulated are seen as value-free, neutral and real.

This orthodox perspective is however now being challenged and the new view of science suggests that the difference between it and other forms of knowledge is not as radical as initially supposed. Discussing the role of theories and beliefs, Polanyi (1946) argues that empirical evidence rests on scientists' taking for granted theories and beliefs concerning what reality consists of. There is no direct relationship between observation and reality. What one sees and accepts as a 'fact' is influenced by the theoretical categories one uses. Mulkay, in support of this view, concludes that scientific knowledge is not so much revealed or discovered but *intellectually constructed*. Thus it is not in their existence, but in the content of its theories and beliefs that science differs. One can also wonder whether a change in the instruments used to observe (empirical) evidence would radically alter our knowledge of reality. If Man's senses (i.e. eyes, nose, ears) possessed other properties, how would the world out there appear to us (Stark 1958)?

On the issue of tacit versus explicit knowledge, it is now believed that much of what the scientist knows is first grasped at the unconscious level and some of it *remains* there. Actual discovery in science is said to require the kind of 'mental leap' observed in other areas of life (such as religion, art). Polanyi (1958) has argued that a lot of knowledge is tacit, or personal knowledge in which an individual unconsciously connects together pieces of evidence to form a configuration. However he may remain unaware of how he arrived at the 'fact'. This argument is supported by a report of a symposium on 'The Creative Process in Science and Medicine' (1975). It was accepted by the discussants that creativity in science, as elsewhere, requires subjective components – sympathetic intuition, imagination, and perhaps boldness. These creative impulses (which are sometimes called 'genius') allow scientists to make the necessary leap. If we apply this argument to the earlier statement about theories, we can see that beliefs and theories will affect the idiom in which the flash of intuition presents itself and is translated to the public at large. Thus the scientist will grasp a fact through the type of imagery that makes sense to him.

Finally, the process of negotiating is now believed to be more integral to science than usually assumed. This is particularly true when new ground is being broken and tests used in validating knowledge have not been standardised (Mulkay pp. 75–6). The importance of negotiated knowledge is already well recognised in clinical medicine (Young 1980, 1981b).

The above review of scientific production places science in closer proximity to what is generally known as non-scientific information. However, most Western-trained physicians still hold the orthodox view of science and feel that much of the knowledge of religious or indigenous healers cannot be classified as facts. Their pronouncements are regarded as merely subjective beliefs. Since a sizeable amount of the healer's knowledge is explained in terms of revelations, dreams, or flashes of intuition, the scientist insists that this non-objective mode of explanation is unacceptable. There is also tacit information gained through practical experience, which the healer is unable to communicate logically to others.

In opposition to the orthodox scientific view of knowledge production, the Yoruba of south-western Nigeria believe that medical knowledge can be produced in a variety of objective and subjective ways. For example, legend has it that medical knowledge was 'produced' by supernatural beings and imparted to Man. One version is that a divine being, originally sent from the spirit world, taught sixteen beings, at Ile-Ife, the secrets of divination. These beings then initiated human beings who were to be known as Babalawo (Diviners) (McClelland 1966). Knowledge can also be obtained in dreams. In this way, ancestors or deities are said to contact individuals. In the production of medical knowledge, the Yoruba readily admit to the use of other 'instruments' besides the five senses used to obtain objective knowledge. Since there is not the sharp dichotomy of body-mind, inner/outer, spiritual/physical realms as in the West (Morakinyo and Akiwowo 1981), evidence can be accepted through internal (unconscious) as well as external instruments (conscious eyes, ears, etc.). Thus the Yoruba still accept a level of knowing which medical science has tried to disown.

In the West, these other knowledge claims are accepted only within certain delimited areas of life. While for example Weber acknowledges the existence of both religious and intuitive knowledge (Gerth and Mills 1946), these are seen as opposed to scientific knowledge. Each type of knowledge develops within a different value milieu and in pursuit of different goals. (While religious knowledge attempts to understand the meaning of things, intuitive knowledge is concerned with the being of things and science seeks to control nature in a technical sense.) There is constant tension between scientific and other forms of knowledge rather than co-operation, in pursuing a single goal (such as medical knowledge). Owing to the emphasis on unity as opposed to dichotomy, the Yoruba do not have the tension between empirical and non-empirical modes of developing knowledge. It is interesting to note that some Western scholars are beginning to wonder whether or not the field of medicine poses a special problem. Medicine deals with Man who exhibits both objective and subjective dimensions. Illness and health states are to a large extent subjective experiences which must somehow be translated into objective knowledge to be used as the basis for treatment. This may need the acceptance of more intuitive and other subjective forms of knowledge (e.g. dreams, folk tales, myths) both by the patient (Baron 1981) and the physician (Popper 1975) than hitherto believed. In addition, collaboration between the two parties leads to negotiated knowledge. In situations of rapid change where various therapeutic alternatives exist, negotiations between practitioners and patients are likely to be frequent. For example, in Nigeria, where colonial penetration led to the growth of Western services alongside indigenous ones, patients of all classes are known to use both types of services as well as the new faith-healing services which have incorporated aspects of the old medical system and the new religious system. I have suggested elsewhere (Pearce 1984) that patients have an input into the development of new medical material. They are not passive onlookers, but carry ideas from one system to another in search of answers to their health problems.

If illness and health are to be understood fully, it is obvious than we must begin to take seriously the non-rational aspects of Man. The problem remains of how to understand these non-rational dimensions. Thus the present interest in the subjective approaches used in many non-Western cultures. Within each culture the 'facts' created about illness will be influenced by the models and beliefs held by the people. Therefore one does not expect that the subjective knowledge developed and used in one cultural setting will be the same as that of another setting. Nevertheless, through all the different subjective insights, Man will perhaps begin to evolve a more comprehensive view of illness causation and the role of non-rational elements.

Besides subjective knowledge, healers also possess empirical medical knowledge. This has been developed through trial and error over the generations. Various techniques (e.g. massage, bonesetting, birth-practices, etc.) or herbal and mineral mixtures which work have been used, although not refined (see Sofowora 1982). In addition, there is the phenomenon of 'frequency interpretations' (Erasmus 1977). From their experience, people often observe correlations between an event and an illness. Preventive health behaviour may arise out of the noted relationship. Thus in Ecuador, it is believed that food which has gone cold must be reheated otherwise illness may result. As Erasmus pointed out, the people were most likely preventing food poisoning (botulism). In Nigeria, pregnant women are not to be frightened or allowed to see frightful animals lest their babies be deformed. Today, there is a lot of interest in the West with regard to the relationship between pregnancy wastage or difficulty and the emotional state of the mother-to-be.

In summarising the arguments on the production of knowledge, one can briefly state that, not only is there much overlap between scientific and non-scientific knowledge, but that in medicine the importance of subjective means of gaining knowledge must be further explored.

THE DISSEMINATION OF KNOWLEDGE

Before knowledge is disseminated, it is stored. It is stored in structures and symbols. In the West, a great deal of medical information is stored in institutions of learning, books (e.g. in libraries) and electronic equipment (computers). From the arguments presented earlier, we now know that a vast amount is also stored in people, in the form of tacit knowledge (in both the preclinical and clinical scientist). The great advantage of Western medicine as compared to indigenous systems in Africa is that the technologies for storage and communication (e.g. writing) have greatly enhanced the growth of its content. Writing allowed 'scientists to effectively pool and expose accumulated facts and conclusions within professional communities that are contiguous in neither time or space' (Young 1981a, p. 381). People always had the option of referring back to fine points of detail which they did not have to retain in their memories. One disadvantage in the oral tradition of storage is attrition of information caused by memory loss or death. Nevertheless, certain steps were taken to safeguard the information. For example, Holzner (1968) has argued that special values and attitudes are one method by which specialists are insulated from the public and their knowledge kept safe. This may help explain the vows of poverty and extreme discipline to which the Ifa priests were expected to adhere in Yorubaland. To have their minds continually harassed by the usual aspirations of the general public would have been counterproductive. Secondly, the very structure of the Ifa verses, and the occurrence of the motif of two in the arrangement of the Odu and Omo-Odu systems, which influence the pattern of recall (Abimbola 1976; McClelland 1966), must have assisted storage. McClelland suggests that the symmetry within the whole system gives a 'certain amount of intellectual satisfaction' and that the priests she interviewed were aware of how everything hung together. Abimbola (1967) also informs us that within a community, Ifa priests met weekly, monthly and yearly. At the yearly meetings, there were recitals in the form of chanting of the Ifa verses. This ensured that the information had been correctly remembered. Mistakes were not tolerated. Finally, in so far as knowledge is stored through (or within) structures, the objects, ceremonies and rituals which the healer must memorise ensure that a lot of information is made visible. The continual recreation of these is important in terms of storage. One should also note that as with the Western-trained physician, much information is stored within the healer, of which he is unconscious.

Both groups of medical workers communicate their knowledge to three categories of people, and the pattern of communication generally differs for each category. There is the immediate production group or partners. At the next level we have other specialists who are part of the professional community. I would include trainees within this category. Lastly, there is the general public who required the application and interpretation of the specialised knowledge. There is some similarity in the way the two types of specialists deal with the three categories. Within the immediate production group, information travels backwards and forwards assisting production itself. Medical scientists working together on a project, or the healer and his novices, can produce new information because they are continuously communicating, either verbally or non-verbally (i.e. by example). What is interesting here, as Mulkay has argued, is that some information is always kept a secret within the confines of this body of people. This puts the workers at a competitive advantage *vis-à-vis* other specialists within the field. Here the secrecy of indigenous medical workers is legendary.

At the next level, workers seek to inform other specialists of their findings and compare data. The codes used are usually difficult for non-initiates to comprehend, and the mode of communication is stylised. There are recognised structures and organisations through which the knowledge claims are disseminated. In the West, the organisations include university halls where lectures, seminars and conferences take place, hospitals and health centres where demonstrations occur and a range of audio-visual as well as telecommunication equipment. In addition material is disseminated in print through journals, periodicals and very specialised books. Thus advantage has been taken of sophisticated organisation systems. Compared to this, the structures for transmitting information within the indigenous system have remained relatively small. Trainees (e.g. Ifa priests) are tutored by the apprenticeship system within the compound of the healer. Within this structure all aspects of their lives are more completely under the authority of the master (see Abimbola 1976, pp. 18–20). Even after initiation, a priest submits himself to another specialist. Since there was always the problem of preserving the material intact, one would imagine that the small size and tight structure of the transmitting group was beneficial. This is not to imply that there were no changes in the Ifa corpus; however, the danger of loss of information was a constant hazard in the oral tradition. Again within the specialist community, the organisation of members remains strictly hierarchical and patterned (with sixteen levels) (Abimbola 1976, pp. 14–15). With such a highly organised group, (cult) secrets are again easier to control. Besides Ifa priests, herbalists and other healers also transmit via the apprenticeship method, although their associations are not as highly organised. Many are just nominal members of these associations. If indigenous medicine becomes 'professionalised', it is obvious that changes are likely to be most radical in this area. The structures through which trainees and other specialists obtain information will be reorganised and expanded.

Lastly, there is the public to which knowledge is communicated via its application and interpretation. Here both groups of practitioners are faced with the important problem of legitimating their knowledge claims. Therefore knowledge is often presented in a particular way – e.g. to instil amazement, fear, respect and so forth. The public also includes funding or politically powerful groups who help support the practitioners (Abimbola 1976; Mulkay 1979). Mulkay notes that the rational and formal way scientific material is presented to the public is often in contrast to the way it was less systematically produced. In the same fashion, the communication of indigenous healers is meant to inspire awe. Each group must get rewards for its knowledge in order to maintain its high status. One can therefore appreciate the fact that the way material is communicated to the public is important for the professional interests and survival of the group (especially where there is competition, as discussed earlier).

No doubt the most fascinating aspect of information dissemination is the mode through which it is communicated. The first point to be made is that all forms of communication depend on the use of symbols. These may be verbal or nonverbal. Symbols can be defined as culturally derived indices which depend 'on a separate (occasional) definition for their correct interpretation' (Mulder and Hervey as quoted by Leach 1976, p. 13). With regard to verbal communication, a major difference between the two types of practitioners lies in the use of the oral and the written traditions. Some of the advantages of the literate tradition for the Western-trained practitioner have already been mentioned. In addition it has also meant that practitioners could 'pass on a legacy of detailed empirical knowledge rather than the sets of conclusions (i.e. theoretical knowledge drawn from practice) to which the oral mode of transmission had here restricted them' (Young 1981a, p. 381). With the oral tradition, when the empirical basis for a piece of knowledge was forgotten, its point of reference became a belief in the conclusion, thus giving the knowledge a mystical appearance. While Western-trained practitioners also make use of oral communication to inform each other and clients, the system itself relies more heavily on the written word.

Within the non-Western oral tradition verbal communication is of particular importance because of the belief in the power of the *spoken* word. In Yorubaland, it is believed that when written, words lose their ability to bring about an effect. There are a number of well-recognised forms in which messages are transmitted orally. Verger (1976) has argued that the format for the transmission of the material is taken as a 'well-tested formula from which it (i.e. the message) borrows all the influential force'. From their work on the Yoruba, various scholars have written about the patterns or forms which different stylized messages take. Verger (1976), for example, details the style of *ọfọ* or incantations (play on words which embody a lot of symbolism). Abimbola (1976) notes the general format of the *ẹsẹ Ifa* (usually in 8 parts). Akiwowo (1982) has also discussed the form of *Aṣẹ* (a verbal command assisted by ingredients which have been placed in a horn of an animal). These formulae all contain medical information about plants and animals, the correct names for symptoms, beliefs about causation and cures and so forth. When presented to clients, much of it needs interpretation since it is highly coded. However, from what was said earlier about unconscious absorption of knowledge, we must assume that besides explicit messages, clients imbibe information through the symbols used in these formats. For example, camwood symbolises blood because of its red colour and is thus implicated in medication for women with menstrual problems (Verger 1976). Again, the mouth symbolises the human community. During sacrifices, it is believed that the goodwill of one's fellows must be sought, otherwise people may work against one's interests. Goodwill is achieved when people are asked to participate in the sacrifice and may even help consume some of the food prepared for the occasion. This is the message put across in the *ẹsẹ Ifa* below. The passage emphasises the need for community solidarity. Indeed the best approach is to work in co-operation with people in general. Thus the passage also reveals the way to mend rifts. However other messages also come across. One is that potential enemies lurk everywhere and one must be vigilant and observe the correct codes of behaviour.

What is it we worship at Ife
People's mouths

I have given to those over there,
Their mouths can no longer fight
against me.
Their mouths cannot.
I have given to those in my household,
I have given to passers-by.
Their mouths cannot.
Their mouths can no longer fight
against me.
Their mouths cannot.
(Abimbola 1976, pp. 39–40).

Finally, one can see here the great emphasis placed on the role of human interaction and emotions in the development of misfortune (e.g. illness) or good fortune (e.g. recovery). This theme will be further investigated in the last section of this paper. As is already well known, a diviner may chant several Ifa verses during a divination session in an effort to give the client additional information. He is expected patiently to interpret these. This information would then filter into the lay community, not in its poetic or stylised form, but in the prose or proverbs that the client understands and repeats. Another method by which medical information filters to the public is in the stipulation of taboos. Among the Yoruba, *eewọ* (that which is forbidden) are numerous and are associated with various aspects of life or social institutions (Olabuju 1978). Many observances are associated with the religious worship of *orisa*, others with membership in particular households or towns (for example pregnancy and childbirth food observances). Again there are some specific to people with known afflictions. Thus people with epilepsy are forbidden to eat *akara*. In some households, the new mother must not eat food with pepper or any solids prepared from corn, yam or cassava flour until the child is named. (Adeoye 1980, p. 248). In addition, it is believed that each human being has his/her own set of *eewọ*. These are revealed through divination. The diviner therefore consults the person's *ori* (one's personal deity) and the individual is advised (Abimbola 1975). The *eewọ* may include both food and behavioural instructions.

Besides verbal channels, information is also tramsitted through non-verbal means. Through ritual activities, the non-linguistic aspects of speech, bodily movements and architectural structures, medical information is passed on to the public. The importance of these channels is only gradually being appreciated within Western medicine. For example, what a physician 'knows' or believes about a particular disease (e.g. cancer – that it is curable/incurable, difficult, dirty, painless, or still an enigma, etc.) can be communicated to the patient through the non-linguistic aspects of speech such as the tone, pitch, speed, pauses and volume of the physician's voice. Argyle (1980) has argued that where the verbal and non-linguistic aspects of speech conflict, people tend to ignore the verbal content of the conversation and remember the non-verbal. Wilson (1975) has also observed that the structures and equipment developed in the West reveal what the medical system is saying about health and disease. He writes that 'Hospitals (and Health Centres) powerfully and insidiously mould people's attitudes to life, death and technology. The buildings shape the beliefs of those who grow up with them, and the language of illness becomes their language . . . ' (1975, p. 93). Thus underlying (tacit) knowledge is absorbed unconsciously by members of the public.

In non-Western societies, non-verbal dissemination occurs through the use of ritual activities (e.g. sacrifices, music, dance, drama, etc.) and architectural items (e.g. pots, statues, masks, divination paraphernalia, etc.). These phenomena bring to our notice the information that is passed on through symbolism. In his work on the Ndembu, Turner (1967) notes that each ritual has its own rhythm, songs, combination of medicinal ingredients, stylised behaviour and apparatus. Rituals contain symbols which come in the form of objects, activities, relationships, events, gestures, spatial arrangements, etc. The actors in the situation are able to interpret the symbols and imbibe the hidden information about health and disease. For example, the fact that health is believed to be a group affair is symbolised among the Bomvana of southern Africa when a patient calls on his people to follow him to the diviner's compound for a divination session. They sit in a semi-circle and actively participate in the questions and answers of the consultation (Jansen 1973). This constrasts very strongly with the privacy created in the encounter between the Western doctor and the patient. The patient is further isolated from his social circle during the process of hospitalisation when he is stripped of his social identity by the removal of personal possessions, such as clothes and cosmetic supplies, which normally give him a sense of self (Goffman 1961, p. 20). He is then ready to be worked on by a group of experts who have been trained to apply scientific principles on different diseases. Thus the theme of individual isolation and passivity are strong. One problem medical personnel continually complain about is the non-compliance of patients, while at the same the surgeon (who operates on sleeping patients) is ranked highest among medical practitioners.

Another example of the way that ritual is used to communicate is in the institution of spirit mediums. An instance of this can be found among Bori practitioners of Northern Nigeria. The female medium becomes the vehicle through which a spirit 'speaks' to an audience. Verbal information is passed on when the priestess has been mounted by the spirit, who then speaks to the lay community. With respect to the non-verbal aspects of behaviour, these are highly stylized and coded (Horn 1981). The medium takes on the characteristics of the particular spirit being approached. These include the preferred colour, dress, articles, bodily movements and tone of voice associated with the spirit. Each of these items symbolises something and a message is thus imparted. Lastly, if we return to the case of *aṣẹ* discussed earlier in this paper, we can also observe the non-verbal aspects of this phenomenon. Akiwowo has pointed out that 'horns must be used as containers for the very potent preparations so that the chemical ingredients cannot destroy or corrode the container' (1982, p. 4). In so far as horns may be seen as symbolising strength and durability, the message concerning the power, seriousness and long-term effect of the *aṣẹ* is put across. With these various examples it is possible to see how knowledge claims are transmitted nonverbally. However, in addition to the information they communicate, the symbols used arouse emotions, an important dimension of the non-rational aspect of Man discussed earlier (Turner 1967; Parry 1967). The recognition and use of emotions appear to be very important in the work of indigenous healers, and will now be considered in the final section.

ASSESSING THE MEDICAL KNOWLEDGE EMBEDDED WITHIN THE INDIGENOUS SYSTEM

Since Turner's famous thesis that in Africa the healer undertakes social analysis of the patient's illness and locates the problem within the configuration of tensions and conflicts within his social environment, social scientists have begun to appreciate the type of model with which healers work. As compared to the *medical model* of Western medicine, the *social model* of the indigenous practitioner has more affinity with the viewpoint of the social sciences. Even though physicians have begun to accept the fate that the manifestation of diseases is the result of socio-cultural and political processes, the extent to which these factors are implicated both in the outbreak of disease and in healing is yet to be fully appreciated. I now wish to scrutinise the social model of the healer more carefully.

I wish to suggest that in the process of social analysis and in the treatment prescribed, the indigenous healer's model takes seriously the *role of emotions* and *the place of emotionality in disease and recovery*. Even though it is believed that some diseases (psychosomatic) have a large psychological component to them, we still need to understand the degree to which other types of diseases are affected by emotions and the social structures which give rise to these emotions. In addition, the role of emotions in successful therapy is yet to be properly understood. The present interest in placebo effects, I believe, may just be scratching the surface. It has been noted that healers understand the 'culture' of the people and effect a cure within a context of beliefs and structures which both they and their clients appreciate (Kleinman and Sung 1979).

One means of understanding this process is through applying some of the insights from the 'sociology of emotions'. In his own contributions to this subspeciality, Kemper (1981) made a number of statements which are important to the present discussion. The first is that we must begin to appreciate the role of social structure and relationships in the development of emotions. Particular types of sentiments or emotions are more likely to exist within one type of structure as opposed to another (e.g. polygyny versus monogamy). If we rearrange the structure and status relations, different emotions will be given expression. Kemper argues that 'it is what our fellow participants do to us and what we do to them – the social relations that constitute the existing social structure – that evoke our emotions' (1981, p. 344). His second point is that since people are socialised into various groups, each with rules for behaviour, the violation of these (or even contemplated violation) will bring out strong emotions. The role that all these emotions play in all categories of illnesses needs full investigation. The concept of stress as presently used does not uncover all the dimensions of the problem. For example, what is a stressor? (Cassel 1977). What is the relationship between a stressor, personality (including emotions), social structure and disease manifestation? Here the work of the healer can be better understood. The social model which he uses pays particular attention to the specific types of social organisation and relationships of his people.

He would be familiar with the types of emotions these arrangements are likely to produce. He is also aware of the discomfort or anxiety violations of prescriptions cause. *Much of this information may remain tacit knowledge to him* as discussed earlier. Apart from the emotions which develop out of particular social relationships, other emotions arise, because in all human communities there are conflicting values. Thus for example, women are caught between the value for life and the cultural emphasis on child-bearing, which in most non-Western societies remains hazardous.

An obvious example of this is brought out in Turner's discussion of the Nkula ritual of birth among the Ndembu. Here the fertility ceremony was seen to be organised around the belief that some women unconsciously reject their female role as child-bearers. Another important source of strong emotions may be located within the individual. Individuals tend to have inner tendencies or characteristics which may conflict with the dominant patterns of behaviour of the group to which a person belongs. In recognition of these problems, many groups have developed schemes for explaining and handling the anxieties. Thus among the Yoruba, such concepts as *Ipori* (the unconscious self) and *Ori-Inu* (the conscious self) allow for a whole range of explanations about anxiety and health (Pearce 1983). Each individual is expected to visit the diviner to consult his *Ori* and align the conflicting aspects of his life. Experienced healers are likely to be aware of all these different sources of emotions within their cultural setting. Their interpretation of the problem should therefore be superior to those of non-specialists. Thus the healer may be viewed as someone who identifies and uncovers emotions. These include both the emotions of the client and of those who stand in particular relationships to him (e.g. spirits, ancestors, co-wives, children, in-laws, etc.).

Besides those emotions which led to the breakdown, there are also emotions associated with illness itself. Various scholars have pointed out the alienating, isolating, and disruptive dimensions of illness. Skultans (1976) for example discusses the emotional aspects of pain, particularly the problem of enforced privacy. The healer helps to interpret these difficult situations, manage the emotions which develop, and mould attitudes towards them. In the West, physicians have been taught to deal mainly with the non-emotional (rational) aspects of illness. The 'socialization of emotionality' (Hearns 1982) has been delegated to the lower occupations such as nursing, social work and health visiting. Yet these occupations do not have the therapeutic authority of the physician. They are considered to be the 'caring' occupations. However, at this point we are unaware of just how much curing takes place as a result of caring. (There is also the issue of emotions and well-being. What type of emotions bring health as opposed to illness? These may not have obvious physical correlates and may be more difficult to study).

In addition to the emotions aroused by illness itself, others are elicited by the healer during therapy. It appears that within the indigenous system, emotions are explicitly used as medicine. In other words, intense emotions are often deliberately aroused during the rituals, ceremonies and verbal transactions. These include fear, love, hope, faith, confidence and awe and so forth. We are only just beginning to understand the extent to which the mind can affect the discharge of substances such as endorphin or control automatic functions in the body. As an expert in rituals, the indigenous healer is able to arouse emotions through the symbols used in therapy. Earlier, I noted that symbols evoke emotions. In the oral tradition there is a lot of emphasis on participation in rituals. Not only is medical knowledge passed to the patient which he will use in the future (i.e. affecting attitude to symptoms, illness behaviour, anxiety, etc.), but he is also taught how the problem can be controlled and the types of emotions which go (or should go) with this activity (of overcoming the illness). In his chapter on the format of the Ifa verses, Abimbola states that patients are informed as to whether the mythical being for whom the divination was originally performed followed all instructions (part V), what happened to him after he complied or refused to comply (part VI), and the emotional reactions of the being to the divination (part VII). These no doubt mould the patient's own feelings. It is also known that healers (e.g. psychiatrists) often shout at patients to force particular reactions, and the belief in the spoken word (e.g. *ọfọ̀*) also arouses emotions.

It may thus be that diviners and other groups of healers are tapping an area of knowledge which science has avoided, since they try to unravel the internal dimensions and inter-subjective aspects of health. Fortes (1976) reminds us that health and illness are *lived experiences*. In science, these problems are not dealt with as lived experience. Thus Cunningham and Tickner have argued that 'germs have no existential value! The irreversible gains of our scientific knowledge involved liberation from the world of spirits, but it is in a sense a knowledge that cannot be lived and, in so far as health is a matter of lived experience, this knowledge is silent' (1981, p. 227). At the present time, the tools used to accumulate this subjective knowledge remain rudimentary. Again, there is no doubt that the idiom through which this type of knowledge is expressed (i.e. mystical/supernatural idiom) is unacceptable to many and often instils extreme fear, so that it becomes difficult to study. Nevertheless, it may be necessary to probe the meanings behind the explicit models that are used, so that the social relevance of the hidden information can be better understood.

In the second section of this paper it was shown that science is no longer seen as a special type of knowledge which cannot be demystified. The same approach needs to be applied to the knowledge of the healer *before* it is forced to 'become scientific' in what may be a premature attempt to rationalise it and professionalise its practitioners. This is particularly important, since, as I have already argued, the interest of the Western-trained physicians in the future activities of indigenous healing will be influenced by their own professional interests. It would seem, therefore, that the task at hand is the understanding of the social knowledge used by the various indigenous practitioners, without too much anxiety about how well it can be translated into a strict biomedical or scientific model. We must try to avoid the problem discovered by Leslie in India, where the professionalising Ayurvedic physicians set out to 'demonstrate that the institutions and scientific theories of cosmopolitan medicine were anticipated in the ancient texts' [1976, p. 365]. I believe it will be a waste of time to set up a kind of competition whereby the myths and beliefs about local deities are used to prove scientific knowledge in a 'me too' campaign. Since Man is not a completely rational creature, problems as profound as health and illness are unlikely to be completely understood from one perspective. In studying other forms of medical knowledge (the so-called non-scientific forms) we may be able to make the kinds of strides in the future which science made for us in the past. The main problem seems to be to find ways of demystifying or demythologising this knowledge.

CONCLUSION

Thus, the present interest in encouraging professional associations, building indigenous schools and clinics, registering the various groups of healers and so forth, should not be principally concerned with how much biomedical (i.e. scientific) knowledge can be salvaged from indigenous practice for Western orthodox medicine. While it is true that new scientific knowledge will be uncovered through the analysis of herbs, this is not likely to be the area where the most interesting type of knowledge is to be found. Insofar as Euro-American medicine has received political and economic support to develop at its own pace, the indigenous system needs to be studied on its own terms. Many aspects of Euro-American medical practice have been put on film and used for teaching and for further studies (e.g. operations, the doctor/patient relationship, group therapy, etc.). These and other methods can be used to understand the inner workings of the indigenous system. Many Western-trained physicians believe that thus to expose the indigenous healer would reveal that nothing lies behind his mysticism. However, given the arguments in this paper, this is not likely to be the case. Nonetheless, one can expect resistance from the healers themselves. Serious probes into their 'secret' knowledge will be in opposition to their professional interests.

REFERENCES

Abimbola, W., (1967), 'Ifa as a body of knowledge and as an academic discipline', *Lagos Notes and Records*, 1, 1, pp. 30–40.
——(1975), *Sixteen Great Poems of Ifa*. UNESCO.
——(1976), *Ifa: an exposition of Ifa literary corpus*. Ibadan: Oxford University Press.
Abrahamson, B., (1972), *Military Professionalization and Political Power*. Beverly Hills: Sage Publications.
Adeoye, C., (1980), *Asa ati Ise YORUBA*. Ibadan: Oxford University Press.
Akintunde, S., (1980), 'Oral Communication in the Treatment of Mental Illness: comparative views of traditional and western healers'. Ile-Ife: BSc. Project submitted to Dept. of Sociology/Anthropology.
Akiwowo, A., (1982), 'Ase: visual and spoken power (incantation) as a creative tool, a sociological perspective'. Paper presented at Joint Conference of Association of Psychiatrists in Nigeria, The African Association and the World Federation of Mental Health, Ile-Ife.
Argyle, M., (1980), 'Verbal and Nonverbal Communication', in Corner, J. and Hawthorn, J., (eds.), *Communication Studies*. London: Edward Arnold, pp. 50–61.
Baron, R., (1981), 'Bridging the clinical distance: an empathic rediscovery of the known', *Journal of Medicine and Philosophy*, 6, 1, pp. 5–23.
Bodunrin, P., 'Witchcraft, Magic and E.S.P.: a defence of scientific and philosophical scepticism', *Second Order*, VII, 1 and 2, pp. 36–50.
Cassel, J., (1977), 'Psychosocial processes and "stress": theoretical formation', (ed.) in Kane, R., *Behavioural Sciences and Preventive Medicine*, Washington: US Govt. Printer.
Cunningham, A. and Tickner, D., (1981), 'Psychoanalysis and Indigenous Psychology', in Heelas, P. and Lock, A. (eds.), *Indigenous Psychologies*. London: Academic Press.
Erasmus, C., (1977), 'Changing folk beliefs and the relativity of empirical knowledge', in Landy, D. (ed.) *Culture Disease and Healing*. New York: Macmillan.
Fortes, M., (1976), 'Foreword' in Loudon, J. B. (ed.) *Social Anthropology and Medicine*. London: Academic Press, pp. ix–xx.
Freidson, E., (1972), *Profession of Medicine*. New York: Dodd, Mead and Company.
Gerth, H. and Mills, C. W., (1946), *From Max Weber: essays in sociology*. New York: A Galaxy Book.
Goffman, E., (1961), *Asylums*. New York: Anchor Books.
Hearns, J., (1982), 'Notes on patriarchy, professionalization and the semi-professions', *Sociology*, 16, 2, pp. 184–202.
Hindess, B., (1982), 'Power interests, and the outcome of struggles', *Sociology*, 16, 4, pp. 498–511.
Holzner, B., (1968), *Reality Construction in Society*. Cambridge, Mass: Schenkman Pub. Company.
Horn, A., (1981), 'Ritual drama and the theatrical: a case of Bori Spirit Medium' in Ogunbiyi, Y. (ed.) *Drama and Theatre in Nigeria: a critical source book*, pp. 181–202.
Hospers, J., (1956), *An Introduction to Philosophical Analysis*. London: Routledge and Kegan Paul.
Hughes, E., 'Professions', in Lynn, K. (ed.), *The Professions in America*. Boston: Beacon Press.
Iginla, J., (1983), 'Problems and prospects of trado-medicine in Nigeria', *Sunday*

Times, (Lagos), 27 February 1975.

Igun, U., (1982), 'Traditional and Western-type medicine in Nigeria: possible patterns of co-existence', in Odekunle, F. (ed.), *Mobilization of Human Researches for National Development*, pp. 253–63.

Jansen, G., *The Doctor-Patient Relationship in an African Tribal Society*, Assen: Van Gorcum and Company.

Kemper, T., (1981), 'Social constructionist and positivist approaches to the sociology of emotions', *American Journal of Sociology*, 87, 2, pp. 336–62.

Kleinman, A. and Sung, L., (1979), 'Why do indigenous practitioners successfully heal?' *Social Science and Medicine*, 13B, pp. 7–26.

Leach, E., (1976), *Culture and Communication*. London: Cambridge University Press.

Lee, R., (1981a), 'Chinese and Western medical care in China's rural commune: a case study', *Social Science and Medicine*, 14A, pp. 137–48.

——(1981b), 'Modernization and health care systems: structural superiority and functional importance'. *Leewenhorst: 7th International Conference on Social Science and Medicine*.

Leslie, C., (1976), 'The ambiguities of medical revivalism in modern India', in Leslie, C. (ed.), *Asian Medical Systems*. Berkeley: University of California.

——(1980), 'Medical pluralism in world perspective', *Social Science and Medicine*, 14B, pp. 191–195.

McClelland, E., (1966), 'The significance of number in the Odu of Ife', *Africa*, 36, 4, pp. 421–31.

Merton, R., (1973), *The Sociology of Science*. Chicago: The University of Chicago Press.

Morakinyo, O. and Akiwowo, A., (1981), 'The Yoruba ontology of personality and motivation: a multidisciplinary approach', *Journal of Social Biol. Struct.*, 4, pp. 19–38.

Morley, P., and Wallis, R., (1978), *Culture and Curing*. London: Peter Owen.

Mulkay, M., (1979), *Science and the Sociology of Knowledge*. London: Allen and Unwin.

Olabuju, O., (1978), *Iwe Asa Ibile Yoruba*. Ibadan: Longman.

Oyarebu, K., (1983), 'Views of mental health professionals, psychiatric patients and traditional healers on pluralistic treatment modalities in Bendel State of Nigeria', *African Journal of Mental Health and Society*, 1, 1, pp. 36–43.

Parry, J., (1967), *The Psychology of Human Communication*. London: of London Press.

Pearce, T. O., (1982), 'Integrating Western orthodox and indigenous medicine; professional interests and attitudes among university-trained nigerian physicians', *Social Science and Medicine*, 16, pp. 1611–17.

——(1983), 'On the concept of health among the Yoruba'. Paper in Progress.

——(1984), 'Social change and the "modernization" of the medical sector' in Afonja, S. A. and Pearce, T. O. (eds.), *Social Change in Nigeria*. London: Longman.

Polanyi, M., (1946), *Science, Faith and Society*. Chicago: University of Chicago Press.

——(1958), *The Study of Man*. Chicago. University of Chicago Press.

Popper, K., (1975), Discussant in Symposium on *The Creative Process in Science and Medicine*, ed. Krebs, A. and Shelley, J., New York: American Elsevier Pub. Co.

Simpson, G., (1980), *Yoruba Religion and Medicine in Ibadan*. Ibadan: Ibadan University Press.

Skultans, V., (1976), 'Empathy and healing: aspects of spiritualist ritual' in *Social*

Anthropology and Medicine, ed. J. B. Loudon. London: Academic Press, pp. 190–222.

Sofowora, A., (1982), *Medicinal Plants and Traditional Medicine in Africa*. Chichester: John Wiley and Sons Ltd.

Stark, W., (1958), *The Sociology of Knowledge*. London: Routledge and Kegan Paul.

Turner, V., (1967), *The Forest of Symbols*. Ithaca: Cornell University Press.

Verger, P., (1976), 'The use of plants in Yoruba Traditional Medicine and its linguistic approach.' Paper presented at Seminar in Dept. of African Languages and Literatures, University of Ife.

Wilson, M., (1975), *Health is for People*. London: Darton, Longman and Todd.

Young, A., (1980), 'The discourse on stress and the reproduction of conventional knowledge', *Social Science and Medicine*, 14B, pp. 133–146.

——(1981a), 'The creation of medical knowledge: some problems in interpretation', *Social Science and Medicine*, pp. 379–386.

——(1981b), 'When rational men fall sick: an inquiry into some assumptions made by medical anthropologists', *Culture, Medicine and Psychiatry*, 5, pp. 317–335.

Conclusion G. L. Chavunduka *and* Murray Last

AFRICAN MEDICAL PROFESSIONS TODAY

INTRODUCTION

Healers have for long been treated like trees on savanna farms – not formally cultivated, yet valued and used, particularly by women and their children. They have remained an essential part of the social landscape, signposts and providers of shade during the day's labour. Yet today, they are being included as an integral part of the field of health: in some countries they are being carefully husbanded by government officials, politicians, planners – these are, to use an evocative Nigerian phrase, 'men of timber and calibre'; elsewhere some healers, if not actually being uprooted as socially 'dead wood', are being pruned back, while others are having new ideas grafted onto their stock of traditions. The essays in this volume have sought to throw light on this new 'husbandry' of traditional medicine. In our conclusion we will not try and summarise or synthesise the disparate views expressed earlier. Rather, we wish to offer the reader some general hypotheses about the process of professionalisation in African medicine to-day – hypotheses derived from the data here but sometimes at odds with our contributors' own conclusions.

For almost a decade now there has been a demand for healers to organise traditional medicine so that it too can participate *formally* in providing a nation's health service. Since official emphasis is put now on primary health care, with its slogan 'Health for All by the Year 2000', and as financial stringency stretches on into the future, the demand today is more urgent: health personnel are needed *now*, and one obvious source are traditional healers. But the air of urgency serves to preclude serious discussion of the various longer-term implications – are healers, remodelled as health personnel, seen as merely a stop-gap till the young are trained in the new ways, or are they instead a medium-term measure, in order to make use of a group the need for which will, by the year 2000, have died out naturally in the course of 'progress' and 'science'? Alternatively, do healers represent a separate school of thought, a science, that needs the recognition and the resources to develop itself?

Although it may be agreed that healers are to organise themselves, the question remains – for what? Primarily to facilitate government action by serving as its administrative and financial agencies in this particular sphere? Or to promote collective action by healers politically in a plural society? To preside over the radical transformation of traditional medicine? Or to ensure for it a future of its own making? The different professional associations that exist in traditional medicine today in part reflect the different answers being given to these – and similar – questions.

PROFESSIONAL ASSOCIATIONS: A TYPOLOGY

To understand the differences between associations, it is essential first to recognise the political dimension of health and its historical role in society. The debate over professions is not solely about health policy or even about the best interests of patients (whatever they may prove to be). For example, one point on which there is wide agreement is that the new organisations ought to be *national*, seeking to bring together in a single forum all the disparate groupings that constitute a nation's traditional medicine. Intended to promote, among other things, unity inside an influential sector of society, the organisations function within the state's immediate political arena. Thus the new organisations are neither profession-wide (uniting *all* personnel engaged in medicine) nor are they continent-wide; for although in the colonial period there had been several attempts to build up healers' associations which shared the regional or pan-African aspirations of that time, these aspirations have tended to fade along with colonialism. Thus in countries like Zimbabwe, where the tradition of resistance to colonialism has been often headed by healers (as mediums or diviners) and whose struggle has been both traumatic and only recently won, the role of these healers is a more complex issue than in, say, Nigeria. The central place of healers in the public health systems of pre-colonial states (described for example by Steven Feierman in Chapter 10) indicates the historical depth to the healer's role in rural society and the powerful tradition on which a profession of traditional medicine can still draw, despite nearly a century's clash with colonialism. That healers have nonetheless survived very well till the present day reflects people's use of medicine as an idiom in which their basic personal autonomy has been expressed. Associations of traditional medicine in Africa thus bring to professionalisation a legacy wholly absent from the formal medical professions of most countries elsewhere.

Despite the complexity of this legacy, and its very varied impact on different medical cultures across the continent, there emerges from the evidence presented in this volume a broad typology of professional associations today. On a national plane there are:

1 The new, purpose-built association modelled on the British or American medical profession and aiming not only to unite both herbalists and diviners, but also to include 'traditional birth attendants' and other practitioners. An autonomous body, legally recognised as a voluntary association (and not as a limited company), it has governmental approval but it nonetheless is self-financed; it is dependent solely on the contributions levied on its members even for such programmes as medical education. Similarly the leadership is elected by the membership rather than appointed by government. Membership is by registration locally after an interview or oral examination. Disciplinary procedures, also carried out locally, are backed ultimately by the sanction of possible de-registration; for although non-registered healers are not prohibited by law from practising, professional recognition is important for colleagues and the public's confidence locally. Thus the association is not (yet?) entrusted with a legal monopoly either over specific techniques or over all kinds of traditional healing, and its members are of course still constrained by statutes governing other medical groups (for example, the various Drugs Acts, or measures controlling surgical interventions). Zimbabwe's ZINATHA, described here in Chapter 1, is an example of this type.

2 Also new, purpose-built and usually all-embracing like the first, the second type of association, however, is not autonomous. More like an agency of the Ministry of Health, it has been set up, and continues to be guided, by ministry officials; its funds, in part at least, derive from government sources. In effect it is a national liaison body for government/healer co-operation, and may be called upon to carry out on government's behalf the procedures for selecting and registering healers; but training, for example, of traditional birth attendants, is done by government. An example of this type is Zambia's THPAZ (mentioned in Chapter 5), or Benin's AGTB (Chapter 6: this association, which excluded midwives, is temporarily suspended).

3 The old-established association, usually re-named and upgraded from being more local, more entrepreneurial an association – and, as such, often registered originally as a limited company. In this type of association, the existing leadership largely retains its power, but now operates as the national representative of healers' interests. Its pre-eminence on the national stage is at the expense of other earlier, sometimes larger associations, and this may reflect the strictly political abilities or ambitions of its leaders. This kind of association is much the most common, though they often have rather a poor record of development. The successful ones, such as Malawi's HAM mentioned in Chapter 4, appear to require help from individuals in the universities or in hospital medicine. Other examples referred to in this volume are Tanzania's now-dissolved UWATA (Chapter

3), Nigeria's NAMH (Chapter 11) or Botswana's Dingaka (Chapter 2).

On the local level (though often as part of a national scheme or network), there are:

4 The new, purpose-built local district or regional association or committee. It has usually been set up as a result of specific actions by government or under the auspices of a project (e.g. with USAID help), as part of the new trend for voluntary, decentralised management of development, and is often experimental. An example is the Kintampo project in Ghana (described in Chapter 5 and by Twumasi in Yoder 1982); it is possible similar groupings are being tried out also in Zaire alongside more centralised institutions for traditional medicine (cf. Bibeau, 1980) – comparable, too, are the plans for Botswana (Chapter 2).

5 The old-established regional association retained (and re-modelled?) to provide strictly local links with government. Larger states like Zaire or more especially Nigeria, with its tradition of considerable local autonomy and its diversity in both religion and medicine, may eventually provide examples of this sort (cf. Chapter 11).

6 The old-established cult-based group, whether formally organised and registered like the Msekwa cult in Tanzania (described by I. A. J. Semali in Chapter 3) or more informally structured and having only periodic fetes and re-unions as the occasion for creating a sense of unity, for exchanging information, recognising new members and disciplining the wayward. An example of the latter is the *isangoma* of Zulu medicine described by Harriet Ngubane in Chapter 9 (and also, at more length, in her article in *Social Science & Medicine*, 15B, 3, 1981).

Faith-healing churches might be put into this last category, despite being simultaneously both local and trans-national organisations. These churches are not primarily medical, and the prophets, *qua* healers or diviners, usually work independently of any centrally imposed discipline. Though the leading churches in this field are perhaps the Zionist or Pentecostal churches in southern Africa and the Aladura and Harris-type churches in western Africa, one should not exclude the therapeutic work, for example, of the former Roman Catholic Archbishop of Lusaka, Emmanuel Milingo. The churches are relevant to this typology partly because they provide therapeutic services yet stay outside any professional medical association – an example which may have to be followed by spirit mediums and diviners in the event of their not being acceptable to professional associations.

THE TREND TOWARDS HERBALISM

At the risk of over-generalising, there are certain features that all these professional associations have in common. Primarily, the associations (local cults excepted) are more strictly herbalist in background – usually their founders have been drawn from the herbalist end of the healing spectrum; and the orientation of these associations is towards developing and spreading the use of herbal medicines. (The distinction between diviner/medium and herbalist is more marked in some medical cultures than in others, and has possibly become sharper in the course of the twentieth century. The legal aspect has been discussed briefly in the introduction). Associations tend to be interested in modernising traditional medicine, incorporating ideas from foreign or colonial pharmacology and taking on some of the styles of medical schools – issuing certificates and diplomas, membership cards, with extensive rules of association, even titles. The model is more often that of a friendly society or club than an Anglo-American-style profession; alternatively, the association may be trading as a company, especially where the association is centred round one prominent healer and his acolytes. In either case – club or company – the entrepreneurial spirit is more marked in the old-established associations than in the more cult-based groupings. As a corollary, these associations tend to be urban- or suburban-biased, with membership drawn from the more mobile healers – immigrants from another state (for example, Malawians in Zimbabwe), or merely from another region in the country. It thus provides a network, as well as a structure, for modes of healing not necessarily embedded within the culture of a local community.

This pre-eminence of herbalism in professional associations in recent decades requires explanation. The most obvious factor has been the legal constraint against practising anything that might be construed as sorcery. The various Witchcraft Regulations, Ordinances and Acts promulgated from 1895 on, particularly in the anglophone territories of Africa, have made healers potentially liable for prosecution, if for nothing more serious than fraud or slander. In areas where illness and other misfortunes were commonly diagnosed as ultimately the result of witchcraft or sorcery (that is, a specific living person was blamed as the cause of the trouble), the Acts made such a diagnosis a criminal offence. In such circumstances, more strictly herbal approaches to treatment were the only obvious alternative for those who practised publicly – as did, necessarily, many itinerant healers. The adoption of Christianity, whether through missions or through independent churches, also favoured the overt use of herbal therapies. Similarly, faith-healing and divining in church drew off some of the clientele who normally patronised more traditional therapies involving spirits or ancestors. In the towns, then, herbalists have remained the most high-profiled representatives of traditional medicine.

With the spread of primary and secondary education – but also, more widely, with people's increased familiarity, for example, with complex applied science and technology (and its need for repair!) – there has, it seems, been a cultural shift of idiom towards a more mechanical 'rationality'. Herbalism, in its present guise as empirical (rather than symbolic) medicine, is a product of this shift, yet it necessarily retains too the symbolic and ritual overtones that add crucially to its potency as a traditional cure. (Such ambivalence, along with the placebo effect, is to be found, of course, in hospital medicine too.) Furthermore there has, it seems, been a persistent demand by some for freedom from the entanglements of village life. Herbalism becomes an increasingly attractive – and efficacious? – alternative where traditional non-herbal therapy is intricately bound up with a community life whose double-binds are beginning to seem needlessly oppressive.

Quite apart from the 'pull' exerted by traditional medicine's changing clientele, herbalists have been 'pushed' by university departments of pharmacology, pharmacognosy and chemistry seeking their collaboration and local expertise; a 'push' too from pharmaceutical companies, foreign and local, in search of 'green' medicine's wonder drugs, as well as from marketplace competition against the pedlars of imported patent medicines. Empirics became especially fashionable in the 1950s, and then again in the 1970s, first as the possibilities of new markets and discoveries opened up for a new generation of researchers in the wake of the post-war boom; the second, as recession and the accompanying disillusion with the existing *modus vivendi* spurred the next generation to seek alternatives. For increasing numbers, then, traditional medicine was coming to be identified with herbalism.

Given the boom in herbalism both as an attitude of mind and as practice, the simultaneous boom in association-building among herbalists may seem anomalous. One reason apparently was the comparatively low status, as individual entrepreneurs, of herbalists. Though their low status may have suited customers seeking relief from the domineering stance of mediums and diviners at home, herbalists were vulnerable despite the boom to competition and to power politics. Unlike the relatively structured cults of the mediums and diviners, the earlier, traditional herbalists apparently had little formal organisation; nor did they have the same alliances with the politically powerful. Along with midwives and barber surgeons, they had been somewhat marginal practitioners, minor tradesmen dependent overtly, not on a special relationship with spirits, but on the public; and they were always competing with a family's own resources for self-medication. Therefore lacking the support of their immediate community and often instead part of a wider society of migrant workers, these associations provided both support for the individual and a basis for a more pan-African sense of community. Other associations, especially those centred round a charismatic practitioner, created medical trade networks not unlike those that existed around regional cults. Indeed the very success of herbalism made these associations possible, and in turn contributed to the modernist style in which the new herbalism operated.

ASSOCIATION INTO PROFESSION?

If this brief historical analysis is correct, then it goes some way to explain the difficulties encountered in adapting these early associations either for use by Ministries of Health or for the development of a traditional medical profession.

Primarily herbalists are unrepresentative of the wider population of healers. Diviners and spirit-mediums, though users of herbs in their treatments, in the countryside tend not to join associations, and certainly not under the leadership of herbalists. Nationwide, despite past presidencies of this or that association, the important herbalists still have a lower status in public esteem than do the major diviners. In consequence, the existing leadership of most of the older associations is unacceptable to others at a national level. Furthermore, a much enlarged association may only accentuate the divisions or fissiparous tendencies already evident within the association, while the opportunities for building a personal reputation on the national stage only intensify the competition for office. Finally, the entrepreneurial origin of most of these early associations is not so easily replaced by an ethic of altruistic service – despite all the rhetoric and the aims stated in the association's constitution. In practice, the economic realities of medical practice tend to be uncongenial to the securely salaried government officials watching over the associations, if not directly inconsistent with the overt ideologies of their political parties and governments. The unhappy history of Tanzania's UWATA, sketched in Chapter 3, illustrates this well.

Thus there is a considerable incentive to start afresh with a wholly new professional association sponsored by government. But this too has had its problems. First, such associations are inevitably bureaucratic in organisation, and most healers – if they really are healers – are inexperienced in committee procedures and the niceties of officialdom. In short, officers of the new association have to be taught a whole new set of skills (if not a new language, plus literacy). Not surprisingly they become pawns of government, liable to lose their posts, or even to find their new association itself abolished, as the tides of political fashion or success come and go. In such a climate few serious healers remain long involved, leaving the jobs (and their perquisites) to economic or political opportunists. Furthermore, where associations are government-funded, there is not even the financial control exerted by members anxious about the misuse of their subscriptions. At least, as Dr Semali shows in Chapter 3, associations registered as limited companies have their shareholders to contend with! In such a situation, a government-run association is liable to be as much an object of suspicion as a vehicle for mobilising the real healers in the community.

Institutions are as hard to create as they are easy to criticise; and they take time. So, too, does leadership. At this early stage, the record of most of the professional associations may not be particularly impressive. But in the opinion of some observers – and of some governments – even experimenting with professional structures is an error, not least because, they argue, there are some altogether better alternatives.

ALTERNATIVES TO PROFESSIONS

There are two fundamental alternatives to a policy of encouraging the development of independent professional associations; these are discussed in this volume particularly in the Chapters 7, 2 and 5. The first is to *incorporate* selected practitioners (most often midwives, or 'traditional birth attendants' as they are called) into the state-run national health services, usually after some training has been given. The degree of formal subordination implied by this is recognised as unacceptable or impracticable for most kinds of healer. The second is to ask selected practitioners to collaborate or at least *co-operate* with the state's hospital-based services, again usually after some training. This latter scheme may involve working in a specially erected traditional health centre, with or without a hospital-trained doctor or dispenser working alongside in another wing of the building. But it is seldom spelt out how far, in practice, co-operation will differ from incorporation: questions, for example, include how the co-operating traditional practitioners will be remunerated (by government?); will they be able to sign medical certificates, will they be fully responsible legally for patients in the event of disagreement over treatment; will they be restricted in the procedures they may perform and in the medicaments they may prescribe? In such circumstances, co-operating healers may need more than ever a professional association to defend their rights as partners in the state's health service.

That a large number of traditional practitioners are willing to try co-operation with the hospital services is clear (the issue is discussed particularly in Chapters 3 and 12). However, apparently willingness in principle is more readily shown by healers in eastern and southern Africa than (Ghana excepted) in West Africa – where co-operation has had a longer history, especially in psychiatry. Indeed, in both anglo- and francophone West Africa there have been considerable reservations expressed by hospital practitioners about the practicalities of co-operation after several years' experience (cf. Asuni 1979; Dores 1981); and it would seem unwise, as outside observers, simply to put it down to professional jealousies. On the other hand, the experimental projects in Ghana have apparently proved a success.

Most of the practitioners selected for involvement with the state's system are recruited singly, *ad hoc*. Only rarely is a system envisaged in which healers' associations play an active part, let alone a controlling part. The implication apparently is that these healers are not expected to act collectively but to remain politically powerless within or alongside a much more powerful system, and accept direction from planners, government and other 'full' professionals. Indeed, the pervasive impression that healers generally are secretive, isolated individuals unwilling to co-operate *with each other* may prove to have been in this context merely a very convenient myth.

The source of this attitude – that professional associations for traditional medicine are at best otiose, at worst disastrous – may lie in one of two assumptions, mentioned earlier, which hinge on presuppositions about the future popularity of, and therefore the long-term need for, traditional medicine. Firstly, the assumption that the employment of healers by the state for its primary health care is only a stop-gap until other personnel are 'properly' trained; or secondly, that in the long run traditional medicine will be phased out by 'progress' and successful competition from the new health personnel. In neither case is a future for traditional healing envisaged, and certainly not as a professional medical practice. For if it were, the crucial problem, that of the transmission or 'reproduction' of traditional medical knowledge – and its future independent development – would be of paramount importance. Yet it is in this area that the possible effects of professionalisation on African medicine need particularly careful thought and research.

MEDICAL KNOWLEDGE

The most obvious difficulty lies in the formal training and certification of healers in the future, and in particular what the content of that training will be. In the light of the data presented in this volume, there is an inherent danger that traditional medical knowledge will be defined simply in terms of its technical herbal expertise, that this experience will in turn be recognised only for its empirical pharmacognosy, without reference to the symbolic and ritual matrix within which it is used – still less, the social matrix in which those rituals and symbols have meaning at any particular time or place. But even within the herbalist tradition, there is, for example, a potential conflict between those developing the allopathic use of herbs (in which the medicine 'poisons' the disease agents) and those who defend the more homoeopathic approach, in which the medicine 'feeds' or stimulates the body's agents in its own defence. Furthermore, offers of outside help in teaching – or indeed even in funding – may result in gradual external dominance over the curriculum or style of instruction that is hard to resist. Only ZINATHA, of associations discussed in the volume, appears to have had experience of confronting this problem.

Traditional medical knowledge, however, is much broader and more subtle than technical herbal expertise. Indeed the very nature of this knowledge may militate against its formal structuring in the way professionalisation might seemingly require, with its objective examinations and tests of efficacy. What is this knowledge, then? All agree that we do not understand nearly enough about the tacit, personal knowledge that lies behind so much of traditional medicine. Harriet Ngubane, in Chapter 9, argues that even the overt, logical structures of traditional medicine are not yet taken into account even when they are readily understandable – in part because they are in apparent contradiction with current socio-medical practice and its own moral premises. Tola Pearce, in Chapter 12, while questioning our existing ideas about the status of conventional medical knowledge, also implies that there is an alternative mode of knowledge underlying traditional healing, and suggests the study of emotion might be an avenue for exploring this mode. From this perspective, then, traditional medicine may be taught as a theoretically informed system as well as a practice; its alternative mode of knowledge can be researched, too, and the insights of its particular approach developed for wider application elsewhere. Indeed some have argued that in medicine, particularly in societies where public belief is still strong and explicit, we can no longer afford to ignore research into parapsychology and psychic phenomena generally, nor to continue treating witchcraft and exorcism as figments to be studied purely sociologically; concepts like 'placebo', 'nocebo', so the argument goes, obscure more than they explain. In this context, professionalisation of knowledge can be seen as potentially positive if it enables research to be carried on, and treated, seriously, with the necessary funds and institutional support and control.

But not all effective medical cultures function on this basis. In her field report on Zimbabwean healers in Chapter 8, Pamela Reynolds points out not just the overt structures but the sometimes contradictory, covert reality that we need to know to understand how traditional knowledge is transmitted. More significantly, she shows how the local community itself acts as the 'professional body', over time validating a new healer's qualifications, disciplining wrongful conduct and participating in the development of new knowledge. In short, professional knowledge is not a simply tacit, personal knowledge but is more a 'common sense' (if not quite 'common knowledge'). A 'common sense' of this sort requires both continuity and a certain transparency of social life; it results, too, in many people understanding how cures are done but only a few actually performing them. Thus there exists a 'therapeutic community' of a particular kind – but one whose expertise is not necessarily articulated or even called upon. Rather, the 'common sense' is implicit, and therefore flexible in a way that both ensures efficacy and allows for adaptation. Thus if accusations of witchcraft prove socially or morally unacceptable, satisfactory explanations for illness can plausibly be shifted onto ancestors or spirits without demur.

Such healers, then, are located in the countryside not because they are some isolated remnant (which socially speaking they certainly are not); but because the system of examination and control still works in the countryside and thus can be trusted by town and country people alike. A therapeutic system like this is manifestly untransferable to a school setting and its short, precise timetable. Yet any profession will have to be flexible enough to include such a community-based system of validation just as it is. One advantage that may accrue to the profession in doing so is that the (artificial?) gap between the new herbalist and the diviner/medium may begin to be bridged.

The politics of medicine, it is argued here, require now a degree of professionalisation among healers of all kinds. And not just for what healers can gain from the share-out of national resources – though this might be very important in the long term – but, paradoxically perhaps, so that they can survive as a relatively disorganised group in an increasingly bureaucratised society: in short, self-professionalisation is needed to forestall a more severe professionalisation-by-others. What is challenging, however, is that associations of traditional medicine in Africa may have to develop, and defend, ways of operating as a *profession* that will differ markedly from models elsewhere. This volume, then, has been an initial report on their progress.

REFERENCES

Asuni, T., (1979), 'The dilemma of traditional healing with specific reference to Nigeria', *Social Science and Medicine*, 13B, 1, pp. 33–9.

Bibeau, G., *et al.* (1980), *Traditional Medicine in Zaire*, Ottawa: IRDC.

Dores, M., (1981), *La Femme Village*, Paris: Harmattan.

Yoder, S., (ed.) (1982), *African Healing Systems*. Los Angeles: Crossroads Press.

INDEX